Debating the Death Penalty

Debating the Death Penalty

SHOULD AMERICA HAVE CAPITAL PUNISHMENT?

THE EXPERTS ON BOTH SIDES MAKE

THEIR BEST CASE

EDITED BY

Hugo Adam Bedau and Paul G. Cassell

UNIVERSITY PRESS

2004

OXFORD
UNIVERSITY PRESS

Oxford   New York
Auckland   Bangkok   Buenos Aires   Cape Town   Chennai
Dar es Salaam   Delhi   Hong Kong   Istanbul   Karachi   Kolkata
Kuala Lumpur   Madrid   Melbourne   Mexico City   Mumbai   Nairobi
São Paulo   Shanghai   Taipei   Tokyo   Toronto

Published by Oxford University Press, Inc., 2004
198 Madison Avenue, New York, New York 10016

www.oup.com

Oxford is a registered trademark of Oxford University Press

Library of Congress Cataloging-in-Publication Data

Debating the death penalty : should America have capital punishment? : the experts on
both sides make their best case / edited by Hugo Adam Bedau & Paul G. Cassell.
p. cm.
Includes index.
ISBN 0-19-516983-2
1. Capital punishment—United States. I. Bedau, Hugo Adam. II. Cassell, Paul G.
HV8699.U5D635 2004
364.66'0973—dc21   2003049868

Printing number: 9 8 7 6 5 4 3 2 1

Printed in the United States of America
on acid-free paper

Contents

———— • ————

Introduction

————— • —————

The death penalty has been a commonplace in Western civilization for more than two thousand years. Not until some two centuries ago, however, was its use and abuse seriously challenged in Italy, France, and England. Since then capital punishment has been a steady topic of debate and controversy, in Europe as well as in the United States. Whether discussing the Nuremberg tribunals of the 1940s in postwar Germany or the Rosenbergs' trial and execution in the 1950s, arguments over the death penalty continue to reverberate in the halls of public debate. Today, opponents of execution point to recent cases in which innocent prisoners—like Rolando Cruz in Illinois in 1995—narrowly escaped being unjustly executed. Supporters of the death penalty point to terrible crimes—such as the mass murder in Oklahoma City by Timothy McVeigh also in 1995—that they believe cry out for the death penalty as the only just punishment.

Among many recent events involving the politics of capital punishment, two in particular have received national publicity.

- In his final days in office early in 2003, Governor George Ryan of Illinois pardoned four death row prisoners and commuted to life imprisonment all 163 of the others on the state's death row. The magnitude of this unprecedented exercise of executive clemency earned the praise of death penalty opponents and simultaneously created a firestorm of protest. Ryan declared that he was deeply troubled by the flaws in the state's criminal justice system that led to sending innocent men to death row. While some of his admirers nominated him for the Nobel Peace Prize, his detractors painted a picture of a corrupt politician seeking public favor and redemption.

- Supporters of the death penalty have found their leading national spokesman in the person of Attorney General John Ashcroft. A dramatic example of his desire to use the death penalty occurred in late 2002. Residents in Washington, D.C., and nearby communities had been terrorized by a mysterious sniper. When suspects were arrested, the attorney general steered their prosecution away from Maryland (where the death penalty has recently been under serious attack) and from the District (an abolition jurisdiction) to Virginia, where the death penalty enjoys widespread support. Ashcroft's admirers praised him for his forthright pursuit of capital punishment; his detractors were outraged at his political rationale for favoring one jurisdiction over the others.

These are but two from scores of events around the country that concern the current use and the status of the death penalty. This volume (which had its origin in a spirited public debate held at the Graduate Center of City College in New York and funded by a grant from the Annenberg Public Policy Center of the University of Pennsylvania) provides the reader with an unusual opportunity to review the whole range of issues raised by any serious discussion of the death penalty. The eight contributing authors bring different perspectives and strengths to the table. Two are judges: Alex Kozinski sits on the federal Court of Appeals for the Ninth Circuit in San Francisco; Paul G. Cassell is on the bench of the federal district court in Salt Lake City. Both judges favor the death penalty. Three of the contributors are practicing attorneys: Bryan A. Stevenson is the executive director of the Equal Justice Initiative of Alabama, in Montgomery, and Steven B. Bright is the director of the Southern Center for Human Rights in Atlanta. Both oppose the death penalty. Joshua K. Marquis, a district attorney in western Oregon, favors it. Two of the contributors are philosophers: Hugo Adam Bedau (against), retired from the faculty of Tufts University, and Louis Pojman (for), on the faculty of the U. S. Military Academy. The eighth contribution is the text of former Illinois Governor George Ryan's January 11, 2003 speech announcing his commutation of all of Illinois's death sentences. Ryan is a recent convert to abolition. The eight essays fall neatly into two groups of four in favor of and four against the death penalty. Taken together, the authors raise all the main questions that deserve to be addressed in any thoroughgoing and reasonably comprehensive discussion of the death penalty in America today.

What are those questions? Here are a dozen of the most important ones:

- Does the death penalty deter better than long-term imprisonment?
- How important is it to decide the question of deterrence?
- Have innocent defendants been convicted, sentenced to death, and executed?
- Are reforms possible that would significantly reduce the risks of wrongful execution?
- If a death penalty system is more expensive than a system of long-term imprisonment, why pay the extra cost?
- Can the death penalty be best defended on retributive (backward-looking) grounds or on utilitarian (forward-looking) grounds?
- Is the death penalty unfair—arbitrary and discriminatory—to racial minorities and the poor?
- How trustworthy is the evidence on which the controversies over deterrence, racial unfairness, and wrongful executions turn?
- Can the death penalty be defended on the ground that nothing else brings closure to the agony of the victim's surviving family?
- Where is the current moratorium movement headed?
- What role should firsthand stories and anecdotes about murders, murderers, and their execution play in a rational discussion of the death penalty?

The strengths of this book will be found in two features. First, the essays together provide a very broad introduction to a very large topic.

This is unlike what one finds in many recent books on the death penalty, confined, for example, to the issue of wrongful convictions, or the issue of racial bias, or the history of this mode of punishment, or a case history of an innocent defendant freed from death row or of a recidivist murderer. Second, the contributors taken together bring to the discussion considerable experience with both the theoretical and the practical aspects of the subject. The result is a set of essays of unusual comprehensiveness, variety, and accessibility for a diverse public audience.

The opening essay by Judge Kozinski confronts the reader with the judge's highly personal reflections, which have arisen from his own experience on the bench. There he has been charged with the responsibility of deciding whether to sustain or vote against the death penalty in cases on the appeals docket of his court. No other essay in the volume approaches his in presenting such an intimate portrait of what it is like to bear such responsibility. (If one wants a comparable story of personal involvement but written by someone who does not favor capital punishment, one will have to turn elsewhere, say, to a testimonial from a member of Murder Victims Families for Reconciliation.)

The next chapter, by Professor Bedau, is divided into three independent parts. First, he briefly sketches the history of the death penalty in this country, thereby providing a background against which to interpret the views of his co-authors. He then turns to considering how defenders and critics of the death penalty diverge in their views of the present state of the death penalty in the United States today. How ought we to respond to the fact that the 15,000 or so criminal homicides annually in recent years so far yield on the average only two or three hundred death sentences per year and even fewer executions? Finally, Bedau offers what he regards as the best (though not the only) argument against the death penalty, based on a fundamental principle of political philosophy that he thinks ought to appeal both to conservatives and liberals alike.

Professor Pojman begins his essay with a direct response to four claims made by Bedau. He then turns to his own pro–death penalty argument, one that rests on retributive as well as preventive grounds. In the context of the latter, Pojman introduces the reader to what has become over the past decade or so the preferred line of defense of the death penalty, at least among philosophers, the so-called Best Bet argument. According to this argument, even if some who are innocent are sentenced to death and executed, society is better off (because more innocent lives are saved) by using the death penalty than by abolishing it.

Three of the next four essays are dispatches from the trenches, observations based on years of experience confronting the challenges of prosecution and defense in capital cases. Death row attorneys Bright and Stevenson address the bulk of their remarks to spelling out what Judge Cassell calls "the administrative challenges" to the death penalty as it is actually implemented by our courts. Unlike Cassell and Marquis (and Kozinski), Bright and Stevenson find these challenges sufficient to discredit the death penalty.

Stevenson presents the reader with several dramatic accounts of "close calls"—in which an innocent defendant was convicted of murder and sentenced to death but spared execution, thanks to timely intervention. The case of Walter McMillian, which Stevenson discusses in some detail, illustrates the disturbing role played by race and inadequate defense counsel in producing the conviction and death sentence of an innocent man. Stevenson's examples and cases are largely confined to Alabama, where he has his office, a state notorious in the annals of the death penalty for the Scottsboro case in the early 1930s. Not every death penalty jurisdiction in the nation has such a legacy, and one is tempted to suggest that racism and inadequate defense counsel are issues peculiar to the South. The evidence suggests otherwise. Research on race undertaken in 2002 by Governor Ryan's commission confirmed for Illinois what extensive research established more than a decade ago for Georgia: Men, white or black, who murder whites are statistically more likely to receive a death sentence than those who kill a nonwhite. The same results were reported early in 2003 for Maryland, in a study commissioned by Governor Parriss N. Glendenning.

Bright opens his essay by defending the proposition that the death penalty in America today violates international human rights standards and thus undermines the worldwide standing and moral authority of our nation. He then takes issue with Cassell over the exoneration of death row convicts. This is followed by a criticism of the discretion prosecutors have in deciding whether to pursue a death penalty in any given case of criminal homicide. He strongly disagrees with Marquis over the issue of racism when the death penalty is involved, and he argues that inept defense counsel is an important source of gross unfairness in capital trials. As with Stevenson, Bright's experience in southern courtrooms leaves an indelible impression on him of the inequities in our current death penalty system.

District Attorney Marquis wrestles with the death penalty whenever he deliberates whether to seek a death sentence and, if so, how to convince a jury that this is the appropriate punishment. The observations in his essay, arising from nearly two decades of experience with capital and non–capital homicide cases, cover a wide range of practical issues. Some of his remarks reinforce the conclusions of Judge Cassell. He counters many arguments made by death penalty opponents, claiming they often stretch the meaning of "innocent" in order to paint the criminal justice system as fatally flawed when it is not. He also argues that whatever may have been true in the past, the current system of capital punishment cannot be fairly criticized as racist. He draws on his own experience to provide examples of horrible murders that he believes deserved the death penalty, and he defends the adequacy of the extensive safeguards available to criminal defendants. Like many supporters of capital punishment, who acknowledge that our criminal justice system is far from perfect, Marquis demonstrates some ambivalence.

Judge Cassell begins his essay (as Stevenson did his) with a case history; for Cassell it is the story of the deadly crimes committed by Kenneth McDuff in Texas, whose death sentence had been commuted under the ruling by the Supreme Court in *Furman v. Georgia* (1972). McDuff was later released on parole, only to kill again—a clear case showing that had he been executed (or sentenced to life without the possibility of parole) several innocent lives would have been saved. The rest of Cassell's essay is divided into two roughly equal parts. In the first he reviews "the intellectual underpinnings of the death penalty," which consist in his view of incapacitation, deterrence, and retribution. This is in effect his reply to Bedau. In the second part Cassell addresses "the new wave of administrative challenges" directed against

1

·

Tinkering with Death[*]

Alex Kozinski

1.

I woke with a start and sat upright in the darkness.

He must be dead by now.

The thought filled my head and gave me a weird sense of relief. But no, it couldn't be. The execution was set for Sunday morning at seven—long after daybreak. The display on the digital clock showed 1:23. I fell back on my pillow and tried to chase Thomas Baal from my mind.

I had first heard his name just three days earlier. My friend and mentor Supreme Court Justice Anthony M. Kennedy had mentioned during a telephone conversation that an execution was scheduled that night somewhere in my jurisdiction. As a judge on the United States Court of Appeals for the Ninth Circuit, I hear cases from nine states and two territories spread over the Western United States and Oceania.

*Originally published in *The New Yorker*, February 10, 1997. Reprinted with the permission of Alex Kozinski.

"Must not be mine," I told him, "or I'd have heard about it by now." And left for lunch. When I returned, the fax was chattering away.

"The clerk's office called," my secretary said. "Guess who's been drawn for that execution?"

"How can it be? A man is scheduled to die tonight and this is the first I hear of it?"

"He doesn't want a stay," my law clerk interjected. "I've been reading the documents and it looks like he's ready to swallow the bitter pill. It's his mom and dad who are trying to stop the execution. They say he's not competent to waive his right to appeal. The district court is holding a hearing even as we speak."

"Oh, good," I muttered. "Maybe the district judge will enter a stay."

"Fat chance," my secretary and my law clerk said in unison. "Better read those papers."

2.

As I drifted back to sleep, I thought that Thomas Baal was not such a bad fellow compared with some of his neighbors on death row. On February 26, 1988, Baal had robbed thirty-four-year-old Frances Maves at knifepoint. Maves gave him twenty dollars, but Baal demanded more. She struggled. "You shouldn't have done that," Baal told her. "Now you pay. I sentence you to death." He stabbed Maves eight times.

I had seen my first death cases shortly after law school, when I clerked at the United States Supreme Court for former Chief Justice Warren E. Burger. That was almost two decades ago now, but I've never quite gotten over the experience. Whatever qualms I had about the efficacy or the morality of the death penalty were drowned out by the pitiful cries of the victims screaming from between the lines of dry legal prose:

> On the afternoon of May 14, 1973, defendant and three others ...
> drove to the residence of Jerry Alday.... The defendant and one
> of his companions entered the mobile home for the purpose of
> burglary. Shortly thereafter two members of the Alday family, Jerry

capital punishment as it is actually practiced in death penalty jurisdictions across the nation. His remarks here are in effect a critique of the views of Bright and Stevenson. He devotes special attention to the claim (which he believes is unsupported by the evidence) that many innocent defendants have been sentenced to death and some executed.

The book closes with the statement by Governor Ryan explaining his decision early in 2003 to extend clemency to all the prisoners in Illinois then on death row. It is unusual for a governor to defend at length (as Ryan did) his exercise of the clemency power to empty (at least temporarily) the death row of his state—and not only because the exercise of clemency for capital offenders is itself rare. Ryan's statement is also unusual because his argument rests squarely on the inherent danger of executing the innocent. He does not claim that Illinois has, to its disgrace, actually executed anyone now known to be innocent. He does acknowledge that Illinois has arrested, tried, convicted, and sentenced to death more than a dozen innocent defendants in the past few years. Whether any other state can show a comparable record of miscarriages of justice in capital cases is unknown; it is fair to say that as of this writing such miscarriages either have not occurred or not been detected in anything like the number found in Illinois. It remains to be seen whether future discoveries of such errors in other jurisdictions will mount up and rival Illinois's unfortunate record.

In the nature of the case, this book raises more questions about the death penalty than it can answer. There is much more to be said on each side of the debate, and the structure of the book does not permit as much by way of rejoinder as did the public debate that preceded it. Readers should use the questions raised in the book to reconsider their own views—pro or con. The following chapters, we hope, will put even the well-informed reader in a much better position to understand and evaluate our death penalty system.

and his father, Ned Alday, arrived in a jeep, were escorted at gunpoint into the trailer, and were shot to death at close range with handguns . . . .

Shortly thereafter a tractor driven by Jerry's brother, Jimmy Alday, arrived at the trailer. After being forced to empty his pockets, he was placed on the living room sofa and killed with a handgun fired at close range.

While one of the four was moving the tractor out of the driveway, Jerry's wife, Mary, arrived at her home by car. . . . Two other members of the Alday family, Aubrey and Chester, Jerry's uncle and brother, arrived in a pickup truck. Mary was forced into the bathroom while Aubrey and Chester were taken at gunpoint into the bedrooms and shot in a manner similar to the first two victims. . . .

Mary Alday was then raped by two or more of the men. . . . She was then taken, bound and blindfolded, in her car about six miles to a wooded area where she was raped by two of the men, was beaten when she refused to commit oral sodomy, and her breasts mutilated. She was then killed with two shots. Her watch was then removed from her nude body.

Sometimes the victims had tiny voices, barely audible as they endured fates so horrible that they defy human comprehension:

Over the . . . latter portion of Kelly Ann's short, torturous life the defendant [her father] did these things to her on one or many occasions:

1. Beat her in the head until it was swollen.
2. Burned her hands.
3. Poked his fingers in her eyes.
4. Beat her in the abdomen until "it was swollen like she was pregnant."
6. Held her under water in both the bath tub and toilet.
7. Kicked her against a table which cut her head then . . . sewed up her wound with needle and thread.
9. On one occasion beat her continuously for 45 minutes.
13. Choked her on the night she died and when she stopped

breathing . . . placed her body in a plastic garbage bag and buried
her in an unmarked and unknown grave.

Brutal facts have immense power; they etched deep marks in my
psyche. Those who commit such atrocities, I concluded, forfeit their
own right to live. We tarnish the memory of the dead and heap needless misery on their surviving families by letting the perpetrators live.

Still, it's one thing to feel and another to do. It's one thing to give
advice to a judge and quite another to *be* the judge signing the order
that will lead to the death of another human being—even a very bad
one. Baal was my first.

3.

Another start. The clock showed 3 A.M. Would this night never end? I
knew I had done the right thing; I had no doubts. Still, I wished it
were over.

The district court had made its decision around 6 P.M. Thursday.
Yes, Baal was competent; he could—and did—waive his right to all
appeals, state and federal. This finding was based on the affidavits of
the psychiatrists who had examined Baal, and on Baal's courtroom
responses:

> THE COURT: Do you want us to stop [the execution], sir, to give
> you an opportunity to appeal . . . ?
> THE DEFENDANT: No, I feel that I've gone through a lot of prob-
> lems in there and I'm just—I feel that the death penalty is needed.
> And I don't feel that I have to stick around ten years and try to fight
> this thing out because it's just not in me.
> THE COURT: You know that your act here in the Courtroom of
> saying, "Don't stop the execution," will result in your death. You're
> aware of that, are you not?
> THE DEFENDANT: Yes. . . .
> THE COURT: Now, you know that the choice that you're making
> here is either life or death. Do you understand that?
> THE DEFENDANT: I understand. I choose death. . . .

THE COURT: Is there anything else?

THE DEFENDANT: Just bring me a hooker.

THE COURT: Obviously the court can't grant requests such as that. Any other requests?

THE DEFENDANT: Just my last meal and let's get the ball rolling.

In desperation, Baal's parents had submitted an affidavit from a psychiatrist who, without examining Baal, could say only that he *might* not be competent. The district judge didn't buy it. Stay denied.

The case officially landed in my lap just as I was leaving the office for dinner at a friend's house. I arranged with the two other judges who had been selected to hear the case for a telephone conference with the lawyers later that evening. Nothing stops the conversation at a dinner party quite like the half-whispered explanation "I have to take this call. It's a stay in a death case. Don't hold dessert."

Last-minute stay petitions in death cases are not unusual; they're a reflex. Except in rare cases where the prisoner decides to give up his appeal rights, death cases are meticulously litigated, first in state court and then in federal court—often bouncing between the two systems several times—literally until the prisoner's dying breath. Once the execution date is set, the process takes on a frantic pace. The death warrant is usually valid only for a limited time—in some states only for a single day—and the two sides battle furiously over that piece of legal territory.

If the condemned man (only one woman has been executed in the last thirty-five years) can delay the execution long enough for the death warrant to expire, he will have bought himself a substantial reprieve—at least a few weeks, sometimes months or years. But, if the state can carry out the execution, the game ends in sudden death and the prisoner's arguments die with him.

The first time I had seen this battle was in 1977, when a platoon of American Civil Liberties Union lawyers descended on the United States Supreme Court in a vain effort to save Gary Gilmore's life. Gilmore's case was pivotal to death-penalty opponents, because he would be the first to be executed since the Supreme Court had emptied the nation's death rows in 1972 by declaring all existing death-penalty statutes unconstitutional. A number of states had quickly retooled their death statutes, but opponents hoped to use procedural delays to stave off all executions for many years. Gilmore upset this calculation by waiving his appeals after he was found guilty.

Gilmore was scheduled to face the firing squad on the morning of January 17, 1977. Efforts to obtain a stay from the lower federal courts during the night had proved unsuccessful, and the lawyers brought a stack of papers to the Supreme Court Clerk's office. The Court was due to hear cases at ten, which was also when the execution was scheduled. In the hour before the Justices took the bench, Michael Rodak, the Clerk of the Supreme Court, carried the petition to them in their chambers—first to one, then to another. The Justices entered the courtroom at the stroke of ten, and Rodak hurried back to his office. A few minutes after ten, he placed a call to the state prison in Draper, Utah, where Gilmore was being held. He first identified himself with a password: "This is Mickey from Wheeling, West Virginia." He continued, "I've presented the stay petition to the Justices, and it was denied. You may proceed with the execution."

Rodak then fell silent for a few seconds as he listened to the response from the other end of the line.

"Oh. . . . You mean he's already dead?"

4.

So as not to wake my wife with my tossing, I went to the kitchen and made myself a cup of tea. As I sipped the hot liquid, I thumbed through the small mountain of papers that had accumulated over the past seventy-two hours.

With the stakes in death cases so high, it's hard to escape the feeling of being manipulated, the suspicion that everything the lawyers say or do is designed to entice or intimidate you into giving them what they want. Professional distance—the detachment that is the lawyers' stock-in-trade in ordinary cases—is absent in death cases. It's the battle of the zealots.

And it's not just the lawyers. Death cases—particularly as the execution draws near—distort the deliberative process and turn judges into advocates. There are those of my colleagues who have never voted to uphold a death sentence and doubtless never will. The view that judges are morally justified in undermining the death penalty, even though it has been approved by the Supreme Court, was legitimatized by the former Supreme Court Justices William J. Brennan, Jr., and Thurgood Marshall, who voted to vacate as cruel and unusual every single death sentence that came before the Court. Just before retiring, in 1994, Justice Harry A. Blackmun adopted a similar view, by pronouncing, "From this day forward, I shall no longer tinker with the machinery of death."

Refusing to enforce a valid law is a violation of the judges' oath—something that most judges consider a shameful breach of duty. But death is different, or so the thinking goes, and to slow down the pace of executions by finding fault with every death sentence is considered by some to be highly honorable. In the words of Justice Brennan, this practice "embod[ies] a community striving for human dignity for all, although perhaps not yet arrived."

Judges like me, who support the death penalty, are swept right along. Observing manipulation by the lawyers and complicity from liberal colleagues, conservative judges often see it as their duty to prevent death-row inmates from diminishing the severity of their sentence by endlessly postponing the day of reckoning.

Armageddon on this question was fought in my court in 1992 when Robert Alton Harris became the first person to be executed in California since the days of Caryl Chessman. Harris killed two teen-age boys because he wanted to steal their car; he then finished off the hamburgers they had been eating. There was no doubt that Harris was guilty—he confessed the same day—yet he and his able lawyers managed to hold the executioner at bay for thirteen years, at a staggering cost to the taxpayers.

With his fifth scheduled execution days away, Harris brought two actions in federal court. In one, he claimed that, regardless of his guilt or innocence, the *method* that California had selected for executing him (lethal gas) was unconstitutional because it inflicted needless suffering. This claim was far from frivolous; another death-row inmate making the same argument later succeeded in closing California's gas chamber. (California now uses lethal injection.) But in Harris's case many judges of my court (I among them) thought there was no reason—other than the hope of manipulating us into granting a last-minute stay—that the claim had not been raised during the many years Harris had spent on death row.

Not all judges saw it that way. To give Harris time to litigate this claim—a process that would have taken years—various judges issued three successive stays in the hours preceding Harris's scheduled mid-night execution, but the United States Supreme Court just as quickly lifted them. Finally, at about 3:30 A.M., Harris was taken into the gas chamber and strapped down to await the dropping of the sodium-cyanide pellets into the sulfuric acid—when his lawyers persuaded a judge of my court to issue yet a fourth stay.

Harris was unstrapped and escorted out of the gas chamber, but the reprieve was brief: less than two hours later, as a new day started in Washington, the Supreme Court lifted the stay in a brusque order that forbade any other federal court to interfere with the execution.

Much has been said about the Supreme Court's final order in the Harris case—one of my colleagues went so far as to accuse the Supreme Court of committing "treason to the Constitution"—but the drama had no other possible outcome. Harris and his supporters (both outside and within the judiciary) were bound and determined to keep California from jump-starting its death penalty. Eventually, the Supreme Court Justices, who had held in numerous opinions that the death penalty is constitutional, said, "Enough is enough."

Harris was again subjected to the grisly gas-chamber ritual, and this time there was no reprieve. At 6:10 A.M., he inhaled the deadly gas as relatives of his victims watched from an observation room only six feet away.

Families of murder victims are among the most fervent supporters of the death penalty. They often use the press and political channels to agitate for the hasty demise of the monster who shattered their lives. Yet no one seems to have given serious thought to whether families are helped or harmed by the process, especially when it is long delayed. Does watching the perpetrator die help the families reach closure, or does the frustrated hope of execution in the face of endless appeals keep the psychological wounds open, sometimes for decades?

5.

Another hour passed, but sleep eluded me. Events of the last three days kept knocking around in my head.

Over my friend's kitchen telephone, the lawyers spoke with great urgency and took predictable positions. Afterward, my colleagues and I conferred. One of them—who has never seen a death sentence he liked—quickly voted to issue a stay. Almost instinctively, I took the opposite view. After some discussion, the third judge voted for a stay, and the execution was halted.

We spent all day Friday and most of that night preparing the stay order and my dissent. My colleagues argued that Baal's parents made a strong showing that he was not competent to surrender his life: he had a long history of "behavioral and mental problems," had attempted suicide on several occasions, and had been found to suffer from a variety of psychiatric disorders. Twice in the past, he had waived his legal remedies but had later changed his mind.

My dissent emphasized the diagnosis of the psychiatrists who had examined him; the state court's finding—just a week earlier—that he was competent; and Baal's lucid and appropriate answers to questions posed from the bench. I ended by arguing that Baal's decision to forgo the protracted trauma of numerous death-row appeals was rational, and that my colleagues were denying his humanity by refusing to accept his decision:

> It has been said that capital punishment is cruel and unusual because it is degrading to human dignity. . . . But the dignity of human life comes not from mere existence, but from that ability which separates us from the beasts—the ability to choose; freedom of will. See Immanuel Kant, "Critique of Pure Reason." When we say that a man—even a man who has committed a horrible crime—is not free to choose, we take away his dignity just as surely as we do when we kill him. Thomas Baal has made a decision to accept society's punishment and be done with it. By refusing to respect his decision we denigrate his status as a human being.

The idea that a long sojourn on death row is itself an excruciating punishment—and violates basic human rights—has gained some notable adherents. In 1989, the European Court of Human Rights refused to order the extradition of a man wanted for murder in the United States on the ground that the delay in carrying out death sentences in this country amounts to inhuman and degrading punishment. Four years later, the British Privy Council vacated a Jamaican death sentence because its imposition had been delayed for fourteen years. The Supreme Court of Zimbabwe reached a similar conclusion with respect to much shorter delays—delays that were, however, coupled with unusually harsh conditions of confinement.

This view has some important followers in the United States as well, notably Supreme Court Justice John Paul Stevens. Justice Stevens argues that such delayed executions violate the Constitution, because they serve no purpose. Living for twenty years under the terror of a death sentence is punishment enough, he argues; moreover, a death sentence so long delayed can have no deterrent value and is therefore capricious. No other Justice has yet embraced this view, but Justice Stephen G. Breyer has shown some sympathy.

There is a lot to be said, of course, for the proposition that the death penalty ought to be carried out swiftly. But swift justice is hard to come by, because the Supreme Court has constructed a highly complex—and mutually contradictory—series of conditions that must be satisfied before a death sentence may be carried out. On the one hand, there must be individual justice: there can be no mandatory death sentence, no matter how heinous the crime. On the other hand, there must be consistent justice: discretion to impose the death penalty must be tightly circumscribed. But individual justice is inherently inconsistent—different juries reach different results in similar cases. And there are scores of other issues that arise in every criminal case but take on special significance when death is involved. Death, as liberal judges keep telling us, is different.

Not surprisingly, a good lawyer (with cover from sympathetic judges) can postpone an execution for many years. When Duncan Peder McKenzie reached the end of the road on May 10, 1995, he had been a fixture of Montana's death row for two decades. A total of forty-one state and federal judges had examined the case (many of them several times) and had issued two dozen published opinions analyzing various claims. In the end, McKenzie argued that he had suffered enough because of this delay and he should be forgiven his death sentence. We rejected this argument, and the Supreme Court refused to stay the execution, with Justice Stevens dissenting.

6.

Dawn broke as I drifted off into fitful sleep, but a part of me kept reaching out to the man I knew was living the last hour of his life. Awareness of death is intrinsic to the human condition, but what is it like to know precisely—to the minute—when your life is going to end? Does time stand still? Does it race? How can you swallow, much less digest, that last meal? Or even think of hookers?

Though I've now had a hand in a dozen or more executions, I have never witnessed one. The closest I came was a conversation with Bill Allen, a lawyer from my former law firm. I ran into him at a reception and his face was gray, his eyes—usually sharp and clear—seemed out of focus.

"Not well," Bill answered when I asked how he was doing. "I lost a client. His name was Linwood Briley. I saw him die in the electric chair a couple of days ago."

"Was it rough?"

"What do you think? It was awful."

"What was it like when they turned on the juice?"

"Oh, by the time they got done strapping him down, putting the goop on his head and the mask on his face, the thing sitting in that chair hardly looked human. But the really strange part was before: looking at him, talking to him, even joking with him, fully aware he'd be dead in half an hour."

"Why did you go?"

"I thought he should have a friend there with him in his final minutes."

The look on Bill's face stayed with me a long time. It was enough to persuade me that I'd never want to witness an execution. Yet I sometimes wonder whether those of us who make life-and-death decisions on a regular basis should not be required to watch as the machinery of death grinds up a human being. I ponder what it says about me that I can, with cool precision, cast votes and write opinions that seal another human being's fate but lack the courage to witness the consequences of my actions.

After filing my dissent, at 2:59 A.M. Saturday, I put Baal out of my mind, figuring that it would be quite some time before I'd have to think about him again. Much to my surprise, however, the Supreme Court issued an order that evening, lifting our stay. The execution was on. The Court had more or less adopted my reasoning—even cited me by name. I felt triumphant.

But, as Saturday turned to night, it began to sink in that Baal really *was* going to die, and that I would have played a part in ending his life. The thought took hold of my mind and would not let go. It filled me with a nagging sense of unease, something like motion sickness.

7.

I finally plunged into a deep sleep from which I awoke long after the execution was over. I was grateful not to have been awake to imagine in real time how Baal was strapped onto a gurney, how his vein was opened, how the deadly fluids were pumped into his body.

Lethal injection, which has overtaken the electric chair as the execution method of choice, is favored because it is sure, painless, and nonviolent. But I find it creepy that we pervert the instruments of healing—the needle, the pump, the catheter, F.D.A.-approved drugs— by putting them to such an antithetical use. It also bothers me that we mask the most violent act that society can inflict on one of its members with such an antiseptic veneer. Isn't death by firing squad, with mutilation and bloodshed, more honest?

8.

Some three hundred and sixty people have been executed since Gary Gilmore. The most we have dispatched in any one year was fifty-six, in 1995. There are thirty-one hundred or so awaiting their date with the executioner, and the number is growing. Impatient with the delays,

Congress last year passed the Effective Death Penalty Act, which will probably hasten the pace of executions. Even then, it's doubtful we have the resources or the will even to keep up with the three hundred or so convicted murderers we add to our death rows every year.

With the pace of executions quickening and the total number of executions rising, I fear it's only a matter of time before we learn that we've executed the wrong man. There have already been cases where prisoners on death row were freed after evidence turned up proving them innocent. I dread the day we are confronted with a case in which the conclusive proof of innocence turns up too late.

And I sometimes wonder whether the death penalty is not an expensive and distracting sideshow to our battle against violent crime. Has our national fascination with capital punishment diverted talent and resources from mundane methods of preventing violent crime? Take William Bonin, the notorious Freeway Killer, who raped, tortured, and murdered fourteen teen-age boys, then dumped their bodies along Southern California's freeways. If anyone deserved execution, surely it was Bonin. And on February 23, 1996, after fourteen years on death row, he went to his death, even then mocking the families of his victims. Asked if he had any regrets, the confessed killer admitted that, indeed, he did: "Well, probably I went in the [military] service too soon, because I was peaking in my bowling career. I was carrying, like, a 186 to a 190 average. . . . I've always loved bowling."

Yet, looking at the record in his case, one can't help noting that Bonin had given us ample warning of his proclivities. While serving in Vietnam, he had sexually assaulted at gunpoint two soldiers under his command. After returning to civilian life, he had been convicted of molesting four boys between the ages of twelve and eighteen. He had served three years for those crimes and, upon his release, molested another boy. Again, he had served only three years and had then been set free to commence his killing spree.

Bonin is not unique. My concurring opinion in his case lists a number of other killers who gave us fair warning that they were dangerous but were nevertheless set free to prey on an unsuspecting and vulnerable population. Surely putting to death ten convicted killers isn't nearly as useful as stopping a single Bonin before he tastes blood.

9.

It's late Saturday night. Another execution is scheduled for next week, and the machinery of death is humming through my fax. And, despite the qualms, despite the queasiness I still feel every time an execution is carried out in my jurisdiction, I tinker away. I do it because I have taken an oath. But there's more. I do it because I believe that society is entitled to take the life of those who have shown utter contempt for the lives of others. And because I hear the tortured voices of the victims crying out to me for vindication.

2

·

An Abolitionist's Survey of the
Death Penalty in America Today

Hugo Adam Bedau

Lest there be any doubt in the reader's mind, let me declare at the outset that I strongly oppose the death penalty no matter what the crime or the criminal. This will be evident enough later as this essay unfolds and especially when I offer an argument against capital punishment. My position to the side, perhaps the best place to begin this discussion of the death penalty in America and the controversies it has provoked is by summarizing its history in our country. That history is largely a story of efforts to limit and abolish it.

I

The first European colonist whose execution on these shores has been recorded is George Kendall, in Virginia's Jamestown colony. He was hanged in 1608 for the crime of "spying for the Spanish."[1] In the subsequent four centuries an uncounted number—perhaps twenty thousand or more—of convicted murderers, rapists, horse thieves, spies, witches, and kidnappers, among others, have met a similar fate. No one should be surprised that the colonists embraced the death penalty (along with other corporal punishments, such as flogging, branding, and the pillory); the Mother Country itself put extensive reliance on such punishments to control an unruly public.

During the Revolutionary era, historian Louis Masur tells us, "a diverse group of Americans considered the death penalty morally and politically repugnant."[2] So they did. Benjamin Rush of Philadelphia—physician, friend of Benjamin Franklin, and one of the Founding Fathers—was second to none as an outspoken opponent of the hangman. In 1797 he published a lecture attacking public executions under the title "Considerations on the Injustice and Impolicy of Punishing Murder by Death"; printed as a pamphlet, it was widely circulated. Rush argued that "The Punishment of Murder by Death is contrary to *reason,* and to the order and happiness of society [as well as] contrary to divine revelation." Rush's lectures and essays mark the beginning of the abolition movement in this country. During the next century and a half—roughly from the 1780s to the 1950s—several developments in the law affecting the death penalty were pioneered in various state legislatures or, in more recent decades, decreed by the Supreme Court. Six of these developments were paramount, and each warrants closer scrutiny.

Introducing Degrees of Murder

The first major accomplishment of the abolition movement consisted in enacting a novel law in 1793 in Pennsylvania to divide murder into two categories, first and second-degree murder, and to confine the punishment of death to offenders convicted of murder in the first degree. (First-degree murder was defined to include both premeditated murder and so-called felony murder, that is, any killing in the course of committing another felony, such as arson, burglary, rape, or robbery.[3]) Quaker abolitionists in the Keystone State had thought complete repeal of their state's death penalty statutes was within their grasp. They were the first, but not the last, abolitionists to learn they had to settle for less.

English law had long recognized a distinction between murder and manslaughter (the killing of another without malice or premeditation) and had confined the death penalty for criminal homicide to the former crime. In America, the creation of degrees of murder and the limitation of a death sentence to offenders guilty of first-degree murder amounted to a recognition that not all murderers are equally bad, dangerous, irredeemable—a proposition long acknowledged by common sense—and that therefore not all murderers were equally deserving of the ultimate punishment.

Applying the distinction in actual practice between the two kinds of murder, however, proved not so easy, neither then nor now. No less a figure than the eminent Supreme Court Justice Benjamin Cardozo (1870–1938) despaired over the distinction, saying it "is much too vague to be continued in our law. . . . Upon [its] basis . . . with its mystifying psychology, scores of men have gone to their deaths."[4]

For the past quarter century, an offender's conviction of first-degree murder has no longer been a sufficient basis for that person to receive a death sentence. The defendant and the crime must also exhibit so-called "aggravating circumstances" in order to be "death-eligible." These circumstances (for example, the victim was a police officer, the offender had a prior felony conviction, the crime was particularly horrible or inhumane) are usually specified by statute and form part of the judge's instruction to the jury. The law typically provides that it is a necessary condition of a death sentence that the jury find at least one such "aggravator." The introduction of this tactic in death penalty sentencing is but another effort to winnow out the worst from the bad and to confine the death penalty to the former alone.

Ending Public Executions

The second major reform, also pioneered by Rush, was ending the spectacle of public executions in favor of carrying out the death penalty behind a specially built stockade or inside an enclosed prison yard. New York in 1834 was the first to adopt this reform; Pennsylvania, New Jersey, and other states soon followed. Yet as legal historian Stuart Banner notes, "Well into the nineteenth century, execution crowds still outnumbered crowds gathered for any other purpose."[5] There was little privacy in actual practice. Not all spectators were prohibited. Reporters, prison officials, and surviving family members of the victim were invited to watch the execution; they still are today. In one of our last public executions, in Owensboro, Kentucky, in 1936, a reporter noted: "Two hundred of the 20,000 people who saw Rainey Bethea, a stunned 22-year-old Negro boy, hanged at dawn here today, swarmed like carrion over the gallows while his body was still suspended through the trap. . . . They tore the hood off his frightened, hunted face to get souvenirs. . . . Bethea dropped to his death . . . as 20,000 cheering fans packed every available spot."[6]

Abolitionists viewed (and still view) the end of public executions with a divided mind. On the one hand, the move indoors was tacit acknowledgment that hanging a helpless convict in public was unsavory and that watching it was voyeuristic. On the other hand, denying the public the right to watch this lawful punishment being administered was viewed by many as contrary to the principles of republican government. In 1836 Bowdoin College's professor of philosophy, Thomas Upham (1799–1872), a staunch opponent of the death penalty, argued: "Our courts of justice must be open to the public; the deliberations of our legislature must be public. . . . If business of this nature is done at all, it must be done in the light of day."[7] These sentiments were recently echoed by civil libertarian Nat Hentoff in the context of the then-forthcoming execution of Timothy McVeigh. "We, as a people," he wrote, "demand accountability of our public officials. Surely we should not shirk our duty to witness—and therefore be accountable for—the executions we permit."[8] Thus continues the debate over whether executions should be truly public.

Introducing Jury Sentencing Discretion

The next important reform consisted of giving the trial jury the power to decide whether the defendant they had just convicted was to be sentenced to death or was to receive "mercy," in the form of a lengthy (usually, a life) sentence in prison. Of all the reforms in America's long-drawn-out affair with the death penalty, none is more significant (or in sharper contrast with English law) than the end of the death penalty as a mandatory punishment.

Exactly where and why this reform first was enacted remains obscure. We do know that in 1838 Tennessee was the first state to empower the trial jury in a capital case to sentence convicted murderers to death or to prison, and that a few years later Louisiana extended this power to juries for all capital offenders, whatever their crime. As a populist reform, granting to the people (in the form of the trial jury) discretionary sentencing power—the power of life and death—could hardly be improved upon. To this day, governors in their public statements denying clemency in a capital case hasten to point out that a jury of 12 citizens has spoken, and that the conviction and then the death sentence are for that reason not easily to be set aside.

Today, thanks to rulings by the Supreme Court, there are no mandatory death penalties anywhere in the nation. Given that in 1987 the Court ruled unconstitutional a mandatory death penalty for a murderer in prison who has been convicted of committing another murder,[9] it is unlikely that the Court would uphold a mandatory capital statute in the future.

Whether capital trial juries today perform their discretionary sentencing task as the Supreme Court believed they would when it enacted reforms in capital punishment law during the 1970s is very doubtful. Beginning in 1980, the Capital Jury Project has interviewed thousands of former capital jurors in several death penalty jurisdictions to determine whether they understood the judge's instructions regarding sentencing and whether they complied with those instructions. The research so far published is thoroughly discouraging on both points.[10]

Humanizing Methods of Execution

The fourth important reform in our jurisprudence of death concerns the effort to make executions more efficient and humane. Difficult as it is to believe today, this was the rationale behind the introduction in 1890 of the electric chair in New York as an improvement over hanging. Whether the electric chair ever lived up to the claims of efficiency and humanity made on its behalf is doubtful. Certainly its faults in actual practice—erupting in fire, slowly burning the condemned man to death, the death chamber reeking of burned flesh—have been well documented and are beyond dispute. Whatever may have seemed true a century ago, today it ought to be impossible not to regard death in the electric chair as a "cruel and unusual punishment," in direct

violation of the prohibition of such punishments in the Eighth Amendment in the Bill of Rights. Only two states (Alabama and Nebraska)
enter the new millennium employing only this method of execution;
nine others still authorize it but give the condemned man the alternative of lethal injection. Much the same kind of humanitarian argument was used on behalf of execution by lethal gas, initiated in Nevada
in 1923. Death in the gas chamber was widely adopted in subsequent
years, but came under attack (so far unsuccessful) on constitutional
grounds in the 1990s.

Dominating all other methods of execution now and for the fore-
seeable future is lethal injection. Oklahoma in 1977 was the first state
to legalize death by this method, but Texas was the first to use it in
1982. It is now authorized in more than two dozen states. No bodily
mutilation, no disfigurement, no delay, no odor, apparently no pain—
what more could a humane defender of the death penalty want? How
can an opponent of the death penalty argue that lethal injection is an
unconstitutional "cruel and unusual punishment"?[11] There is no doubt
that widespread adoption in the United States of this method of execution during the past quarter century has helped preserve and protect
the death penalty.

Federal Appellate Intervention

A century ago, a capital offender might well go to his death without
ever having an appellate court (especially a federal court) review his
conviction and sentence. By the 1950s, however, it was not uncommon
for both state and federal appellate courts to review a defendant's capital conviction. In recent years, review by the higher courts, state and
federal, has become routine. This heightened scrutiny has resulted in
many reversals and in some cases a retrial or a sentencing rehearing
ordered by the courts. Apparently there is much to remedy. Recent
research conducted by law professor James F. Liebman and his associates established that "More than two out of every three capital judgments reviewed by the courts during the 23-year study period [from
1973 through 1995] were found to be seriously flawed." These flaws
were not mere "technical" violations; they were such as to "seriously

undermine the reliability of the outcome or otherwise 'harmed' the defendant."[12]

On the other hand, since the mid-1990s the federal courts have been severely hampered by Congress and by Supreme Court decisions aimed at reaching "finality" and greater "efficiency" in death penalty cases from carrying out an appropriate degree of close scrutiny. The prospect for the future is discouraging. Critics have pointed out that the Supreme Court's rulings beginning as far back as 1983 have signaled what law professor Robert Weisberg aptly has called the "deregulation of death"—leaving each state to chart its own way within broad limits, never mind the price being paid in arbitrariness, unpredictability, and uncontrolled discretion. It is as though the Court had decided that "it no longer wants to use constitutional law to foster legal formulas for regulating moral choice at the penalty trial."[13]

As of early 2002, abolitionists were pressing for rulings by the Supreme Court on two issues of long-standing concern. One involves limiting the death penalty to persons over 18 at the time of the crime; current law in several jurisdictions permits youths as young as 16 to be executed. The other issue concerns excluding offenders who are mentally retarded from the reach of the death penalty; current law permits (but does not require) defense counsel to lay before the jury during the sentencing phase evidence (if there is any) of the defendant's deficient mental abilities as a mitigating factor. The latter concern has recently been dropped from the abolitionist's agenda because in June 2002 the Supreme Court ruled in *Atkins v. Virginia* that a mentally retarded murderer cannot be held fully responsible for his crime, thus overruling *Penry v. Lynaugh*, decided in 1989. When the Supreme Court will prohibit states from sentencing a murderer to death for a crime committed while he was under 18 cannot be foreseen; nonetheless, it is a likely development in the near future.

Abolition of the Death Penalty

By the middle of the nineteenth century the number of death penalty statutes enacted and enforced in America was being reduced by state legislatures. The reduction came in one of two forms: selective repeal in the variety of capital statutes, and complete abolition of all such laws. The first state to reduce the number of its capital statutes was Pennsylvania in 1786; the legislature abolished the death penalty for robbery, burglary, and sodomy and reserved executions for those convicted of first-degree murder. The first states to repeal the death penalty entirely—Michigan (except for treason), Wisconsin, and Rhode Island—did so just prior to the Civil War. Abolition nearly succeeded in several other states, only to have the war interrupt the trend, not to be resumed until the end of the century. During the Progressive Era, a substantial number of states entered the abolition column: Arizona, Colorado, Kansas, Minnesota, Missouri, Oregon, North Dakota, South Dakota, Tennessee, Washington. All but two restored the executioner within a few years. (The two exceptions were Minnesota and North Dakota.)

Already by more than a century ago, the death penalty in this country had been effectively regionalized. The only part of the nation that has had no experience with even temporary abolition is the South, the Old Confederacy, the Bible Belt. As Stuart Banner soberly notes, "The South has always been a more violent place than the North, and one may suppose that the continued employment of violent punishments for slaves acclimated white southerners to violent punishments generally."[14] This remains true today. Death sentences and executions join high homicide rates as a way of life in Texas, Florida, and other southern states, as they have for generations. Voices opposing the death penalty in these states have never remotely approached a majority, as they have from time to time elsewhere in the nation. It is all too tempting to see a bloody continuity from lawless lynching of blacks by whites just two generations ago to the drum-head "justice" meted out even today in southern courtrooms when a black man is on trial for murdering a white victim. The testimony of Bright and Stevenson on this theme in their contribution to this book is as appalling as it is irrefutable.

As of 1960, and apart from the capital crime of murder, no two American death penalty jurisdictions had the same statutory catalogue of crimes subject to the death penalty. In one jurisdiction or another, more than three dozen different crimes were made punishable by death. Most popular, after murder, were kidnapping (34 jurisdictions), treason (21), rape (18), carnal knowledge (15), armed robbery (10), and perjury in a capital case (10).[15] In those years Georgia alone had 16 statutory capital offenses.

In the mid-1960s, the abolition movement underwent a major transformation. Up to that point, reduction in capital statutes and their complete abolition had been undertaken exclusively by state legislatures and Congress. Beginning in 1967, lawyers attacked the death penalty on constitutional grounds, arguing that it violated "due process of law," "equal protection of the law," and especially the prohibition against "cruel and unusual punishment."[16] These challenges resulted in a de facto moratorium on executions, as the Supreme Court wrestled with their arguments.

In *Furman v. Georgia* (1972), the Court ruled that the typical death penalty statute was so arbitrary that it violated the Eighth and Fourteenth Amendments and that if a state wished to preserve the death penalty it must refashion its statutes accordingly. One effect of that ruling was that hundreds of the nation's death row prisoners had to be resentenced to prison terms. Four years later, however, in *Gregg v. Georgia* (1976), the Court ruled that the death penalty per se was not unconstitutional. This ruling marked the defeat of the campaign to abolish the death penalty nationwide, all at once, and on constitutional grounds. It also marked the beginning of the effort by the Court to supervise the way the death penalty states administered this punishment, tolerating here and repealing there dozens of different provisions in the law.

Not all the Court's rulings in the 1970s sustained the death penalty. In 1976, the mandatory death penalty was declared unconstitutional (*Woodson v. North Carolina*). A year later the death penalty for rape was ruled unconstitutional (*Coker v. Georgia*); indeed, all but a few federal nonhomicidal capital statutes (such as for espionage and treason) quietly died with hardly a trace. The only death penalty statutes to survive constitutional challenge since 1976 are those punishing some form of criminal homicide. Whether the nonhomicidal provisions of Congress's Anti-Terrorism and Effective Death Penalty Act (1996) will be upheld as constitutional remains to be seen.

As for complete abolition, 25 states, Puerto Rico, and Washington, D.C., have each abolished the death penalty for murder at one time or another. As of 2002, 14 jurisdictions belong in the abolition column:

Alaska, Hawaii, Iowa, Maine, Massachusetts, Michigan, Minnesota, North Dakota, Rhode Island, Vermont, West Virginia, Wisconsin, District of Columbia, and Puerto Rico. But statutory abolition of the death penalty has run a checkered course. The number of American jurisdictions that have abolished the death penalty, only to restore it a few years later, is only slightly smaller than the number that have abolished it once and for all (at least up to the present).

II

What lessons can be learned from this brief history? Contemplating the record, some extremist friends of the death penalty are bound to feel frustrated and discouraged. Just look at what they are denied! Nasty and protracted methods of carrying out the death penalty. Mandatory death penalties for murder. A wide variety of nonhomicidal capital crimes. Infliction of the death penalty in public for all to see. Capital punishment flanked by other lawful modes of corporal punishment. Using a method of execution more appropriate than lethal injection to the brutality and horror of the crime. Swift execution after conviction and sentencing, without procedural delays at both the state and federal levels.

The changes wrought by these developments show that the death penalty in America today is but a shadow of its former self; abolitionists are not the only ones likely to believe there is no serious prospect of breathing much life into the practice of capital punishment in the future. As historian Thomas Laqueur has remarked, "The death penalty as it is carried into practice today is like an endangered species brought back from the brink of extinction, a creature from an earlier age making its way in a very different time from when it ruled the earth."[17] Thus it should not be surprising that when abolitionists look at this same record, they draw support from what they see and remain confident that it is just a matter of time before the death penalty in this country is completely abolished.

But is that true? One might equally well argue that the lesson to be drawn from history is rather this: *Each of these reforms has entrenched ever deeper what remains of the death penalty*, which makes what remains of it more resistant to complete repeal. Reform legislation does this by making those who are sentenced to death under its authority seem more deserving of such a penalty. Every step toward greater fairness in death penalty sentencing makes it just that much harder to dismantle what's left. For example, lethal injection surely qualifies as a humane way to put a human being to death. If so, then this method of carrying out lawful executions is all but immune from attack. Of all possible capital crimes, first-degree murder is at the head of everyone's list of crimes that "deserve" the death penalty. Repealing or allowing to fall into desuetude nonhomicidal capital statutes leaves the capital crime of murder standing virtually alone. Shielding from risk of the death penalty all offenders other than those convicted of first-degree murder effectively defines the class of those guilty of the worst crime and so deserving of the severest punishment. (The capital statutes enacted by Congress in the mid-1990s are, with very few exceptions, defined by reference to some form of homicide, e.g., killing a federal witness.) Allowing the death sentence to be issued not by a trial judge but by a fairly drawn panel of ordinary citizens with the discretionary power to sentence the offender to life in prison is democracy in action. Ending the execution of juveniles and of the mentally retarded (rejected by the Supreme Court in 2002) makes executing ordinary adults all the more acceptable, despite evidence that "almost all murderers . . . studied show evidence of brain damage."[18] Eliminating the racist aspects of the death penalty would do no more than make capital punishment an equal opportunity destroyer.

For the past few years, the abolition movement has devoted considerable energy to obtaining a nationwide moratorium on executions. The ostensible purpose has been to make possible a careful study of the practices and procedures governing the administration of the death penalty, with an eye to reducing the risk of error and introducing greater fairness throughout the system. So far the movement has succeeded only in one capital jurisdiction—Illinois—although it claims endorsement from nearly 2,000 organizations and half a hundred city and county jurisdictions.[19] What is it reasonable to expect from the moratorium movement? For one thing, Illinois is unique in the nation in having more persons on death row exonerated in recent years than it has executed. No other state has such an incentive for reform.

Second, the judicially imposed moratorium from 1967 through 1976 enabled the Supreme Court to evaluate the constitutional status of the death penalty and to support major changes in the administration of this punishment. But the moratorium had little or no effect in bringing the public closer to embracing abolition. Third, supporters of the death penalty tend to see the moratorium movement as a stalking horse for abolition. They argue that the proponents of the moratorium are not really interested in improving the administration of the death penalty. Most of the agitation to create a moratorium comes from those who are really interested in using it as a tactic to advance the cause of abolition, and so their efforts are really disingenuous. Finally and most troubling, a widespread moratorium might succeed—that is, end up by introducing various procedural reforms that would give an even more convincing seal of approval to whatever death sentences and executions were imposed under their aegis. (The same problem haunts the Innocence Protection Act, pending in Congress.) Only time will tell whether the friends or the opponents of the death penalty will be happier with the way the moratorium movement unfolds.

III

So much by way of history and its lessons. Let us turn now to look at the current death penalty in the context of our criminal justice system. What we need to see can be neatly described by means of the following set of seven numbers.

1. 22,000
2. 15,000
3. 13,500
4. 10,000
5. 2–4,000
6. 300
7. 55

Each of these numbers is an average annual estimate for the decade of the 1990s.[20] The first is the number of *criminal homicides* reported by the FBI in its category of "murder and non-negligent manslaughter." In the past decade, something more than twenty thousand "murders and non-negligent manslaughters" were recorded each year by the nation's police forces. The second is the number of *arrests* reported by the police of persons charged with criminal homicide. Notice the attrition, from 22,000 to 15,000. (Criminal homicide has always had the highest arrest rate of any felony, yet that rate is only about 65 percent.) The third number estimates the volume of *homicide cases actually prosecuted*, which according to the FBI is about 90 percent of all those arrested for this crime. The fourth number is an estimate of the number of *homicide convictions*, again about two-thirds of those arrested and nearly three-fourths of those prosecuted. The fifth number—2–4,000—is a rough estimate of the so-called *death-eligible defendants*, that is, all and only the offenders convicted of first-degree murder who are at risk of a death sentence because their crime in a death penalty jurisdiction involved one or more "aggravating circumstances" on which the jury could decide to rest its decision to impose a death sentence. Here the attrition is considerable, a drop of about two-thirds of the remaining cases at the higher end of the rough estimate (80 percent at the lower end). The sixth number, the average of *death sentences* annually, is about one-tenth of the death-eligible defendants. In other words, nine out of ten convicted defendants who are death-eligible do not get sentenced to death. And the final number is the average number of *executions* per year. At this point the attrition is nothing short of remarkable: Out of more than twenty thousand criminal homicides per year (assuming roughly one victim for each offender), only 300 perpetrators are sentenced to death and only 55 are actually executed.

With these numbers before us, let us ask how they might be interpreted by friends and opponents of the death penalty.

The friends divide into two groups. The angrier and more vindictive see these figures and argue: We must reduce the number of those murdered, and the best way to do that is to use the death penalty more frequently, much more frequently. For of course there will be little or no special deterrent effect with such a tiny fraction of murderers executed—only one out of about 500. Likewise, we must protect society and express our horror at murder by executing as many of the death-eligible defendants as we can. The two aspects of prevention—individual incapacitation and general deterrence—require no less. And for the same reasons we must increase the number of arrests, the number prosecuted, the number convicted, and especially the number sentenced to death—now, only one out of about 70.

To put it bluntly, these desires are doomed to frustration. For a variety of reasons, the criminal justice system is not capable of making the kinds of changes these extreme friends of the death penalty would like. Only those with little or no familiarity with death penalty jurisprudence can hold out hopes for such a complete reversal of present practice. I note with satisfaction that Judge Kozinski himself has pointed this out in recent writings on the subject.[21]

Those in the other group favoring the death penalty—I think it includes Judge Kozinski, Judge Cassell, and prosecutor Marquis—look at these numbers very differently. They argue: The death penalty was never intended to apply to *all* murderers, but only to the worst. What these numbers and their attrition show is that the criminal justice system is winnowing out the worst from the bad. Three hundred or so of the worst murderers are sentenced to death each year on average—that sounds about right. Half a hundred are executed on average each year—that, too, looks about right (give or take adding another dozen or so). And we know that these are the worst murderers because in every case since the mid-1970s the death sentence rests on the jury's having found one or more "aggravating" circumstances, as defined by statute, and no "mitigating" circumstances (or at least none weightier). Complacent defenders of the death penalty see little if any reason for introducing extensive or fundamental changes in the system; they recognize the insuperable obstacles to significant reduction in the attrition at each step of the way. Probably most defenders of the death penalty today in America hold views more or less like those portrayed here.

Death penalty supporters of this sort are also bound to be disappointed, if they confront political reality candidly. Absolutely essential to their argument is the belief that the system really does segregate the worst from the bad and that it does so in a manner that respects fundamental justice for the accused offender and the convicted prisoner. Yet no one acquainted with the facts can rest comfortably in such a belief. This is especially true where racial factors enter, as they typically do in the Death Belt firmly buckled across the South. On this subject I refer and defer again to my colleagues in this symposium, Bright and Stevenson. Here, I will add only three observations.

First, some states—Texas in particular—base a death sentence (to quote from the Texas statute) on the jury's decision that "the defendant would commit criminal acts of violence that would constitute a continuing threat to society." How a jury is able to make such a prediction, on which their choice of punishment depends, is a mystery. Making reliable predictions of future dangerousness is all but impossible, if we can believe several decades of social science research.[22] (The late law professor Charles Black, Jr., made the difficulty of doing so abundantly clear a generation ago in his superb monograph, *Capital Punishment: The Inevitability of Caprice and Mistake* [1981]). And isn't the whole idea—punishing someone not for what he has done but for what a dozen laypersons predict he will do—morally objectionable? Second, in a few states—Florida is the prime example—the jury's sentencing decision is only advisory; and the trial judge is empowered to decide the sentence by reference to whatever considerations he deems appropriate regardless of whether they are defined by statute as aggravating circumstances. More than a few convicts whom the jury wanted sentenced to life in prison were instead sentenced to death by the arbitrary authority of the trial judge.[23] Third, most death penalty jurisdictions cite as an aggravating circumstance that the murder was "heinous, depraved, and cruel"—a vague criterion that almost any murder could be said to satisfy. The truth is, as the extensive research conducted by the Capital Jury Project has shown, that the statutory guidelines enacted since *Furman* and ratified in *Gregg* are seldom fully understood by the trial jury; even when they are, the jurors often disregard them and sentence the defendant to death or to prison for whatever reasons they find compelling.[24]

Let us turn now to see how abolitionists view the set of seven numbers cited above. They, too, divide into two classes.

One group believes that the elusive goal of complete abolition is out of reach at present but will soon be grasped. In their view the moratorium movement is a vehicle through which friends and nominal supporters of the death penalty will see the error of their ways, as they discover the virtual impossibility of the task they have undertaken to satisfy the mandate of the moratorium. These opponents of the death penalty are cheered by the knowledge that the rest of the civilized world openly and increasingly condemns our death penalty practices, pointing out that such practices violate international human rights law.[25] They notice the unsavory company we keep in continuing to use the death penalty—China, Iran, Saudi Arabia, the Democratic Republic of the Congo—nations whose human rights record leaves much to be desired. These critics note with approval the way foreign countries refuse to extradite persons accused in the United States of a capital crime unless there is prior assurance that the prosecution will not seek the death penalty.[26] They note with satisfaction the steady progress made in persuading the states and federal government to prohibit execution of the mentally retarded and of persons who were juveniles (under 18) at the time of their crime. In their view, support for abolition is growing in the nation's religious communities, especially in the Roman Catholic Church, where the papal encyclical, *Evangelium Vitae* (1995), strongly argues for ending executions. Finally, they believe that the general public has absorbed the message that our death penalty system is bound to make errors, not all of them caught in time, some of them fatal, and that the marginal gains of a death penalty system—if any—are outweighed by the risks.

Others who also oppose the death penalty (I include myself here) are less optimistic. We see the posture of the current Supreme Court as a massive and virtually insurmountable obstacle. We believe that nationwide repeal of the death penalty depends on the Court, since neither the executive nor the legislative branch of the federal government has the authority to overturn state death penalty legislation. We believe that it's bad enough that the Court should tolerate the procedural abuses and disregard for equal protection so well described by Bright and Stevenson (see their remarks later in this volume). It is even worse that the Court should embrace the idea (as it did in *Gregg*) that there is no substantive objection to the death penalty on constitutional grounds because this form of punishment is not "cruel and unusual" in the sense of those words as used in the Constitution. Nationwide abolition is simply inconceivable without a change of heart and mind (and personnel) on the Court. As for the recent shift of public opinion on the death penalty, the drop in 2001 from nearly 80 percent support to 63 percent[27] is surely welcome, but it is too recent to be a clear-cut trend. Finally, the death penalty is deeply entrenched in Texas, Florida, and other states of the Old Confederacy, where lynching was once the preferred way to deal with black men accused of the murder or rape of a white female. No one has any idea how the death penalty in these states—where the vast proportion of all death sentences and executions in the United States takes place—is to be ended or even seriously reduced in the near future.

The anti-death penalty movement led by the lawyers in the mid-1960s was a direct product of the civil rights movement of the late 1950s and early 1960s. Perhaps there is further affinity between the two. After the Supreme Court ruled in *Plessy v. Ferguson* (1896) that "separate but equal" was constitutionally permissible, it took half a century before the Court reversed itself in *Brown v. Board of Education* (1954), with the argument that separate was "inherently" unequal. If abolition of the death penalty by the Supreme Court is on a similar schedule, perhaps we abolitionists can hope for a favorable ruling from the Court, overturning the decision in *Gregg* and allied cases (1976) in another two or three decades.

IV

Abolitionists attacking the death penalty typically employ a wide variety of moral arguments. The value of human life, respect for human life—these norms play a decisive role for some. Others object on the ground that the state has no right to kill any of its prisoners. Some oppose it because they regard it as an affront to human dignity. Many others object on the ground that the death penalty violates the offender's right to life. Some will insist that it is the unfair administration of the death penalty, and the impossibility of making it fair, that warrants abolishing it. Still others insist that the risk of executing the innocent outweighs whatever alleged benefits the death penalty provides, or that, all things considered, a policy of selective death sentences has less overall social utility—in particular, it squanders scarce resources—than does a policy of no death sentencing. Or (to borrow language from the Supreme Court) "evolving standards of decency" condemn the death penalty today, even if they did not a century ago. Some oppose the death penalty not so much for what it does to the offender as for what it reveals about *us* in tolerating, not to say advocating, such killings. These and perhaps other moral concerns can be connected in various ways; they show that there is much to think about from the moral point of view in evaluating and criticizing the death penalty.[28]

This occasion does not present the opportunity to develop an adequate review and critique of all the arguments implied by these varied moral norms. For that reason I propose to present and discuss only one argument—the one I now think is the best argument against the death penalty. Its lineage can be traced back to the little book by Cesare Beccaria, *An Essay on Crimes and Punishments* (1764), the tract usually credited with inspiring the abolition movement during the period of the Enlightenment in Europe and a version of which reappears in the recent papal encyclical, *Evangelium Vitae*. The argument rests on a fundamental principle that neither Beccaria nor the Pope explicitly formulated: Given a compelling state interest in some goal or purpose, the government in a constitutional democracy built on the principle of equal freedom and human rights for all must use the least restrictive means sufficient to achieve that goal or purpose. More expansively, the principle (a near-neighbor to what students of constitutional law would recognize as the principle of "substantive due process") holds that if individual privacy, liberty, and autonomy (or other fundamental values) are to be invaded and deliberately violated, it must be because the end to be achieved is of undeniable importance to society, and no less severe interference will suffice. For convenience of reference, let us henceforth call this the Minimal Invasion argument against the death penalty and the principle that generates it the Minimal Invasion principle.

The Minimal Invasion argument is unlike most arguments against the death penalty in two important respects. First, it does not rely on such familiar values as the right to life, values that either are not widely shared or are widely shared but at the cost of excessive vagueness. Second, the argument (with the exception of the debate over deterrence) does not hinge on establishing the usual faults that plague this form of punishment as actually administered. Thus, this argument sidesteps worries about the risk of executing the innocent, the arbitrariness of death sentencing and executions, the demonstrable effects of racial bias (especially in the South), the evident vulnerability of the poor, the unavoidable economic costs that exceed those of imprisonment. Opponents of the death penalty are often challenged to declare where they would stand were these flaws to be corrected. Despite the current interest in reforming our several systems of capital punishment, it is doubtful whether all or even most of the reforms so far proposed will be adopted. In any case, the Minimal Invasion argument does not depend on such contingencies. While it is a far cry from a philosopher's a priori argument, it comes close to sharing with such arguments immunity to a wide variety of factual considerations.

If an argument against the death penalty is to be constructed around the Minimal Invasion principle, at least three further propositions must be accepted. First, punishment for crime must be judged to be a legitimate practice in society under a constitution such as ours. Second, the death penalty by its very nature must be judged to be more severe, invasive, and irremediable than the alternative of some form of long-term imprisonment. Third, the death penalty must be judged not to play a necessary role in securing public safety either by way of general deterrence or specific incapacitation. If these three propositions are true, as I think they are, then in conjunction with the principle with which we began they lead to the conclusion that we ought to abolish the death penalty for all crimes and all offenders. Restating this argument in semi-formal style, this is what we get:

The principle. Invasions by the government of an individual's privacy, liberty, and autonomy (or other fundamental value) are justified only if no less invasive practice is sufficient to achieve an important social goal.

1. Punishment is justified only if it is necessary as a means to some socially valid end.
2. The death penalty is more severe—more invasive—than long-term imprisonment.
3. Long-term imprisonment is sufficient as an invasion of individual liberty, privacy, and autonomy (and other fundamental values) to achieve valid social goals.

4. Society ought to abolish any lawful practice that imposes more violation of individual liberty, privacy, or autonomy (or other fundamental value) when it is known that a less invasive practice is available and is sufficient.

The conclusion. Society ought to abolish the death penalty.

There's the argument. What can be said on behalf of the truth of each of its premises? Consider first the Minimal Invasion principle (and its corollary, step [4]). How much defense does it require? Surely it is clear that only extreme socialists, fascists, theocrats, or other totalitarians who for various reasons want to extend state power and intervention into the lives of citizens as far as possible will quarrel with this principle. Liberals and conservatives alike, who accept the basic tenets of constitutional democracy and believe in human rights, should readily embrace it.[29] The only issue calling for further discussion among these supporters is whether this principle might ever conflict with other principles worthier of respect in certain cases, so that it must yield to them. What might such an incompatible but superior principle be? What sort of case might arise where such a conflict occurs? A fuller account of the rationale behind this principle would require us to connect it with more fundamental principles of social justice, a topic that cannot be pursued here. As for the three other steps in the argument, each warrants a closer look.

The first premise. Affirming the legitimacy of a system of punishment poses no problem for supporters of the death penalty nor for any but a few of its opponents. No one disputes that public security—protection against criminal victimization—is a salient value and that intervention by government into the behavior of its citizens to achieve that goal is warranted. But pursuit of such a goal is subject to constraints. Not every imaginable weapon to fight crime is morally permissible. Principles of various sorts (e.g., due process of law) restrict the tactics of intervention. These constraints to the side, as things stand, society needs recourse to punitive methods as a necessary condition of public safety.

This is not, however, because punishment is an end in itself; it is because we know of no less invasive responses to individual behavior sufficient as a means to achieve the purpose. If we did, then it would be difficult and perhaps impossible to defend punishment as a morally permissible practice.[30] After all, punishment by its very nature involves deliberately inflicting deprivations and hardships on persons that, if inflicted by private citizens, would be crimes. So punishment needs to be justified, and the only justification available is that it is a necessary means to a fundamental social goal. For present purposes, then, we can say that there is little dispute over the truth of the first proposition.

The second premise. Few will deny the greater brutality and violence of the death penalty when compared to imprisonment. From time to time one hears a friend of the death penalty—and even on occasion some of its enemies—claiming that life in prison is a much more severe punishment than death. Beccaria and his English admirer, Jeremy Bentham (1748–1832), both pioneering abolitionists, believed that life in prison involved more suffering than a few moments on the gallows. I think it is sufficient by way of a reply to point out that those in the best position to know behave in a manner that suggests otherwise.

Few death row prisoners try to commit suicide and fewer succeed. Few death row prisoners insist that all appeals on their behalf be dropped. Few convicted murderers sentenced to life in prison declare years later that they wish they had been sentenced instead to death and executed. Few if any death row prisoners refuse clemency if it is offered to them. No doubt prison life can be made unbearable and hideous; no doubt death row can be managed by the authorities in an inhumane fashion. But none of this is necessary. No doubt not all life-term prisoners find ways to make their imprisonment something more than an inhumane endurance test. So it should hardly come as a surprise that the vast majority of friends of the death penalty as well as its opponents believe that death is worse than imprisonment. This is why its opponents want to abolish it—and why its supporters want to keep it. So we can accept the second proposition without further ado.

The third premise. The third proposition affirms that whatever the legitimate purposes of punishment are, imprisonment serves them as well as or better than the death penalty. This proposition rests on a variety of kinds of empirical evidence, ranging from statistical research on deterrence, the behavior in prison and on parole of convicted murderers not sentenced to death and executed, and above all on the experience of jurisdictions such as Michigan that have gone without the death penalty for decades.

Here is what the record shows: There is no evidence that prison officials, guards, or visitors in prisons where there is no death penalty are more at risk than are their counterparts in the death penalty states. There is no evidence that residents of abolition jurisdictions are at greater risk of murderous victimization than are residents in the death penalty jurisdictions. (The District of Columbia in recent years has had a very high homicide rate and is an abolition jurisdiction; but there is no research that connects the one fact with the other. Most other abolition jurisdictions have a noticeably lower homicide rate than do neighboring death penalty jurisdictions.) To be sure, some convicted murderers commit another murder while in prison or after release— the U.S. Bureau of Justice Statistics reports that 9 percent of those currently on death row had a previous homicide conviction.[31] But not all of these recidivist murderers were guilty in their first homicide of a death-eligible murder. For these murderers, their second homicide could not have been prevented by inflicting the death penalty on them for the first homicide, since their first homicide was not death-eligible. Furthermore, there is no way to predict in advance which convicted murderers are likely to recidivate; the predictions of future dangerousness are plagued with false positives. If we could make accurate and reliable predictions of which prisoners would be dangerous in the future, these offenders could be kept under confinement, just as a typhoid carrier may be quarantined as a public health menace. The only way to prevent such recidivism would be to execute *every* convicted murderer—a policy that is politically unavailable and morally indefensible. Today's defenders of the death penalty must accept a pick-and-choose system of death sentences and executions, with all the adverse effects—as they see it—that such a system has on prevention and retribution.

It is also true that opponents of the death penalty who want to rest their case on the argument under discussion would be vulnerable to evidence—if there were any—showing that the death penalty is a better deterrent than imprisonment. Were there such evidence, opponents would have to rely on some other argument. (I have not claimed that the Minimal Invasion argument is the only argument for abolition; I claim only that I find it the most persuasive.[32]) But since there is so little reason to suppose that the death penalty is ever a marginally superior deterrent over imprisonment, or that such superiority (if any) can be detected by the currently available methods of social science, this "what-if" counterargument can be put to the side and disregarded. (Below, I return to the issue of deterrence.)

With worries about prevention, deterrence, and incapacitation behind us (for the moment), what might we reasonably expect to be the public response in quarters where the death penalty currently has wide support? Is there reason to believe that if the death penalty were abolished, the police would take to administering curbstone justice and the public would revolt? Would the clamor of surviving family members of murder victims force the authorities to restore the death penalty? Would outspoken abolitionists become targets for violent rage, as have some doctors in abortion clinics? Nothing of the sort has happened in any current abolition jurisdiction. However, given the utter lack of political leadership on all aspects of the death penalty in states in the Deep South, where the death penalty has been so conspicuously used, I must admit to some uneasiness over what might happen if Texas were told—say, by a Supreme Court ruling—that it could no longer use the death penalty. The heirs of those who plastered the South in the 1950s with billboards shouting "Impeach Earl Warren" would rise to the occasion and denounce whatever political leadership brought about abolition. Fundamentalist Christians, Mormons, and others who have persuaded themselves that the Bible decrees the death penalty for murder pose a somewhat different problem. How members of these religious groups—clergy and laity, concentrated in (but by no means confined to) the Bible Belt across the South—would behave is far from obvious.

The upshot is that the third premise in the argument under discussion is reasonably supported by the available facts; and that suffices to prove the conclusion.

V

Nevertheless, many friends of the death penalty will not be persuaded by my argument. They will advance at least two objections, one empirical and the other conceptual and normative. First, they will insist on the superiority of the death penalty as a deterrent. Second, they will object that my argument simply ignores a crucial conceptual element and normative principle that, when properly taken into account, leads to a different conclusion.

As to the first, they will point to a quarter century of research by econometricians, pioneered by Isaac Ehrlich in the mid-1970s; continued by one of his students, Stephen Layson in the mid-1980s; and recently revived by other econometricians.[33] Judge Cassell confidently directs our attention to this line of research, but he seems unaware of its well-known weaknesses. First, the Layson and Ehrlich research has been thoroughly criticized (some would say discredited) in public print. Layson has made no effort at reply, to the best of my knowledge. Second, the new deterrence research (in the form available on the Web, as of early 2003) fails to take into account all the major criticisms directed at the earlier research. To trust those who currently advocate a measurable deterrent effect from executions simply ignore the trenchant criticisms of the very idea of trying to use multiple regression analysis to shed light on how individual would-be murderers behave. As this critique has been widely publicized and is easily available,[34] purporting to show a measurable deterrent effect in favor of the death penalty is simply to ignore the trenchant criticism of the very idea of trying to use methods of multiple regression analysis to shed light on how individual would-be murderers behave. One can only speculate why it is so conspicuous by its absence in the discussions by the econometricians on which Judge Cassell relies. It is not I but Nobel Laureate economist Lawrence R. Klein who said "we see too many plausible explanations of [Ehrlich's] finding a deterrent effect other than the theory that capital punishment deters murder."[35] What Klein said in 1978 remains true today. Criminologists William C. Bailey and Ruth D. Peterson have this to say after evaluating 60 published articles on the deterrence question: "The available evidence remains 'clear and abundant' that, as practiced in the United States, capital punishment is not more effective than imprisonment in deterring murder."[36] I predict that the latest research now available will not cause us to alter this conclusion.

Third, the econometric argument for a deterrent effect entirely misses the fundamental point. The question that defenders of the death penalty need to answer is not "Does the death penalty deter?" Common sense assures us that punishments generally serve to deter some persons from some crimes on some occasions. There is no reason to think that the death penalty is an exception. As for measuring how much it deters, as econometricians try to do, that is a side issue. Answering the question above would be dispositive only if opponents of the death penalty favored *no* punishment for capital crimes. But of course they don't favor no punishment (with the exception, perhaps, of some pacificists). The question that death penalty advocates need to answer is this: "Does the death penalty deter *as well as or better than* imprisonment?" To date, no one has even tried to determine the extent to which imprisonment is a deterrent to murder. For all we know, it is as good a deterrent as death, or even better. For all we know, the alleged deterrent effect detected by econometric methods is owing to increases in the use of long-term imprisonment concurrent with executions. Defenders of the death penalty who want to rest their case in whole or in part on the alleged deterrent effect of the death penalty at best refute those abolitionists who think (erroneously) that the death penalty never deters. They leave untouched those abolitionists who think there is no evidence that the death penalty is marginally a better deterrent than executions.

But for the sake of the argument, let us suppose that the death penalty as currently employed does have a marginally superior deterrent effect. Such an effect is of little use in defending the death penalty because the supposed benefit is obtained at an unacceptable cost. The cost comes in the many ways our death penalty system is dysfunctional. The latest study by James S. Liebman and his associates documents this conclusion in alarming detail. Perhaps their most disturbing finding was that the more a jurisdiction uses the death penalty, the greater the likelihood that it will make mistakes—notably, the mistake of convicting the innocent or the mistake of sentencing to death offenders whose crimes should not have made them death-eligible. Everyone agrees that the deterrent effect of a penalty is a function of the frequency with which it is employed; Liebman's research shows that the more courts strive for a deterrent effect by increasing the frequency of death sentences, the more likely they are to err in their judgments and sentences.[37] We have no right to secure a benefit for some (innocents protected by superior marginal deterrence), *knowing* that we do so by methods that impose injustice on others—defendants who may not be guilty (or not guilty of first-degree murder) and whose guilt is determined by violations of due process and equal protection of the law.

Today, would-be defenders of the death penalty no longer rely, as they once did, mainly on the claim of superior deterrence. And that is just as well. Quite apart from the difficulties just discussed in defending the death penalty on grounds of deterrence, those who rely on the principle that severe punishments are justified by their superior deterrent and incapacitative effects are implicitly invited to go further. If death deters more than imprisonment, then death preceded by torture presumably deters more than death alone. If so, on what ground is the defender of the death penalty able to resist embracing torture as well as death? Surely, all sides agree that morality and politics require that there be some upper bound to the permissible severity of punishments no matter what their deterrent effect might be. The dispute is not over whether there is such a limit, but where to place that limit and why. The Minimal Invasion argument provides a reasonable solution to that problem. Preferring the death penalty because of its allegedly superior deterrent effects does not.

VI

In place of deterrence, now that murder has become virtually the only capital crime in the United States, the principal defense of the death penalty is retribution: "Murderers deserve to die," we are told. Accordingly, the second objection to the Minimal Invasion argument is that it completely ignores the role of retribution in a system of punishment, and so ignores the proper, even unique, role that the death penalty plays in providing appropriate retribution for the gravest of wrongs: murder. I think these objections are misguided. First, punishment in any case is a retributive act, insofar as the only persons deemed eligible for punishment are persons judged to be guilty of a crime and thought to be deserving of punishment because of their guilt. A system of inflicting deprivations on persons in the name of punishment that lacked this retributive feature would be a danger to us all.

Second, I do not believe that it is rational to assign as one of the legitimate goals of a system of punishment the exaction of retribution, in some special fashion or further degree that goes beyond the inherently retributive nature of any system of punishment, as described above. Thus, life imprisonment for murder is every bit as retributive as the death penalty for murder, even if it is less severe. Its failure to imitate the crime does not make it less retributive. It provides no support for the notion that a lawful punishment of death could wipe out or cancel the lawless wrongdoing in murder. The doctrine of punishment as cancellation or annulment of wrongdoing has had its distinguished supporters (notably, Hegel), but I do not believe it will withstand scrutiny. No act of punishment as such can undo the harm of the crime; and any plausible punishment suffices to display (and in that sense, annul) the wrongness of the crime. Annulling the crime by proper punishment in a more literal sense might work in some cases— for example, where a thief is punished by being required to return what he stole and in addition to compensate the owner for his trouble. But neither death nor imprisonment can serve in this way to annul a murder.

I will not quarrel with appeal to a general principle of desert: "Wrongdoers deserve to be punished." But by itself, this principle provides no defense of the death penalty; it is fully satisfied by a lesser punishment, such as imprisonment. The proposition that "murderers deserve to die" obviously does support the death penalty, but it does so by essentially begging the question. Why do murderers deserve to die when rapists do not deserve to be raped (or do they? and by whom?)? Why do murderers deserve to die when we haven't the faintest idea what punishment traitors or embezzlers or kidnappers deserve? Retributive considerations rightly tell us *who* deserves to be punished—it is the guilty. But it does not tell us *what* their punishment ought to be. Relying on some version of *lex talionis* is of no help in building a systematic and comprehensive schedule of punishments for crimes.

We could safely and sensibly say that offenders deserve whatever punishment the law provides. But that would land us in the awkward position of maintaining that murderers in Michigan deserve life in prison, but next door in Indiana they deserve death. What they deserve today may turn out not to be what they deserved yesterday, or tomorrow. What we need to know is not what the law provides by way of "deserved" punishment, but what the principles of morality tell us offenders deserve as their punishment. This is precisely what our principles fail to tell us in anything like a uniform and nonarbitrary manner. The attempt to rescue the death penalty for murder as an exception just begs the question.

A similar conclusion is reached if we invoke another retributive principle: "The graver the crime, the greater the punishment deserved." No doubt some such principle of proportionality will be incorporated into any reasonable theory of punishment. By itself, however, this principle does not defend the death penalty. If murder is the gravest crime, then under this principle it warrants the severest punishment. But that punishment could surely be (as it is in the typical abolition jurisdiction) some form of long-term imprisonment. Other schemes of trying to make the punishment fit the crime have also been developed by philosophers in recent years, but without conspicuous success.[38]

I conclude that defenders of retribution face a trilemma. Conceived after the fashion of *lex talionis*, retribution does not yield a coherent and comprehensive system of punishment. Understood as a necessary feature of any system of punishment, it is trivially satisfied by whatever punishment we decree for murder. Singled out as a requirement for the punishment of murder, it is arbitrary and begs the question.

Why life imprisonment is thought to be inadequate retribution for the crime of murder is far from clear. Are we to believe that the many jurisdictions in this country and worldwide that have enacted laws repudiating the death penalty have done so without noticing that they thereby have embraced an inadequately retributive punishment? Are they to be judged to lack a proper sense of the value of innocent human life by their unwillingness to put guilty lives to death? Are American defenders of the death penalty prepared to pronounce such judgment on the English, the French, the Spaniards, the Italians, the Canadians, the Mexicans, and dozens of other peoples around the world? "Inadequate retribution" seems to me to be little more than a euphemism for punishment not as severe as the complainant desires.

There is a certain irony that retributivist defenders of the death penalty tend to overlook. Deserved retribution as punishment presupposes that the offender is fully responsible for his crime. In the United States we currently have several juveniles on death row, yet few of us are prepared to argue that juveniles are always fully responsible for the harms they cause. We also regularly execute offenders who suffer from various forms of incapacitating mental illness, disability, or retardation. (Remember Rickey Ray Rector in Arkansas in 1992, who in all seriousness during his last meal asked the guards to set aside some of his dessert, so that he could have it "later"?) If retribution is such a crucial and fundamental consideration in shaping the punishment a convicted criminal deserves, why don't retributivists use their theory to protest the execution of the young and the abnormal offenders, as they do to demand the execution of adult offenders who are normal by their standards? One is tempted to conclude either that retributivists do not take the consequences of their own theory very seriously or that they are prepared to be wildly inconsistent in its applications.

Moreover, if it is true (as some have persuasively argued) that a retributive theory of punishment requires us to impute to society no small responsibility for the violence, child abuse, and negligence that provides the context in which young men (especially) grow up in our ghettos, then it may be that even normal adult murderers do not deserve to be executed. If, as this reasoning implies, murderers themselves are victims first and offenders only later, then our entire criminal justice system is badly in need of a radical overhaul. Nothing of the required sort will be accomplished by executing two or three hundred murderers each year.[39]

VII

Unquestionably, the killers who most trouble us and who are first and foremost believed to deserve the death penalty are those who commit recidivist murder (such as Gary Gilmore, executed in Utah in 1977), or serial murder (such as John Wayne Gacy, executed in Illinois in 1994), or multiple murder (such as Timothy McVeigh, executed in 2001, having killed 168 people in Oklahoma). Cases such as these pose the greatest challenge to abolitionists. On occasion I have said that if it were up to me, I would be willing to let defenders of the death penalty execute killers of this stripe, provided they were willing to have resentenced to life imprisonment all other death row convicts. This would mean in the United States today that out of some 3,700 prisoners currently on our death rows, all but a tiny fraction, perhaps no more than 2 percent, would evade the executioner's summons. I would consider that a major gain, even though I favor complete abolition. My point in this hypothetical concession is to bring out how unusual the recidivist, serial, or multiple murderer is and to that extent how unreasonable it is to focus argument over the death penalty on such cases; the vast majority of death row convicts present a very different picture—as the sample of cases recounted by Bright and Stevenson show. It is as absurd as trying to shed light on the merits of the death penalty in the United States by insisting that the convicted Nazi war criminals at Nuremberg in 1945 deserved to be executed (as many of them were); there are no Hitlers or Görings or Himmlers on America's death rows. Nevertheless, something needs to be said here about the McVeigh case and others (*horribile dictu*) that could arise to present a similar challenge.

What can a dedicated abolitionist say about the death sentence and execution of McVeigh? Surely, there is something to the comment made by many, including Judge Kozinski, that McVeigh is a poster boy for the death penalty. Yet those who favor complete abolition are unwilling to make an exception for McVeigh or for others like him—notably terrorists of the sort who destroyed the World Trade Center and damaged the Pentagon on 9/11/01. On what grounds can abolitionists argue against their execution? What good would it do to fail to execute such offenders and instead to confine them behind bars for the rest of their lives?

Let us put aside a variety of lesser considerations that came to the surface in the McVeigh case: the inequity of sentencing McVeigh to death and his co-defendant to life in prison; the lost opportunity to learn from McVeigh, had he been sentenced to prison, more about how he committed the crime, his motivation, and his associates; the denial to the defense of a mass of documents in the government's custody bearing on the case; the millions of dollars spent on prosecuting this federal death penalty case; and the transformation of his execution in the federal prison at Terre Haute, Indiana, into a multimedia entertainment event. (Similar considerations apply to other terrorists whom we might arrest, try, and convict.)

Instead, let us notice first the harm that his execution did. McVeigh's execution is a perfect example of a violation of the Minimal Invasion principle. If that principle is sound and thus deserves our respectful compliance, then this execution is a thumb in the eye. There is no reason to doubt that McVeigh could have been kept in safe confinement indefinitely had the government wanted to do that. There is also no reason to believe that other violent ideologues will refrain from using weapons of mass violence because they have been deterred by the example of McVeigh's execution. There is no argument to support that killing McVeigh provides adequate retribution—how could killing him possibly serve as adequate retribution for his murdering scores and severely injuring dozens more? Retribution, incapacitation, deterrence—none was fostered by executing McVeigh. The harm that executing him did in the face of these facts is the harm of miseducating the public, obscuring the truth, cultivating a violent outlet for public anger, and fostering a pattern of official government conduct that climaxes in deliberately inflicting death without necessity.

Those who favored the execution of McVeigh, including Attorney General John Ashcroft, pointed to the "closure" the execution would give the hundreds of bereaved survivors, a consolation and assuagement for them that lifelong imprisonment for McVeigh (they believe) could never provide. May I suggest that the evidence shows that closure sought by this route is rarely found? Carroll L. Pickett, chaplain to death row prisoners in Huntsville, Texas, informs us that his encounters with survivors seeking closure convinced him that "almost without exception . . . the feeling of relief so long anticipated was not realized."[40] The same lesson is taught in vivid detail by Sister Helen Prejean, in her powerful book, *Dead Man Walking* (1993). She recounted to journalist Garry Wills the way prosecutors urge surviving family members to attend the trial: "They learn new details of the crime, and with each new turn of the trial and its aftermath the media call them to get a reaction." Wills commented sardonically, "This is less like healing than like tearing scabs open again and again."[41] In her book, Prejean relates the experience of one victim's father who witnessed the execution of Robert Willie in Louisiana in 1984. "He had walked away from the execution chamber with his rage satisfied but his heart empty."[42] Hardly a lesson in closure of the sort anyone would seriously recommend.

What is so distinctive about the McVeigh case is not just the magnitude of the harm he caused; the publicity surrounding the crime and the way it was motivated by McVeigh's antigovernmental ideology helped make it a crime unlike others. His death at the hands of the government he professed to despise could in time make him a martyr to the cause, another feature of this case that illustrates how atypical it was. Of course no one knows the consequences that will accrue from McVeigh's execution, but it is a sobering thought that by executing McVeigh, the government could have helped turn a poster boy for the death penalty into a poster boy for the thousands of his ideological companions on the violent anarchist fringe who seek a role model.

What good, then, could have come from not executing McVeigh? Abstractly, the abolitionist can say that it is the good of doing the right thing. That it *is* the right thing to do is presumably settled on other grounds, such as those offered in the Minimal Invasion argument. Concretely, however, it is quite difficult to specify with precision any good that might come out of sparing McVeigh (and the few others who might be said to be like him) from death. Murderers serving a life term in prison have been known to make major contributions to educating other prisoners, helping them draft legal documents, cooling racial tensions, and so forth. Is it reasonable to have hoped that McVeigh behind bars might have made comparable contributions to the welfare of others? I do not know enough about him or the prison conditions that might have been imposed on him to speak to the point, but I do know that it is impossible to rule out all such future developments. Were such good things to take place, would they make amends for the harm done? Of course not. Good deeds do not cancel out evil deeds in any such tit-for-tat fashion. McVeigh was a person, as we are, even if he is unlike us in having committed a terrible and unforgivable crime. And being a person, he ought to be treated by us not solely in light of his awful crime. He may not deserve better from us, but even so we ought not to be guided solely—in this case or others—by reference to what punishment we think he deserves for his crime.

Desert, in any case, is not the only morally relevant consideration in determining how we ought to treat others. To conclude that we had to execute McVeigh because that is what he deserved requires us to show that there were no other weighty moral considerations against giving him what he deserved. But supporters of deserved death rarely if ever even try to show this; it is a conspicuous piece of argument missing from the usual philosophies of punishment. If abolitionists invoke the Minimal Invasion argument at this point, they will say that retribution is not an essential feature of the purposes or goals of a system of punishment—except in the uncontroversial sense of the term noted earlier, to the effect that all punishments are retributive. The punishment that McVeigh or others like him *deserve* does not tell us how we *ought* to punish him. We learn that—what we ought to do to him by way of punishment—by figuring out what is the minimally invasive punishment sufficient to achieve the goal of public safety. Killing killers is not minimally invasive.

NOTES

1. Victoria Schneider and John Oritz Smykla, "A Summary Analysis of Executions in the United States, 1608–1987: The Espy File," in Robert H. Bohm, ed., *The Death Penalty in America: Current Research*, Cincinnati, Oh., 1991, p. 4.

2. Louis P. Masur, *Rites of Execution: Capital Punishment and the Transformation of American Culture, 1776–1865*, New York, Oxford University Press, p. 61.

3. E. R. Keedy, "History of the Pennsylvania Statute Creating Degrees of Murder," *University of Pennsylvania Law Review*, 97 (1949), pp. 759–77.

4. Benjamin N. Cardozo, *Law and Literature*, New York, Harcourt, 1931, p. 101.

5. Stuart Banner, *The Death Penalty: An American History*, Cambridge, Mass., Harvard University Press, 2002, p. 25.

6. "There Was a Reason They Outlawed Public Executions," *New York Times*, May 6, 2001, p. wk5.

7. Masur, *Rites of Exectuion*, p. 110.

8. E. J. Dionne Jr., "McVeigh's Punishment Is a Test for All of Us," *Boston Globe*, April 18, 2001, p. A17.

9. *Sumner v. Shuman*, 483 U.S. 66 (1987).

10. See "Symposium: How the Death Penalty Works," *Cornell Law Review*, 83 (1998), pp. 1431–1820; and "Symposium: The Capital Jury Project," *Indiana Law Journal*, 70 (1995), pp. 1033–1270.

11. Elsewhere I have tried to answer that objection; see "Thinking about the Death Penalty as a Cruel and Unusual Punishment," *U. C. Davis Law Review*, 18 (1985), pp. 873–925.

12. James S. Liebman, Jeffrey Fagan, and Valerie West, *A Broken System: Error Rates in Capital Cases, 1973–1995*, New York, Columbia Law School, 2000, pp. 1, 4.

13. Robert Weisberg, "Deregulating Death," *The Supreme Court Review 1983*, p. 395.

14. Banner, *The Death Penalty*, p. 143.

15. H. A. Bedau, ed., *The Death Penalty in America: An Anthology*, New York, Doubleday, 1964, p. 46.

16. See Michael Meltsner, *Cruel and Unusual: The Supreme Court and Capital Punishment*, New York, Random House, 1973.

17. Thomas Laqueur, "Festival of Punishment," *London Review of Books*, October 5, 2000, p. 20

18. Laura Mansnerus, "Damaged Brains and the Death Penalty," *New York Times*, July 7, 2001, p. A15.

19. "Moratorium News," fall 2001, a publication of Equal Justice U.S.A.

20. Each of the first four numbers is larger than it would be if we subtracted the cases that arise in abolition jurisdictions, roughly about one-fifth of those listed here. We might compare the figures in the text with a more accurate set of figures derived from the research of James Liebman et al., *A Broken System*, p. 77. For the 23 years, 1973 through 1995, they report the following national aggregate figures: 331,949 criminal homicides; 300,257 persons arrested; 181,265 cases prosecuted; 118,992 convictions; 5,826 death sentences; and 350 executions. The numbers differ from those in the text but the pattern and magnitude of the attrition does not.

21. Alex Kozinski, "Tinkering with Death," *The New Yorker*, February 10, 1997.

22. See, e.g., John Monahan, "The Prediction of Violent Criminal Behavior," in Alfred Blumstein, Jacqueline Cohen, and Daniel Nagin, eds., *Deterrence and Incapacitation: Estimating the Effects of Criminal Sanctions on Crime Rates*, Washington, D.C., National Academy of Sciences, 1978, pp. 244–66; F. Dutile and C. Foust, *The Prediction of Criminal Violence*, 1987.

23. Michael L. Radelet, "Rejecting the Jury: The Imposition of the Death Penalty in Florida," *U. C. Davis Law Review*, 18 (1985), pp. 1409–33.

24. See "Symposium: The Capital Jury Project," *Indiana Law Journal*, 70 (1995), pp. 1033–1270.

25. See William A. Schabas, *The Abolition of the Death Penalty in International Law*, 2d ed., Cambridge University Press, 1997.

26. See, e.g., John Kifner, "France Seeks Assurance before Extraditing Suspect," *New York Times*, March 31, 2001, p. A13.

27. *ABC World News Tonight*, May 2, 2001.

28. Elsewhere I have discussed some of these issues; see "Abolishing the Death Penalty Even for the Worst Murderers," in Austin Sarat, ed., *The Killing State: Capital Punishment in Law, Politics, and Culture*, New York, Oxford University Press, 1999, pp. 40–59. For a discussion of other moral arguments against the death penalty, see especially Stephen Nathanson, *An Eye for an Eye*, 2d ed., Lanham, Md., Rowman and Littlefield, 2001, and Jeffrey Reiman's contribution to the volume he wrote with Louis Pojman, *The Death Penalty: For and Against*, Lanham, Md., Rowman and Littlefield, 1998.

29. The principle will be found implicitly if not explicitly in John Rawls, *Justice as Fairness*, Cambridge, Mass., Harvard University Press, 2000.

30. I have discussed this issue at greater length elsewhere; see "Punitive Violence and Its Alternatives," in James B. Brady and Newton Garver, eds., *Justice, Law, and Violence*, Philadelphia, Temple University Press, 1991, pp. 193–209.

31. U.S. Department of Justice, Bureau of Justice Statistics, "Capital Punishment 1998," Washington, D.C., 1999, p. 10 U.S. Department of Justice.

32. A strong candidate for an argument equally as concise as but otherwise very different from mine is the "knockdown argument" offered by Stephen Nathanson, *An Eye for an Eye*, p. 175. Here it is, addressed to a death penalty supporter: "You accept justice and respect for human life as fundamental values; the death penalty is inconsistent with these values; therefore, based on your own values, you ought to reject the death penalty."

33. Paul H. Rubin, Hashem Dezhbakhsh, and Joanne Mehlhop, "Capital Punishment and Deterrence: County Level Estimates Using Recent Execution Data," Department of Economics, Emory University, Atlanta, Ga., no date; Hashem Dezhbakhsh, Paul H. Rubin, and Joanna Mehlhop Shepherd, "Does Capital Punishment Have a Deterrent Effect? New Evidence from Post-moratorium Panel Data," *American Law and Economics Review*, forthcoming; H. Nanci Mocan and R. Kaj Gittings, "Pardons, Executions and Homicide," Department of Economics, University of Colorado, Denver, October 2001; and Dale O. Cloninger and Roberto Marchesina, "Execution and Deterrence: A Quasi-controlled Group Experiment," *Applied Economics*, 33 (2001), pp. 569–76.

34. See William C. Bailey and Ruth D. Peterson, "Murder, Capital Punishment, and Deterrence: A Review of the Literature," in H. A. Bedau, ed., *The Death Penalty in America: Current Controversies*, Oxford, New York 1997, pp. 135–61; and Ruth D. Peterson and William C. Bailey, "Is Capital Punishment an Effective Deterrent to Murder? An Examination of Social Science Research," in James R. Acker, Robert M. Bohm, and Charles S. Lanier, eds., *America's Experiment with Capital Punishment*, Durham, N.C., Carolina Academic Press 1998, pp. 157–82.

35. Laurence R. Klein, Brian Forst, and Victor Filatov, "The Deterrent Effect of Capital Punishment: An Assessment of the Estimates," in Alfred Blumstein, Jacqueline

Cohen, and Daniel Nagin, eds., *Deterrence and Incapacitation: Estimating the Effects of Criminal Sanctions on Crime Rates,* Washington, D.C., National Academy of Sciences, 1978, p. 358.

36. Bailey and Peterson, "Murder, Capital Punishment, and Deterrence," p. 155.

37. James S. Liebman et al., *Why There Is so Much Error in Capital Cases, and What Can Be Done about It*, New York, Columbia Law School, February 2002.

38. See, e.g., Michael Davis, *To Make the Punishment Fit the Crime*, Boulder, Colo., 1992; Andrew von Hirsch, *Doing Justice: The Choice of Punishments*, New York, Hill and Wang, 1975.

39. See especially the argument of Jeffrey Reiman, in Louis P. Pojman and Jeffrey Reiman, *The Death Penalty: For and Against*, Lanham, Md., Rowman and Littlefield, 1996, pp. 67–132, 151–63.

40. Carroll L. Pickett, "No Deterrent, No Closure—Just More Victims," *Boston Globe*, April 1, 2001, p. E8.

41. Gary Wills, "The Dramaturgy of Death," *New York Review of Books*, June 21, 2001, p. 10.

42. Helen Prejean, *Dead Man Walking: An Eyewitness Account of the Death Penalty in the United States*, New York, Random House, 1993, p. 226.

3

Why the Death Penalty Is Morally Permissible*

Louis P. Pojman

The death penalty as punishment for the most serious crimes is morally justified. Honest people and philosophers may disagree on these matters, but I will present my reasons for supporting the retention of this practice. I have no illusions about my ability to change the minds of my ardent abolitionist opponents, but I can hope to clear the air of misperceptions and help those with an open mind come to an informed judgment of this crucial matter.

First, let me briefly comment on specific claims in Hugo Bedau's essay "An Abolitionist's Survey of the Death Penalty in America Today."[1] (1) Bedau contends that "today it ought to be impossible not to regard death in the electric chair as 'cruel and unusual punishment' in direct violation of such punishments in the Eighth Amendment in

*Some of the material in the section on deterrence is adapted from my essay "For the Death Penalty" in *The Death Penalty: For and Against* by Louis P. Pojman and Jeffrey Reiman (Rowman & Littlefield, 1998). That book contains a defense of the theory of punishment discussed in this essay. It also includes a fuller defense of my theory of desert. I am indebted to Stephen Kershnar and Michel Levin for comments on an earlier draft of this essay.

the Bill of Rights" (p. 5). Why? I take it that the idea of "cruel and unusual" simply means morally unjustified and unconscionable. If so, we need an argument for this conjunction. I fail to see that death in the electric chair is either "immoral or unconscionable." After all, the criminal has committed a heinous act of violence with malice afore-thought. I would argue that the electric chair, far from being uncon-scionable, is completely justified. Painless lethal injection, which is the process of choice in many states, seems too good for someone who in callous disregard for his victim shed innocent blood. Hanging or the firing squad or a painful electric shock seem more fitting to most acts of murder. (2) Along these same lines, Bedau notes that until the mid-twentieth century many jurisdictions imposed the death penalty for numerous crimes besides murder, including rape, kidnapping, and treason (p. 7). I take it that the implicit argument is that as we become more enlightened and recognize the inherent dignity of human beings, we gradually will narrow the scope of the death penalty until it covers the set of fewer crimes, to the point where it is abolished altogether. I have a different interpretation. We have suffered a loss of confidence in the ability of our society to carry out justice, a failure of nerve. A society that is inured to watching violence in movies and TV but con-demns parents for spanking their children as an act of discipline may not have the inner moral resources to discriminate between morally permissible and impermissible use of force. I suspect that a growing awareness of the sociological influences on criminals has resulted in a tendency to minimize the responsibility of criminals. Child molesters often were molested themselves, abusive people were victims of abuse. "To understand all is to forgive all." There is some truth in these generalizations, but it is a gross fallacy to infer that because we are influenced by our upbringing or heredity, we should not be held re-sponsible for our behavior. A more robust notion of personal respon-sibility might lead us to extend the death penalty to those who grossly violate the public trust, to include CEOs who actively destroyed the pension plans of their employees, as was the case in 2002 with Enron and WorldCom. In 2002 Enron Corporation declared bankruptcy. It announced that thousands of lower-ranking employees would lose their retirement programs, while 29 top executives took in $1.1 billion, selling shares of company stock, with CEO Kenneth Lay scoring $101.4

million. Around the same time, at WorldCom, chief financial officer
Scott Sullivan sold $45.4 million in company stock, quietly shifting $3.9
billion in expenses to make the company look more profitable. The
bubble bursts; the firm declares bankruptcy and lays off 17,000 workers.
The leaders of these large companies probably did more overall harm
to their employees than a murderer. While it is evil to take the life of
one innocent person, it is also grossly evil to destroy the pension plans
of thousands of employees due to greed and dishonesty, while securing
millions of dollars for oneself. The cumulative effect of such deliberate
deception and disregard for one's employees may be worse than that
of the single murder. If the death penalty is an appropriate punishment
for those who commit treason, it is applicable to business executives
who violate the public trust and undermine faith in our economic
system. In applying the death penalty to white collar crimes, we would
be applying it more fairly.[2] The rich, who seldom are tempted to murder, would be subject to the same capital punishment as now is usually
reserved for the poor. Some cases of rape, kidnapping, treason, and
white collar crimes like embezzlement of the savings of elderly and
vulnerable people may well merit the death penalty. Perhaps our an-
cestors erred on the side of being too hard on offenders. We may be
erring in being too soft on them. The goal is to seek the right golden
mean, giving the criminal what he or she deserves.

(3) Bedau quotes with approval Laura Mansnerus's contention that
"almost all murderers . . . studied show evidence of brain damage"
(p. 10). That is too broad a category, hardly a sufficient condition to
abolish punishment. Probably most adults have experienced some
brain damage during their lives brought on by alcohol consumption
and drug use, strokes, injuries to the head, and chemical imbalances.
I read of one study in England showing that many soccer players had
incurred brain damage (presumably brought on by hitting the ball with
their heads). Unless we can establish a correlation between the specific
brain damage and the specific crimes committed, we ought to presume
that people are responsible for their behavior, that including their violent acts. Mansnerus's thesis, if confirmed, would prove too much—
namely, that no one should be punished for murder since such brain-
damaged people cannot be held accountable for their acts. Where we
have evidence of brain damage or impaired ability, such as in the case

of a retarded or (temporarily) insane criminal, we do mitigate or cancel the proposed punishment.

(4) Bedau appeals to Beccaria's principle of Minimal Invasion that given a state interest the government "must use the least restrictive means sufficient to achieve that goal or purpose" (p. 19). Bedau admits that punishment for a crime is a legitimate practice, but opts for the Minimal Invasion principle as a constraint on that punishment. I too agree that we ought to minimize suffering, all things being equal, but sometimes things are not equal, for the criminal may deserve more than a minimal punishment, deserving, in fact, the death penalty. So the Minimal Invasion principle may be overridden in the name of justice. Bedau wants to place a *ceiling* on punitive desert, but there may also be a *floor* on punishment. Sometimes nothing less than harsh punishment is justified. (5) Bedau argues against those like Attorney General John Ashcroft who hold that the death penalty produces closure in the families of the victims. He rightly notes that sometimes it doesn't bring that sense of cathartic relief (p. 33). I agree with Bedau here and do not use the closure argument in my defense, though the families of victims often do express satisfaction that the murderer has been executed. So much the better. But this is not a sufficient argument for the death penalty. I turn now to my case for the death penalty.

A DEFENSE OF THE DEATH PENALTY

Who so sheddeth man's blood, by man shall his blood be shed. (Genesis 9:6)

There is an ancient tradition, going back to biblical times, but endorsed by the mainstream of philosophers, from Plato to Thomas Aquinas, from Thomas Hobbes to Immanuel Kant, Thomas Jefferson, John Stuart Mill, and C. S. Lewis, that a fitting punishment for murder is the execution of the murderer. One prong of this tradition, the *backward-looking* or deontological position, epitomized in Aquinas and Kant, holds that because human beings, as rational agents, have dignity, one who with malice aforethought kills a human being forfeits his right to life and deserves to die. The other, the *forward-looking* or consequentialist, tradition, exemplified by Jeremy Bentham, Mill, and Ernest van den Haag, holds that punishment ought to serve as a deterrent, and that capital punishment is an adequate deterrent to prospective murderers. Abolitionists like Bedau and Jeffrey Reiman[3] deny both prongs of the traditional case for the death penalty. They hold that long prison sentences are a sufficient retributive response to murder and that the death penalty probably does not serve as a deterrent or is no better deterrent than other forms of punishment. I will argue that both traditional defenses are sound and together they make a strong case for retaining the death penalty. That is, I hold a combined theory of punishment. A backward-looking judgment that the criminal has committed a heinous crime plus a forward-looking judgment that a harsh punishment will deter would-be murderers is sufficient to justify the death penalty. I turn first to the retributivist theory in favor of capital punishment.

RETRIBUTION

The small crowd that gathered outside the prison to protest the execution of Steven Judy softly sang, "We Shall Overcome" . . . But it didn't seem quite the same hearing it sung out of concern for someone who, on finding a woman with a flat tire, raped and murdered her and drowned her three small children, then said that he hadn't been "losing any sleep" over his crimes. . . .

I remember the grocer's wife. She was a plump, happy woman who enjoyed the long workday she shared with her husband in their ma-and-pa store. One evening, two young men came in and showed guns, and the grocer gave them everything in the cash register.

For no reason, almost as an afterthought, one of the men shot the grocer in the face. The woman stood only a few feet from her husband when he was turned into a dead, bloody mess.

She was about 50 when it happened. In a few years her mind was almost gone, and she looked 80. They might as well have killed her too.

Then there was the woman I got to know after her daughter was killed by a wolfpack gang during a motoring trip. The mother called me occasionally, but nothing that I said could ease her torment. It ended when she took her own life.

A couple of years ago I spent a long evening with the husband, sister and parents of a fine young woman who had been forced into the trunk of a car in a hospital parking lot. The degenerate who kidnapped her kept her in the trunk, like an ant in a jar, until he got tired of the game. Then he killed her.[4]

Human beings have dignity as self-conscious rational agents who are able to act morally. One could maintain that it is precisely their moral goodness or innocence that bestows dignity and a right to life on them. Intentionally taking the life of an innocent human being is so evil that absent mitigating circumstances, the perpetrator forfeits his own right to life. He or she deserves to die.

The retributivist holds three propositions: (1) that all the guilty deserve to be punished; (2) that only the guilty deserve to be punished; and (3) that the guilty deserve to be punished in proportion to the severity of their crime. Thomas Jefferson supported such a system of proportionality of punishment to crime:

> Whosoever shall be guilty of rape, polygamy, sodomy with man or woman, shall be punished, if a man, by castration, if a woman by cutting through the cartilage of her nose a hole of one half inch in diameter at the least. [And] whosoever shall maim another, or shall disfigure him . . . shall be maimed, or disfigured in the like sort: or if that cannot be, for want of some part, then as nearly as may be, in some other part of at least equal value.[5]

Criminals like Steven Judy, Jeffrey Dahmer, Timothy McVeigh, Ted Bundy (who is reported to have raped and murdered over 100 women), John Mohammed and John Lee Malvo, who murdered 12 people in the killing spree of 2002, and the two men who gunned down the grocer (mentioned in the quotation by Royko, above) have committed capital offenses and deserve nothing less than capital punishment.[6] No doubt malicious acts like the ones committed by these criminals deserve worse punishment than death, and I would be open to suggestions of torture (why not?), but at a minimum, the death penalty seems warranted.

People often confuse *retribution* with *revenge*. Governor George Ryan, who recently commuted the sentences of all the prisoners on death row in the State of Illinois, in his essay in this volume quotes a letter from the Reverend Desmond Tutu that "to take a life when a life has been lost is revenge, it is not justice."[7] This is simply false. While moral people will feel outrage at acts of heinous crimes, such as those described above by Mike Royko, the moral justification of punishment is not *vengeance*, but *desert*. Vengeance signifies inflicting harm on the offender out of anger because of what he has done. Retribution is the rationally supported theory that the criminal deserves a punishment fitting the gravity of his crime.

The nineteenth-century British philosopher James Fitzjames Stephens thought vengeance was a justification for punishment, arguing that punishment should be inflicted "for the sake of ratifying the feeling of hatred—call it revenge, resentment, or what you will—which the contemplation of such [offensive] conduct excites in healthily constituted minds."[8] But retributivism is not based on hatred for the criminal (though a feeling of vengeance may accompany the punishment). Retributivism is the theory that the criminal *deserves* to be punished and deserves to be punished in proportion to the gravity of his or her crime, whether or not the victim or anyone else desires it. We may all deeply regret having to carry out the punishment, but consider it warranted.

On the other hand, people do have a sense of outrage and passion for revenge directed at criminals for their crimes. Imagine that someone in your family was on the receiving end of Stephen Judy's violent acts. Stephens was correct in asserting that "[t]he criminal law stands to the passion for revenge in much the same relation as marriage to the sexual appetite."[9] Failure to punish would no more lessen our sense of vengeance than the elimination of marriage would lessen our sexual appetite. When a society fails to punish criminals in a way thought to be proportionate to the gravity of the crime, the danger arises that the public would take the law into its own hands, resulting in vigilante justice, lynch mobs, and private acts of retribution. The outcome is likely to be an anarchistic, insecure state of injustice. As such, legal retribution stands as a safeguard for an orderly application of punitive desert.

Our natural instinct is for *vengeance,* but civilization demands that we restrain our anger and go through a legal process, letting the outcome determine whether and to what degree to punish the accused. Civilization demands that we not take the law into our own hands, but it should also satisfy our deepest instincts when they are consonant with reason. Our instincts tell us that some crimes, like McVeigh's, Judy's, and Bundy's, should be severely punished, but we refrain from personally carrying out those punishments, committing ourselves to the legal processes. The death penalty is supported by our gut animal instincts as well as our sense of justice as desert.

The death penalty reminds us that there are consequences to our actions, that we are responsible for what we do, so that dire consequences for immoral actions are eminently appropriate. The death penalty is such a fitting response to evil.

DETERRENCE

The second tradition justifying the death penalty is the utilitarian theory of deterrence. This holds that by executing convicted murderers we will deter would-be murderers from killing innocent people. The evidence for deterrence is controversial. Some scholars, like Thornstein Sellin and Bedau, argue that the death penalty is not a deterrent of homicides superior to long-term imprisonment. Others, such as Isaac Ehrlich, make a case for the death penalty as a significant deterrent.[10] Granted that the evidence is ambiguous, and honest scholars can differ on the results. However, one often hears abolitionists claiming the evidence shows that the death penalty fails to deter homicide.[11] This is too strong a claim. The sociological evidence doesn't show either that the death penalty deters or that it fails to deter. The evidence is simply inconclusive. But a commonsense case can be made for deterrence.

Imagine that every time someone intentionally killed an innocent person he was immediately struck down by lightning. When mugger Mike slashed his knife into the neck of the elderly pensioner, lightning struck, killing Mike. His fellow muggers witnessed the sequence of events. When burglar Bob pulled his pistol out and shot the bank teller through her breast, a bolt leveled Bob, his compatriots beholding the spectacle. Soon men with their guns lying next to them were found all across the world in proximity to the corpses of their presumed victims. Do you think that the evidence of cosmic retribution would go unheeded?

We can imagine the murder rate in the United States and everywhere else plummeting. The close correlation between murder and cosmic retribution would serve as a deterrent to would-be murderers. If this thought experiment is sound, we have a prima facie argument for the deterrent effect of capital punishment. In its ideal, prompt performance, the death penalty would likely deter most rational criminally minded from committing murder. The question then becomes how do we institute the death penalty so as to have the maximal deterrent effect without violating the rights of the accused.

We would have to bring the accused to trial more quickly and limit the appeals process of those found guilty "beyond reasonable doubt." Having DNA evidence should make this more feasible than hitherto. Furthermore, public executions of the convicted murderer would serve as a reminder that crime does not pay. Public executions of criminals seem an efficient way to communicate the message that if you shed innocent blood, you will pay a high price. Bedau cites Nat Hentoff's advocacy of a public execution of Timothy McVeigh in terms of being accountable for such actions (p. 4). I agree with Hentoff on the matter of accountability but also believe such publicity would serve to deter homicide.

Abolitionists like Stephen Nathanson argue that because the statistical evidence in favor of the deterrent effect of capital punishment is indecisive, we have no basis for concluding that it is a better deterrent than long prison sentences.[12] If I understand these opponents, their argument presents us with an exclusive disjunct: Either we must have conclusive statistical evidence (i.e., a proof) for the deterrent effect of the death penalty, or we have no grounds for supposing that the death penalty deters. Many people accept this argument. Recently, a colleague said to me, "There is no statistical evidence that the death penalty deters," as if to dismiss the argument from deterrence altogether. This

is premature judgment, for the argument commits the fallacy of supposing that only two opposites are possible. There is a middle position
that holds that while we cannot prove conclusively that the death penalty deters, the weight of evidence supports its deterrence. Furthermore, I think there are too many variables to hold constant for us to
prove via statistics the deterrence hypothesis, and even if the requisite
statistics were available, we could question whether they were cases of
mere correlation versus causation. On the other hand, commonsense
or anecdotal evidence may provide insight into the psychology of human motivation, providing evidence that fear of the death penalty deters some types of would-be criminals from committing murder.[13]
Granted, people are sometimes deceived about their motivation. But
usually they are not deceived, and, as a rule, we should presume they
know their motives until we have evidence to the contrary. The general
commonsense argument goes like this:

1. What people (including potential criminals) fear more will
   have a greater deterrent effect on them.
2. People (including potential criminals) fear death more than
   they do any other humane punishment.
3. The death penalty is a humane punishment.
4. Therefore, people (including criminals) will be deterred more
   by the death penalty than by any other humane punishment.

Since the purpose of this argument is to show that the death penalty
very likely deters more than long-term prison sentences, I am assuming
it is *humane*—that is, acceptable to the moral sensitivities of the majority in our society. Torture might deter even more, but it is not
considered humane. I will say more about the significance of hu-
maneness with regard to the death penalty below.

Common sense informs us that most people would prefer to remain
out of jail, that the threat of public humiliation is enough to deter
some people, that a sentence of 20 years will deter most people more
than a sentence of two years, that a life sentence will deter most would-
be criminals more than a sentence of 20 years. I think that we have
commonsense evidence that the death penalty is a better deterrent than
prison sentences. For one thing, as Richard Herrnstein and James Q.

Wilson have argued in *Crime and Human Nature*, a great deal of crime is committed on a cost-benefit schema, wherein the criminal engages in some form of risk assessment as to his or her chances of getting caught and punished in some manner. If he or she estimates the punishment mild, the crime becomes inversely attractive, and vice versa.[14] The fact that those who are condemned to death do everything in their power to get their sentences postponed or reduced to long-term prison sentences, in the way *lifers* do not, shows that they fear death more than life in prison.

The point is this: Imprisonment constitutes one evil, the loss of freedom, but the death penalty imposes a more severe loss, that of life itself. If you lock me up, I may work for a parole or pardon, I may learn to live stoically with diminished freedom, and I can plan for the day my freedom will be restored. But if I believe that my crime may lead to death, or loss of freedom followed by death, then I have more to fear than mere imprisonment. I am faced with a great evil plus an even greater evil. I fear death more than imprisonment because it alone takes from me all future possibility.

I am not claiming that the fear of legal punishment is all that keeps us from criminal behavior. Moral character, good habit, fear of being shamed, peer pressure, fear of authority, or the fear of divine retribution may have a greater influence on some people. However, many people will be deterred from crime, including murder, by the threat of severe punishment. The abolitionist points out that many would-be murderers simply do not believe they will be caught. Perhaps this is true for some. While the fantastic egoist has delusions of getting away with his crime, many would-be criminals are not so bold or delusionary.

Former Prosecuting Attorney for the State of Florida, Richard Gernstein, has set forth the commonsense case for deterrence. First of all, he claims, the death penalty certainly deters the murderer from any further murders, including those he or she might commit within the prison where he is confined. Second, statistics cannot tell us how many potential criminals have refrained from taking another's life through fear of the death penalty. He quotes Judge Hyman Barshay of New York: "The death penalty is a warning, just like a lighthouse throwing its beams out to sea. We hear about shipwrecks, but we do not hear about the ships the lighthouse guides safely on their way. We do not have proof of the number of ships it saves, but we do not tear the lighthouse down."[15]

Some of the commonsense evidence is anecdotal, as the following quotation shows. British member of Parliament Arthur Lewis explains how he was converted from an abolitionist to a supporter of the death penalty:

> One reason that has stuck in my mind, and which has proved [deterrence] to me beyond question, is that there was once a professional burglar in [my] constituency who consistently boasted of the fact that he had spent about one-third of his life in prison. . . . He said to me "I am a professional burglar. Before we go out on a job we plan it down to every detail. Before we go into the boozer to have a drink we say 'Don't forget, no shooters'—shooters being guns." He adds "We did our job and didn't have shooters because at that time there was capital punishment. Our wives, girlfriends and our mums said, 'Whatever you do, do not carry a shooter because if you are caught you might be topped [executed].' If you do away with capital punishment they will all be carrying shooters."

It is difficult to know how widespread this reasoning is. My own experience corroborates this testimony. Growing up in the infamous Cicero, Illinois, home of Al Capone and the Mafia, I had friends who went into crime, mainly burglary and larceny. It was common knowledge that one stopped short of killing in the act of robbery. A prison sentence could be dealt with—especially with a good lawyer—but being convicted of murder, which at that time included a reasonable chance of being electrocuted, was an altogether different matter. No doubt exists in my mind that the threat of the electric chair saved the lives of some of those who were robbed in my town. No doubt some crimes are committed in the heat of passion or by the temporally (or permanently) insane, but some are committed through a process of risk assessment. Burglars, kidnappers, traitors and vindictive people will sometimes be restrained by the threat of death. We simply don't know how much capital punishment deters, but this sort of commonsense, anecdotal evidence must be taken into account in assessing the institution of capital punishment.

John Stuart Mill admitted that capital punishment does not inspire terror in hardened criminals, but it may well make an impression on prospective murderers. "As for what is called the failure of the death punishment, who is able to judge of that? We partly know who those are whom it has not deterred; but who is there who knows whom it has deterred, or how many human beings it has saved who would have lived to be murderers if that awful association had not been thrown round the idea of murder from their earliest infancy?"[16] Mill's points are well taken: (1) Not everyone will be deterred by the death penalty, but some will; (2) the potential criminal need not consciously calculate a cost-benefit analysis regarding his crime to be deterred by the threat. The idea of the threat may have become a subconscious datum "from their earliest infancy." The repeated announcement and regular exercise of capital punishment may have deep causal influence.

Gernstein quotes the British Royal Commission on Capital Punishment (1949–53), which is one of the most thorough studies on the subject and which concluded that there was evidence that the death penalty has some deterrent effect on normal human beings. Some of its evidence in favor of the deterrence effect includes these points:

1. Criminals who have committed an offense punishable by life imprisonment, when faced with capture, refrained from killing their captor though by killing, escape seemed probable. When asked why they refrained from the homicide, quick responses indicated a willingness to serve life sentence, but not risk the death penalty.
2. Criminals about to commit certain offenses refrained from carrying deadly weapons. Upon apprehension, answers to questions concerning absence of such weapons indicated a desire to avoid more serious punishment by carrying a deadly weapon, and also to avoid use of the weapon which could result in imposition of the death penalty.
3. Victims have been removed from a capital punishment State to a non-capital punishment State to allow the murderer opportunity for homicide without threat to his own life. This in

itself demonstrates that the death penalty is considered by some would-be-killers.[17]

Gernstein then quotes former District Attorney of New York, Frank S. Hogan, representing himself and his associates:

> We are satisfied from our experience that the deterrent effect is both real and substantial . . . for example, from time to time accomplices in felony murder state with apparent truthfulness that in the planning of the felony they strongly urged the killer not to resort to violence. From the context of these utterances, it is apparent that they were led to these warnings to the killer by fear of the death penalty which they realized might follow the taking of life. Moreover, victims of hold-ups have occasionally reported that one of the robbers expressed a desire to kill them and was dissuaded from so doing by a confederate. Once again, we think it not unreasonable to suggest that fear of the death penalty played a role in some of these intercessions.
>
> On a number of occasions, defendants being questioned in connection with homicide have shown a striking terror of the death penalty. While these persons have in fact perpetrated homicide, we think that their terror of the death penalty must be symptomatic of the attitude of many others of their type, as a result of which many lives have been spared.[18]

It seems likely that the death penalty does not deter as much as it could due to its inconsistent and rare use. For example, out of an estimated 23,370 cases of murder, nonnegligent manslaughter, and rape in 1949, only 119 executions were carried out in the United States. In 1953, only 62 executions out of 27,000 cases for those crimes took place. Few executions were carried out in the 1960s and none at all from 1967 to 1977. Gernstein points out that at that rate a criminal's chances of escaping execution are better than 100 to 1. Actually, since Gernstein's report, the figures have become even more weighted against the chances of the death sentence. In 1993, there were 24,526 cases of murder and nonnegligent manslaughter and only 56 executions; and in 1994, there were 23,305 cases of murder and nonnegligent manslaughter and only 31 executions—for a ratio of better than 750 to 1. The average length of stay for a prisoner executed in 1994 was 10 years and two months. If potential murderers perceived the death penalty as a highly probable outcome of murder, would they not be more reluctant to kill? Gernstein notes:

> The commissioner of Police of London, England, in his evidence before the Royal Commission on Capital Punishment, told of a gang of armed robbers who continued operations after one of their members was sentenced to death and his sentence commuted to penal servitude, but the same gang disbanded and disappeared when, on a later occasion, two others were convicted of murder and hanged.[19]

Gernstein sums up his data: "Surely it is a common sense argument, based on what is known of human nature, that the death penalty has a deterrent effect particularly for certain kinds of murderers. Furthermore, as the Royal Commission opined, the death penalty helps to educate the conscience of the whole community, and it arouses among many people a quasi-religious sense of awe. In the mind of the public there remains a strong association between murder and the penalty of death. Certainly one of the factors which restrains some people from murder is fear of punishment and surely, since people fear death more than anything else, the death penalty is the most effective deterrent."[20]

I should also point out that *given the retributivist argument* for the death penalty, based on desert, the retentionist does not have to prove that the death penalty deters *better* than long prison sentences, but if the death penalty is deemed at least as effective as its major alternative, it would be justified. If evidence existed that life imprisonment were a *more effective* deterrent, the retentionist might be hard pressed to defend it on retributivist lines alone. My view is that the desert argument plus the commonsense evidence—being bolstered by the following argument, the Best Bet Argument, strongly supports retention of the death penalty.

The late Ernest van den Haag has set forth what he called the Best Bet Argument.[21] He argued that even though we don't know for certain whether the death penalty deters or prevents other murders, we should bet that it does. Indeed, due to our ignorance, any social policy we take is a gamble. Not to choose capital punishment for first-degree murder is as much a bet that capital punishment doesn't deter as choosing the policy is a bet that it does. There is a significant difference in the betting, however, in that to bet against capital punishment is to bet against the innocent and for the murderer, while to bet for it is to bet against the murderer and for the innocent.

The point is this: We are accountable for what we let happen, as well as for what we actually do. If I fail to bring up my children properly so that they are a menace to society, I am to some extent responsible for their bad behavior. I could have caused it to be some-what better. If I have good evidence that a bomb will blow up the building you are working in and fail to notify you (assuming I can), I am partly responsible for your death, if and when the bomb explodes. So we are responsible for what we omit doing, as well as for what we do. Purposefully to refrain from a lesser evil which we know will allow a greater evil to occur is to be at least partially responsible for the greater evil. This responsibility for our omissions underlies van den Haag's argument, to which we now return.

Suppose that we choose a policy of capital punishment for capital crimes. In this case we are betting that the death of some murderers will be more than compensated for by the lives of some innocents not being murdered (either by these murderers or others who would have murdered). If we're right, we have saved the lives of the innocent. If we're wrong, unfortunately, we've sacrificed the lives of some murderers. But say we choose not to have a social policy of capital punishment. If capital punishment doesn't work as a deterrent, we've come out ahead, but if it does work, then we've missed an opportunity to save innocent lives. If we value the saving of innocent lives more highly than the loss of the guilty, then to bet on a policy of capital punishment turns out to be rational. Since the innocent have a greater right to life than the guilty, it is our moral duty to adopt a policy that has a chance of protecting them from potential murderers.

It is noteworthy that prominent abolitionists, such as Charles Black, Hugo Adam Bedau, Ramsey Clark, and Henry Schwartzchild, have admitted to Ernest van den Haag that even if every execution were to deter a hundred murders, they would oppose it, from which van den Haag concludes, "To these abolitionist leaders, the life of every murderer is more valuable than the lives of a hundred prospective victims, for these abolitionists would spare the murderer, even if doing so will cost a hundred future victims their lives." Black and Bedau said they would favor abolishing the death penalty even if they knew that doing so would increase the homicide rate 1,000 percent.[22] This response of abolitionists is puzzling, since one of Bedau's arguments against the death penalty is that it doesn't bring back the dead. "We cannot do anything for the dead victims of crime. (How many of those who oppose the death penalty would continue to do so if, *mirabile dictu*, executing the murderer might bring the victim back to life?)"[23] Apparently, he would support the death penalty if it brought a dead victim back to life, but not if it prevented a hundred innocent victims from being murdered.

If the Best Bet Argument is sound, or if the death penalty does deter would-be murderers, as common sense suggests, then we should support some uses of the death penalty. It should be used for those who commit first-degree murder, for whom no mitigating factors are present, and especially for those who murder police officers, prison guards, and political leaders. Many states rightly favor it for those who murder while committing another crime, such as burglary or rape. It should be used in cases of treason and terrorist bombings. It should also be considered for the perpetrators of egregious white collar crimes such as bank managers embezzling the savings of the public. The savings and loan scandals of the 1980s, involving wealthy bank officials absconding with the investments of elderly pensioners and others, ruined the lives of many people. This gross violation of the public trust warrants the electric chair. Such punishment would meet the two conditions set forth in this paper. The punishment would be deserved and it would likely deter future crimes by people in the public trust. It would also make the death penalty more egalitarian, applicable to the rich as well as the poor.

Let me consider two objections often made to the implementation of the death penalty: that it sometimes leads to the death of innocents and that it discriminates against blacks.

Objection 1: Miscarriages of justice occur. Capital punishment is to be rejected because of human fallibility in convicting innocent parties and sentencing them to death. In a survey done in 1985 Hugo Adam

Bedau and Michael Radelet found[24] that of the 7,000 persons executed in the United States between 1900 and 1985, 25 were innocent of capital crimes. While some compensation is available to those unjustly imprisoned, the death sentence is irrevocable. We can't compensate the dead. As John Maxton, a member of the British Parliament puts it, "If we allow one innocent person to be executed, morally we are committing the same, or, in some ways, a worse crime than the person who committed the murder."

Response: Mr. Maxton is incorrect in saying that mistaken judicial execution is morally the same as or worse than murder, for a deliberate intention to kill the innocent occurs in a murder, whereas no such intention occurs in wrongful capital punishment.

Sometimes the objection is framed this way: It is better to let ten criminals go free than to execute one innocent person. If this dictum is a call for safeguards, then it is well taken; but somewhere there seems to be a limit on the tolerance of society toward capital offenses. Would these abolitionists argue that it is better that 50 or 100 or 1,000 murderers go free than that one innocent person be executed? Society has a right to protect itself from capital offenses even if this means taking a finite chance of executing an innocent person. If the basic activity or process is justified, then it is regrettable, but morally acceptable, that some mistakes are made. Fire trucks occasionally kill innocent pedestrians while racing to fires, but we accept these losses as justified by the greater good of the activity of using fire trucks. We judge the use of automobiles to be acceptable even though such use causes an average of 50,000 traffic fatalities each year. We accept the morality of a defensive war even though it will result in our troops accidentally or mistakenly killing innocent people.

The fact that we can err in applying the death penalty should give us pause and cause us to build a better appeals process into the judicial system. Such a process is already in most places in the American and British legal systems. That an occasional error may be made, regrettable though this is, is not a sufficient reason for us to refuse to use the death penalty, if on balance it serves a just and useful function.

Furthermore, abolitionists are simply misguided in thinking that prison sentences are a satisfactory alternative here. It's not clear that we can always or typically compensate innocent parties who waste away in prison. Jacques Barzun has argued that a prison sentence can be worse than death and carries all the problems that the death penalty does regarding the impossibility of compensation:

> In the preface of his useful volume of cases, *Hanged in Error*, Mr. Leslie Hale refers to the tardy recognition of a minor miscarriage of justice—one year in jail: "The prisoner emerged to find that his wife had died and that his children and his aged parents had been removed to the workhouse. By the time a small payment had been assessed as 'compensation' the victim was incurably insane." So far we are as indignant with the law as Mr. Hale. But what comes next? He cites the famous Evans case, in which it is very probable that the wrong man was hanged, and he exclaims: "While such mistakes are possible, should society impose an irrevocable sentence?" Does Mr. Hale really ask us to believe that the sentence passed on the first man, whose wife died and who went insane, was in any sense *revocable*? Would not any man rather be Evans dead than that other wretch "emerging" with his small compensation and his reason for living gone?[25]

The abolitionist is incorrect in arguing that death is different from long-term prison sentences because it is irrevocable. Imprisonment also takes good things away from us that may never be returned. We cannot restore to the inmate the freedom or opportunities he or she lost. Suppose an innocent 25-year-old man is given a life sentence for murder. Thirty years later the error is discovered and he is set free. Suppose he values three years of freedom to every one year of life. That is, he would rather live 10 years as a free man than 30 as a prisoner. Given this man's values, the criminal justice system has taken the equivalent of 10 years of life from him. If he lives until he is 65, he has, as far as his estimation is concerned, lost 10 years, so that he may be said to have lived only 55 years.

The numbers in this example are arbitrary, but the basic point is sound. Most of us would prefer a shorter life of higher quality to a longer one of low quality. Death prevents all subsequent quality, but imprisonment also irrevocably harms one by diminishing the quality of life of the prisoner.

Objection 2: The second objection of ten made against the death penalty is that it is unjust because it discriminates against the poor and minorities, particularly African Americans, over rich people and whites. Stephen B. Bright makes this objection in his chapter. Former Supreme Court Justice William Douglas wrote that "a law which reaches that [discriminatory] result in practice has no more sanctity than a law, which in terms provides the same."[26] Nathanson argues that "in many cases, whether one is treated justly or not depends not only on what one deserves but on how other people are treated."[27] He offers the example of unequal justice in a plagiarism case. "I tell the students in my class that anyone who plagiarizes will fail the course. Three students plagiarize papers, but I give only one a failing grade. The other two, in describing their motivation, win my sympathy, and I give them passing grades." Arguing that this is patently unjust, he likens this case to the imposition of the death penalty and concludes that it too is unjust.

Response: First of all, it is not true that a law that is applied in a discriminatory manner is unjust. Unequal justice is no less justice, however uneven its application. The discriminatory application, not the law itself, is unjust. A just law is still just even if it is not applied consistently. For example, a friend once got two speeding tickets during a 100-mile trip (having borrowed my car). He complained to the police officer who gave him his second ticket that many drivers were driving faster than he was at the time. They had escaped detection, he argued, so it wasn't fair for him to get two tickets on one trip. The officer acknowledged the imperfections of the system but, justifiably, had no qualms about giving him the second ticket. Unequal justice is still justice, however regrettable. So Justice Douglas is wrong in asserting that discriminatory results invalidate the law itself. Discriminatory practices should be reformed, and in many cases they can be. But imperfect practices in themselves do not entail that the laws engendering these practices themselves are unjust.

With regard to Nathanson's analogy with the plagiarism case, two things should be said against it. First, if the teacher is convinced that the motivational factors are mitigating factors, then he or she may be justified in passing two of the plagiarizing students. Suppose that the one student did no work whatsoever, showed no interest (Nathanson's motivation factor) in learning, and exhibited no remorse in cheating, whereas the other two spent long hours seriously studying the material and, upon apprehension, showed genuine remorse for their misdeeds. To be sure, they yielded to temptation at certain—though limited—sections of their long papers, but the vast majority of their papers represented their own diligent work. Suppose, as well, that all three had C averages at this point. The teacher gives the unremorseful, gross plagiarizer an F but relents and gives the other two D's. Her actions parallel the judge's use of mitigating circumstances and cannot be construed as arbitrary, let alone unjust.

The second problem with Nathanson's analogy is that it would have disastrous consequences for all law and benevolent practices alike. If we concluded that we should abolish a rule or practice, unless we treated everyone exactly by the same rules all the time, we would have to abolish, for example, traffic laws and laws against imprisonment for rape, theft, and even murder. Carried to its logical limits, we would also have to refrain from saving drowning victims if a number of people were drowning but we could only save a few of them. Imperfect justice is the best that we humans can attain. We should reform our practices as much as possible to eradicate unjust discrimination wherever we can, but if we are not allowed to have a law without perfect application, we will be forced to have no laws at all.

Nathanson acknowledges this latter response but argues that the case of death is different. "Because of its finality and extreme severity of the death penalty, we need to be more scrupulous in applying it as punishment than is necessary with any other punishment" (p. 67). The retentionist agrees that the death penalty is a severe punishment and that we need to be scrupulous in applying it. The difference between the abolitionist and the retentionist seems to lie in whether we are wise and committed enough as a nation to reform our institutions so that they approximate fairness. Apparently, Nathanson is pessimistic here, whereas I have faith in our ability to learn from our mistakes and reform our systems. If we can't reform our legal system, what hope is there for us?

More specifically, the charge that a higher percentage of blacks than whites are executed was once true but is no longer so. Many states have made significant changes in sentencing procedures, with the result that currently whites convicted of first-degree murder are sentenced to death at a higher rate than blacks.[28]

One must be careful in reading too much into these statistics. While great disparities in statistics should cause us to examine our judicial procedures, they do not in themselves prove injustice. For example, more males than females are convicted of violent crimes (almost 90% of those convicted of violent crimes are males—a virtually universal statistic), but this is not strong evidence that the law is unfair, for there are biological/psychological explanations for the disparity in convictions. Males are on average and by nature more aggressive (usually tied to testosterone) than females. Simply having a Y chromosome predisposes them to greater violence. Nevertheless, we hold male criminals responsible for their violence and expect them to control themselves. Likewise, there may be good explanations why people of one ethnic group commit more crimes than those of other groups, explanations that do not impugn the processes of the judicial system nor absolve rational people of their moral responsibility.

Recently, Governor George Ryan of Illinois, the state of my childhood and youth, commuted the sentences of over 150 death row inmates. Apparently, some of those convicted were convicted on insufficient evidence. If so, their sentences should have been commuted and the prisoners compensated. Such decisions should be done on a case-by-case basis. If capital punishment is justified, its application should be confined to clear cases in which the guilt of the criminal is "beyond reasonable doubt." But to overthrow the whole system because of a few possible miscarriages is as unwarranted as it is a loss of faith in our system of criminal justice. No one would abolish the use of fire engines and ambulances because occasionally they kill innocent pedestrians while carrying out their mission.

Abolitionists often make the complaint that only the poor get death sentences for murder. If their trials are fair, then they deserve the death penalty, but rich murderers may be equally deserving. At the moment only first-degree murder and treason are crimes deemed worthy of the death penalty. Perhaps our notion of treason should be expanded to include those who betray the trust of the public: corporation executives who have the trust of ordinary people, but who, through selfish and dishonest practices, ruin their lives. As noted above, my proposal is to consider broadening, not narrowing, the scope of capital punishment, to include business personnel who unfairly harm the public. The executives in the recent corporation scandals who bailed out of sinking corporations with golden, million-dollar lifeboats while the pension plans of thousands of employees went to the bottom of the economic ocean, may deserve severe punishment, and if convicted, they should receive what they deserve. My guess is that the threat of the death sentence would have a deterrent effect here. Whether it is feasible to apply the death penalty for horrendous white-collar crimes is debatable. But there is something to be said in its favor. It would remove the impression that only the poor get executed.

CONCLUSION

While the abolitionist movement is gaining strength due in part to the dedicated eloquence of opponents to the death penalty like Hugo Adam Bedau, Stephen Nathanson, and Jeffrey Reiman, a cogent case can be made for retaining the death penalty for serious crimes, such as first-degree murder and treason. The case primarily rests on a notion of justice as desert but is strengthened by utilitarian arguments involving deterrence. It is not because retentionists disvalue life that we defend the use of the death penalty. Rather, it is because we value human life as highly as we do that we support its continued use. The combined argument based on both backward-looking and forward-looking considerations justifies use of the death penalty. I have suggested that the application of the death penalty include not only first-degree murder but also treason (willful betrayal of one's country), including the treasonous behavior of business executives who violate the public trust.

The abolitionists in this book point out the problems in applying the death penalty. We can concede that there are problems and reform is constantly needed, but since the death penalty is justified in principle, we should seek to improve its application rather than abolish a just institution.[29] We ought not throw out the baby with the dirty bathwater.

NOTES

1. The numbers in parentheses refer to the page numbers in Bedau's essay, "An Abolitionist's Survey of the Death Penalty in America Today."

2. It seems that the former mayor of New York City, Fiorello LaGuardia, had this in mind when he said, "I would hang a banker who stole from the people." Quoted in Alyn Brodsky, *The Great Mayor: Fiorello LaGuardia and the Making of the City of New York* (Truman Talley Books, 2003).

3. See Hugo Adam Bedau, *The Death Penalty in America* (Oxford University Press, 1982) and his "Capital Punishment," in *Matters of Life and Death*, ed. Tom Regan, (Random House, 1980); see also Jeffrey Reiman, "Why the Death Penalty Should Be Abolished in America," in *The Death Penalty: For and Against*, ed. by Louis P. Pojman and Jeffrey Reiman (Rowman & Littlefield, 1998).

4. Mike Royko, quoted in Michael Moore, "The Moral Worth of Retributivism," in *Punishment and Rehabilitation,* 3rd ed., ed. Jeffrie G. Murphy (Wadsworth, 1995): 98–99.

5. Thomas Jefferson, *Bill for Proportioning Crime and Punishments* (1779), quoted in Ernest van den Haag, *Punishing Criminals: Concerning a Very Old and Painful Question* (Basic Books, 1975): 193. I do not agree with all of Jefferson's claims, but the principle is correct.

6. These are the most notorious of recent murders, but if you agree that these culprits deserve the death penalty, the case has been made against the abolitionist who wants to abolish the death penalty altogether.

7. See his speech in this volume announcing his commutation of all of Illinois's death sentences. I will comment on this toward the end of my essay. Joshua Marquis also makes some pertinent comments on this commutation in his essay in this volume.

8. Sir James Fitzjames Stephens, *Liberty, Equality, Fraternity* (Cambridge University Press, 1967): 152.

9. Sir James Fitzjames Stephens, *A History of Criminal Law in England* (Macmillan, 1863): 80.

10. Thorstein Sellin, *The Death Penalty* (1959), reprinted in *The Death Penalty in America,* ed. Hugo Bedau (Anchor Books, 1967). Isaac Ehrlich, "The Deterrent Effect of Capital Punishment: A Question of Life and Death," *American Economic Review,* 65 (June 1975): 397–417.

11. Sophisticated abolitionists argue that the death penalty doesn't deter better than long-term prison sentences, but their less sophisticated disciples often make the broader claim. I hear the charge regularly from students that the death penalty fails to deter.

12. Nathanson, *An Eye for an Eye?* (Rowman & Littlefield, 1987): chap. 2.

13. Michael Davis offers a similar commonsense argument for the deterrent effect of the death penalty. His article is especially useful as it shows just how little the statistics of social science demonstrate and why we should take the common sense data as weightier. See his "Death, Deterrence, and the Method of Common Sense," *Social Theory and Practice,* vol. 7, no. 2 (Summer 1981).

14. Herrnstein and Wilson conclude, "To increase the disutility of crime for people in general, society must increase either the speed, the certainty, or the severity of punishment, or some combination of all three." *Crime and Human Nature* (Simon & Schuster, 1985): 397.

15. Richard E. Gernstein, "A Prosecutor Looks at Capital Punishment," *Journal of Criminal Law: Criminology and Police Science*, vol. 51, no. 2 (1960).

16. *Parliamentary Debates*, third series, April 21, 1868. Reprinted in Peter Singer, ed., *Applied Ethics* (Oxford University Press, 1986): 97–104.

17. Quoted in Gernstein, "A Prosecutor Looks at Capital Punishment."

18. Ibid.

19. Ibid.

20. Ibid.

21. Ernst van den Haag, "On Deterrence and the Death Penalty," *Ethics*, 78 (July 1968).

22. Cited in Ernest van den Haag, "The Death Penalty Once More," *unpublished manuscript*. In "A Response to Bedau," *Arizona State Law Journal*, 4 (1977), van den Haag states that both Black and Bedau said that they would be in favor of abolishing the death penalty even if "they knew that its abolition (and replacement by life imprisonment) would increase the homicide rate by 10%, 20%, 50%, 100%, or 1000%. Both gentlemen continued to answer affirmatively." Bedau confirmed this in a letter to me (July 28, 1996).

23. Hugo Adam Bedau, "How to Argue about the Death Penalty," in *Facing the Death Penalty*, ed. Michael Radelet (Temple University Press, 1989): 190.

24. Hugo Adam Bedau and Michael Radelet, *Miscarriages of Justice in Potential Capital Cases* (1st draft Oct. 1985, on file at Harvard Law School Library), quoted in E. van den Haag, "The Ultimate Punishment: A Defense," *Harvard Law Review*, vol 99, no. 7 (May 1986): 1664.

25. Jacques Barzun, "In Favor of Capital Punishment" *The American Scholar*, vol. 31, no. 2 (Spring 1962).

26. Justice William Douglas in *Furman v Georgia*, 408 U.S. 238 (1972).

27. Nathanson, *An Eye for an Eye?* (Rowman & Littlefield, 1987): 62.

28. The Department of Justice's *Bureau of Justice Statistics Bulletin* for 1994 reports that between 1977 and 1994, of those arrested for murder 2,336 (51%) were white, 1,838 (40%) were black, 316 (7%) were Hispanic. Of the 257 who were executed, 140 (54%) were white, 98 (38%) were black, 17 (7%) were Hispanic, and 2 (1%) were other races. In 1994, 31 prisoners—20 white men and 11 black men—were executed although whites made up only 7,532 (41%) and blacks 9,906 (56%) of those arrested for murder. Of those sentenced to death in 1994, 158 were white men, 133 were black men, 25 were Hispanic men, 2 were Native American men, 2 were white women, and 3 were black women. Of those sentenced, relatively more blacks (72%) than whites (65%) or Hispanics (60%) had prior felony records. Overall the criminal justice system does not seem to favor white criminals over black, though it does seem to favor rich defendants over poor ones.

4

Close to Death: Reflections on Race and Capital Punishment in America

Bryan Stevenson

Even before I began representing people on death row, I was opposed to capital punishment. The logic of gratuitously killing someone to demonstrate that killing is wrong eluded me. We don't rape those who rape, nor do we assault those who have assaulted. We disavow torturing those who have tortured. Yet we endorse killing those who have killed.

The death penalty has always seemed to me to be a punishment rooted in hopelessness and anger. My own moral and religious background caused me to believe that each of us is more than the worst thing we've ever done. No one is just a crime. Punishment must be constrained by basic human rights. I also recognized before I became a lawyer that the criminal justice system was replete with arbitrary and unfair decision making, particularly for the poor and people of color.

In the almost two decades that I have been working as an attorney for condemned prisoners,[1] I have developed a far more direct and personal understanding of the degree to which this country's capital punishment system is riddled with flaws and tainted with injustice.[2] I have represented dozens of death row prisoners, most of whom were unconstitutionally convicted and unfairly sentenced to death. I've defended men, women, and children accused of capital crimes and had to confront the intense anger and complex issues these cases present. I have sat with scores of people who have been victimized by violence and death: family members of murder victims who have lost loved ones to crime, the mothers, fathers, sons, and daughters of executed prisoners, and an increasing number of decision makers who have become disillusioned by the process of state governments executing human beings. I have come to believe that whatever one's views of the death penalty in the abstract, reasonable people of goodwill, if armed with the facts about how the death penalty is actually administered in this country, ought to conclude that the death penalty should be abolished.

Criminal justice policy has been incident driven in the United States for many years. Crimes, sensationalized by the media, have resulted in policies that are uninformed by analysis and research. Policy makers have defended ill-conceived and irrational sentencing schemes by invoking public support for tougher sentences. The broader, long-term implications of these policy choices are rarely considered. This approach to sentencing has made the death penalty immune to rational analysis and discourse. Most supporters of capital punishment are not affected by its implementation in any practical way. They do not perceive the death penalty as a threat to their taxes or their pocketbooks, which results in a costless assessment of its value.[3] When executions are impersonal and unexamined, Americans are free to consider capital punishment in a disembodied manner in which death-sentenced prisoners are stereotyped villains with no discernible humanity. Unless something sensational or atypical occurs, the condemned are executed out of sight with little attention and ever diminishing legal scrutiny. The family members of homicide victims are expected to perform a public role as active pl—   on and the implementation
                                                   unishment of an offender
                                                   ate tragedy of a particular
                                                   nt depending on the vic-
                                                   thiness."

                                                   has taken shape in Amer-
                                                   nal justice in the United

However, in recent years, media accounts of exonerations of death row inmates[5] and reports about the unreliability of the capital punishment system[6] have begun to bring some of the realities of the death penalty to the public consciousness. There is evidence that this new information is beginning to transform the public's and decision makers' views about the death penalty.[7] In the last several years, dozens of innocent people have been released from death row after narrowly escaping execution. For every eight executions that have occurred in the United States since resumption of capital punishment in the 1970s, one innocent person has been discovered on death row and exonerated.[8] The shockingly high error rate has prompted a retreat from the death penalty in some circles, even wholesale commutation of every death sentence by the governor of Illinois. But, perhaps inevitably, the national debate continues to focus on abstract concepts: Personal tragedies of unjustly condemned individuals are transformed into empirical data, which are then subjected to debates about the generalizability of the samples and the reliability of the survey techniques.[9] Although such scrutiny of scientific method is self-evidently appropriate and valuable, what is often lost in the process are the vivid, personal narratives that can provide a crucial context for public understanding of the actual workings of the capital punishment system.

The reality is that capital punishment in America is a lottery. It is a punishment that is shaped by the constraints of poverty, race, geography, and local politics. It is a punishment that has become notorious for its unreliability and unfairness. The death penalty in the United States has increasingly come to symbolize a disturbing tolerance for error and injustice that has undermined the integrity of criminal justice administration and America's commitment to human rights.

In this chapter, I describe the cases of some of the people I have represented and discuss what these cases reveal about capital punishment in America. I speak in particular about the influence of conscious and unconscious racial bias in the administration of the death penalty. I discuss some of my experiences in Alabama, the state in which I have represented many condemned prisoners and capital defendants. However, I draw on national studies to show that the problems I have witnessed are representative of the situation in other death penalty states as well.

I begin with the case of Walter McMillian, which illustrates how the actions of the police, prosecutors, the bench, and a jury selected in a racially discriminatory manner can combine to produce a capital murder conviction and sentence of death for a person who was innocent.

THE DEATH PENALTY IN OPERATION:
STATE V. WALTER MCMILLIAN

On June 7, 1987, Walter McMillian, a black 45-year-old pulpwood worker with no prior felony convictions, was stopped by Monroe County Sheriff Tom Tate and nearly a dozen law enforcement officers while driving his pickup truck on a county road in Alabama. Mr. McMillian was surrounded by police with their weapons drawn and pointed, and he was arrested on a charge of sodomy.[10] The victim was alleged to be Ralph Myers, a white convicted felon with a lengthy criminal record who was in the sheriff's custody as a suspect for murder in another county. During the arrest, Sheriff Tate, who is also white, made several threatening and racist remarks about his belief that Mr. McMillian had previously had an affair with a young white woman in the community.[11]

Mr. McMillian's arrest, it turned out, was a pretext for taking him to the county jail. Sheriff Tate had arranged for an inmate in his custody to examine Mr. McMillian's truck and falsely claim that he had seen the truck at the scene of a fatal shooting of a woman named Ronda Morrison.[12] Seven months earlier, Ms. Morrison had been murdered while working at a dry cleaning store in Monroeville, Alabama. The shooting of a young white college student sent shock waves throughout Monroe County, a rural area in southwest Alabama. After several months of widespread attention to the case, law enforcement officers had failed to make an arrest or solve the crime.

Two days after his arrest, Mr. McMillian was charged with the capital murder of Ronda Morrison based on a statement by Ralph Myers that Mr. McMillian may have been involved in the murder. Myers made several recorded statements to the police prior to Mr. McMillian's arrest in which he told investigators that Mr. McMillian had nothing to do with the murder of Ronda Morrison. During these re-corded interviews, Myers was threatened with the electric chair if he did not implicate Mr. McMillian. These recorded statements were never disclosed to Mr. McMillian's defense counsel.

At the time Ronda Morrison was killed, Walter McMillian was at his home several miles away from the crime scene. Mr. McMillian had been working on his truck for several hours while surrounded by fam-ily and friends, who had gathered at his home to raise money for his sister's church. Church members were selling sandwiches and fried fish to passers-by, some of whom contacted Sheriff Tate after Mr. Mc-Millian's arrest and confirmed his innocence.

On July 31, 1987, while Mr. McMillian was still a pretrial detainee awaiting trial at the Monroe County Jail, Sheriff Tate again made threatening and racist remarks. At one point Sheriff Tate told Mr. McMillian, "I ought to take you off and hang you like we done that nigger in Mobile, but we can't stand that suit."[13] A couple of years before Mr. McMillian's arrest, a black man named Michael Donald was abducted in Mobile, Alabama, and lynched by members of the Ku Klux Klan. The Klan was successfully sued in court by Mr. Donald's family and ordered to turn over all property and assets.

The day after the sheriff's threatening remarks, Mr. McMillian was taken to Holman State Prison and placed on Alabama's death row among nearly 100 condemned men who had been convicted of capital murder and were awaiting execution. Ralph Myers, who later testified against Mr. McMillian at trial but had not yet given law enforcement officers a full statement accusing Mr. McMillian of the murder, was also taken to death row to coerce him to further implicate Mr. McMillian. Placing a pre-trial detainee on death row is illegal.[14]

The transfers to death row came shortly before the previously sched-uled execution of a death row inmate at the prison. Within a month after the men were transferred to death row, Wayne Ritter was executed in Alabama's electric chair less than 100 feet from where Mr. McMillian and Myers were being held. On the day after the execution, Ralph Myers contacted Sheriff Tate and agreed to give law enforcement of-ficials a complete, false statement accusing Mr. McMillian of the Ronda Morrison murder. After agreeing to testify against Mr. McMillian, My-ers was removed from death row and returned to the Monroe County

Jail. Mr. McMillian spent the next 13 months on Alabama's death row awaiting trial.[15]

Prior to trial, a great deal of exculpatory evidence was concealed by law enforcement officers. In addition to recorded statements of Myers that made clear that his testimony was false, law enforcement investigators suppressed exculpatory evidence from witnesses whose information about the timing of the murder directly contradicted Myers' false testimony and the case against Walter McMillian.[16]

Mr. McMillian's capital murder trial took place in just two days. The trial began at 1:15 P.M. on Monday, August 15, 1988, and was completed by 1:52 P.M. on Wednesday, August 17. The penalty phase of Mr. McMillian's trial was conducted in less than two hours. Jury selection, which in many jurisdictions takes days and can go on for weeks in serious or complex cases, began at 9:00 in the morning on August 15 and was completed by noon. Mr. McMillian was convicted of capital murder—based solely on the testimony of Ralph Myers.[17] Race clearly played a role in the prosecution of the case and in the jury's consideration of the evidence. Although the crime took place in Monroe County, which has an African American population of over 40 percent, the judge transferred the case to Baldwin County, Alabama, which has a black population of less than 15 percent. Only one African American served on Mr. McMillian's jury after the state excluded other qualified black jurors by means of peremptory strikes. The district attorney also improperly told the jury the story of Mr. McMillian's rumored affair with a young white woman.[18] The introduction of this evidence had no purpose or relationship to this case other than inflaming racial prejudice against Mr. McMillian. Evidence from over a half-dozen black witnesses who testified that Mr. McMillian was at home working on his truck at the time of the crime was simply ignored. The testimony of Ralph Myers was apparently regarded by the jury as more credible despite the fact that Myers had a lengthy criminal record.

Mr. McMillian was sentenced to death by Monroe County Circuit Court Judge Robert E. Lee Key, Jr., on September 19, 1988. Judge Key imposed a death sentence on Mr. McMillian despite the fact that the jury had returned a sentencing verdict of life imprisonment without parole.[19] Although Judge Key changed the venue of the jury trial and sentencing hearing to a location outside Monroe County, he held the final sentencing hearing—in which he overrode the jury's life verdict and imposed a death sentence—back in Monroe County in a courtroom packed with local residents and local media.

I began representing Mr. McMillian shortly after he was sentenced to death. Sixteen months later, Mr. McMillian's conviction and sentence were affirmed by the Alabama Court of Criminal Appeals.[20]

In July 1991, Ralph Myers contacted me from prison where he was serving time for another crime. He informed me that he had been pressured to testify falsely against Walter McMillian, and he recanted his trial testimony.[21] A post-conviction challenge was filed in state court and the ensuing investigation led to the discovery of other evidence of Mr. McMillian's innocence.[22] The recorded statements of Sheriff Tate and law enforcement officers threatening Myers were buried in a case file in another county, as was other exculpatory evidence that had been suppressed. After several evidentiary hearings and four years of intensely contentious litigation, the Alabama Court of Criminal Appeals finally overturned Mr. McMillian's conviction and death sentence based on the state's failure to disclose favorable evidence.[23]

The Alabama Bureau of Investigation launched a new investigation into the case. During this investigation, the other two witnesses who had testified against Mr. McMillian recanted and admitted that their trial testimony was false. The state finally acknowledged that Mr. McMillian was innocent. On March 3, 1993, all charges against Mr. McMillian were dismissed. After nearly six years on death row, he was free.

CAPITAL PUNISHMENT AND THE LEGACY OF RACIAL BIAS IN AMERICA

At the end of 2002, there were 3,692 people on death row in the United States. Thirty-eight of the 50 states have death penalty statutes.[24] Since the death penalty was resurrected in 1976, there have been over 800 executions, 89 percent of which have occurred in the American South.[25] Women, juveniles, and the mentally ill are among the hundreds who have been shot, electrocuted, asphyxiated, hanged, and injected with lethal poisons by state governments in America. Most of these exe-

Friends, family members and community residents gathered at the courthouse to greet Walter McMillian on the day that the state acknowledged his innocence and he was released from death row. Mr. McMillian (left) and I (right) are joined by his wife and granddaughter. (Photo courtesy of The Equal Justice Initiative of Alabama.)

cutions have taken place in the last ten years, as support for capital punishment has acquired greater political resonance and as federal courts have retreated from the degree of oversight and review that existed in the early 1980s. In the last year of the twentieth century, the world's "leading democracy" executed close to 100 of its residents. All of the executed were poor, a disproportionately high number were racial minorities convicted of killing white victims, many of the executed were mentally ill, and some were juveniles at the time their crimes occurred. There is no meaningful assurance that all of the executed were guilty.

Injustices such as those that occurred in Walter McMillian's case unfortunately are far from rare. In recent years, there has been a steady drumroll of exonerations of erroneously convicted criminal defendants.[26] These revelations have served to focus attention on the various actions of judges, prosecutors, and police officers that may cause or contribute to erroneous convictions or improper death sentences. Instances where exculpatory evidence has been withheld by the police or prosecutors, reliance on jailhouse informants or snitches, erroneous jury instructions, bias on the part of judges or jurors, incompetent or corrupt forensic "experts," and ineffective assistance from defense counsel have all been documented as causing innocent people to be wrongly convicted and sentenced to death.

Closer scrutiny of the operation of the death penalty has also resulted in greater awareness of some of the capital punishment system's other abuses. These include the imposition of capital punishment on the most vulnerable offenders—the mentally retarded, the mentally ill, juveniles and foreign nationals.[27] Although the Supreme Court declared in June 2002 that execution of mentally retarded persons violates the Eighth Amendment,[28] the United States remains among the small number of nations that permit the execution of individuals who were under the age of 18 at the time of the crime.[29] Most of my practice has been in Alabama, which has the largest number of death-sentenced juveniles per capita in the country. I have frequently dealt with the especially troubling issues generated by legal representation of 16- and 17-year-old children who have been sentenced to death. At present, 7 percent of Alabama's death row—14 people—were sentenced for crimes they were convicted of committing at the age of 16 or 17. In

Texas, 6 percent of death row is made up of juveniles. Alabama and Texas have 51 percent of all juveniles currently sentenced to death in America.[30] A less examined but equally troubling aspect of the juvenile death penalty are the hundreds of even younger children, many 13 and 14 years of age, who have been prosecuted for capital crimes and "mercifully spared of the death penalty" and sentenced to life imprisonment without parole. It is only in a country in which the juvenile death penalty exists that a sentence of life imprisonment without parole for a 14-year-old could be considered "lenient."

Serious problems plague the administration of the death penalty in the United States. The inability of the poor to receive adequate legal representation is the core problem surrounding capital punishment. However, the pervasive and indelible taint of racial discrimination also reveals a fundamental problem endemic to capital punishment that implicates American society in a significant way that transcends the administration of criminal justice. Although the capital punishment system's other systemic problems are certainly worthy of discussion as well, the endemic racial bias issues provide a particularly useful vehicle for demonstrating that the death penalty should be abandoned in this country.

The most glaringly obvious symptom of the dysfunctions of the American criminal justice process, readily apparent to even the most casual observer, is the stark overrepresentation of people of color (primarily African Americans and Latinos) in the ranks of those who are prosecuted for crimes in the United States.[31] One out of three African American men between the ages of 18 and 35 is in jail, in prison, on probation, or on parole in the United States.[32] Evidence of disparate treatment of racial minorities becomes more pronounced at each juncture of the criminal justice process (arrest, filing of charges, pretrial detention, conviction, and incarceration) as systemic decision makers (police officers, prosecutors, and judges), who tend to be predominantly white,[33] frequently exercise their discretion in ways that disfavor people of color.[34] Even though there is evidence of disproportionately high involvement by African Americans and Latinos in some criminal offense categories,[35] the disparities in arrest, sentencing, and incarceration persist even when offender rates are racially proportionate. For example, people of color are disproportionately represented among those arrested, prosecuted, convicted, and sentenced to prison for drug offenses. While African Americans make up 13 percent of the nation's monthly drug users, they represent 35 percent of those arrested for drug possession, 53 percent of those convicted of drug offenses, and 75 percent of those sentenced to prison in this offense category.[36]

When the Supreme Court struck down the use of capital punishment in 1972 in *Furman v. Georgia*,[37] some of the Justices frankly acknowledged the existence of racial bias in this country's administration of the death penalty.[38] When the Court thereafter upheld the constitutionality of capital punishment in 1976 in *Gregg v. Georgia*[39] and its companion cases, the Court refused to presume that historic racial bias could not be remedied. On being presented with the relevant empirical data in *McCleskey v. Kemp*[40] in 1987—data that documented the existence of racial bias in Georgia's use of the death penalty[41]—the Court did not deny the taint of racial bias. Indeed, the Court freely admitted that race-based sentencing disparities are "an inevitable part of our criminal justice system."[42] Expressing the concern that responding to racial bias in death penalty cases might necessarily require confronting racial bias in other criminal cases,[43] the Court concluded that the Constitution does not place such "totally unrealistic conditions" on the use of capital punishment or the administration of criminal justice.[44]

It seems unimaginable that the Supreme Court of the United States, an institution vested with the responsibility to achieve "equal justice under the law," could issue an opinion that condones the existence of racial bias in the criminal justice system, particularly in the application of a penalty as grave and irrevocable as capital punishment.[45] However, it is precisely this acceptance of bias and the tolerance of racial discrimination that has come to define America's criminal justice system, including the administration of the death penalty.

In the years since the *McCleskey* decision was issued in 1987, the evidence of racial bias in the capital punishment system has continued to mount. A report by the United States General Accounting Office in 1990 concluded that 82 percent of the empirically valid studies on the subject show that the race of the victim has an impact on capital charging decisions or sentencing verdicts or both.[46] A 1998 study by David Baldus, whose earlier data had been presented to the Court in *McCleskey*, found—on the basis of data from 27 of the 37 states that have employed the death penalty since the *Furman* decision in 1972—that more than 90 percent of these jurisdictions exhibit patterns of racial bias in capital charging or sentencing of defendants accused of killing white victims.[47] In 2000, a review of the federal death penalty revealed similar racial disparities in sentencing and charging decisions.[48] President Clinton and Attorney General Janet Reno concluded that a moratorium on federal executions was necessary to conduct a further study of the problem.[49] That study was abandoned in 2001 by newly appointed Attorney General John Ashcroft, who asserted that a supplemental study[50] showed "no evidence of racial bias in the administration of the federal death penalty" and who declared that the Department of Justice would not suspend executions on the basis of doubts about racial fairness.[51]

In some capital cases, the existence of racial bias is overt and graphic. The Supreme Court vacated the death sentence of Victor Saldano in 2000[52] after the attorney general of Texas conceded that the "prosecution's introduction of race as a factor for determining 'future dangerousness' constituted a violation of the appellant's right to equal protection and due process."[53] At trial, the state's expert testified at the penalty phase that one of the factors associated with a defendant's future dangerousness was his race or ethnicity.[54] The state's "expert" identified the Argentinean defendant as Hispanic and relied on the overrepresentation of black and brown people in prison to support his assumption about the correlation between race and dangerousness.[55] After the United States Supreme Court vacated the sentence based on the Texas attorney general's confession of error, the Texas Court of Criminal Appeals reinstated the death sentence. The Texas court concluded that the attorney general had no authority to confess error in a death penalty case appealed to a federal court.[56]

Many appellate courts have shown a willingness to excuse overt racial bias in death penalty cases. Anthony Ray Peek, an African American, was wrongly convicted of capital murder and sentenced to death in Florida after a white trial judge improperly admitted evidence and expedited the penalty phase proceedings by stating from the bench, "Since the nigger mom and dad are here anyway, why don't we go ahead and do the penalty phase today instead of having to subpoena them back at cost to the state."[57] Mr. Peek was sentenced to death. On appeal, the Florida Supreme Court reversed Mr. Peek's conviction on evidentiary grounds not directly related to the racist comments made by the judge. With regard to the defendant's arguments concerning the racial bigotry exhibited by the judge, the court, in a one-paragraph analysis, merely admonished state trial court judges to "convey the image of impartiality."[58] Mr. Peek was retried in front of a different judge and acquitted.

In 1989, a federal judge found that Wilburn Dobbs was tried by a state court judge who had spent his life and career defending racial segregation and who would only refer to Mr. Dobbs at trial as "colored" or "colored boy."[59] Dobbs was convicted by a jury, some of whom later revealed that they believed that the Ku Klux Klan did good things in the community and that black people are more violent than whites.[60] Mr. Dobbs was defended by an attorney whose racist views included a belief that black people are morally inferior, less intelligent, and biologically destined to steal.[61] The District Court and the Eleventh Circuit nevertheless affirmed Mr. Dobbs's conviction and death sentence. The lower court rulings eventually were reversed by the United States Supreme Court on other grounds.[62]

THE ALABAMA STORY

When one turns the lens to Alabama, evidence of racial bias in the use of the death penalty is readily apparent. There are 190 people currently sentenced to death in Alabama. Alabama has the largest death row per capita in the United States and the seventh largest in raw numbers. Alabama's death row population has doubled since 1990. Since 1998, Alabama has sentenced more people to death per capita than any other state in the country.[63] The death sentencing rate in Alabama is 3 to 10 times greater than in other southern states.

One of the reasons the number of death sentences is so high in Alabama is that the state has one of the most expansive capital murder statutes in the country. The statute has been expanded six times since the original statute was modified in 1981. Each year, legislation is introduced to make application of the death penalty more widespread. For example, in the last several years the governor and various legislators have introduced bills calling for the death penalty for rape, sodomy, acts of terrorism, and other nonhomicide offenses.[64] In recent years, bills have been introduced that would permit capital prosecutions of children as young as 12, people who deal drugs, or someone charged with child abuse.

Another factor that contributes to Alabama's extraordinarily high death sentencing rate is the state's unrestricted judicial override practice. Alabama is the only state in the country that permits elected trial judges to override a jury's sentencing verdict of life imprisonment without parole and instead impose a sentence of death without limitation.[65] Over 20 percent of Alabama's current death row prisoners received life without parole verdicts from sentencing juries, which were then overridden by elected trial judges.[66]

Of the persons executed in Alabama between 1975 and 2000, 70 percent have been African American.[67] Although nearly 65 percent of homicide victims in Alabama are African American,[68] 80 percent of Alabama's death row prisoners have been sentenced for crimes involving victims who are white.[69] Race of the defendant and race of the victim are significant predictors of who is sentenced to die in Alabama.

In Alabama, overt bias is frequently evident at capital proceedings as well. Herbert Richardson was executed in 1989 after the prosecutor urged the sentencing judge to impose the death penalty, in part, because of Mr. Richardson's alleged association with the "Black Muslim organization."[70] Samuel Ivery, an African American, was tried by a nearly all-white jury that was told by the prosecutor that the defendant's lifelong history of mental illness, which included a prior commitment to a state mental hospital,[71] was nothing more than "niggeritous"[72]—an effort to fake mental illness to avoid criminal prosecution and punishment. The jury sentenced Mr. Ivery to death and the Alabama Court of Criminal Appeals found no error in the trial prosecutor's comments.[73] The appeals court stated: "The regrettable fact that the prosecutor couched this statement in racially offensive language does not . . . 'so infect the trial with unfairness as to make the resulting conviction a denial of due process.' "[74]

The prosecutor at Demetrius Frazier's trial told the jury that the victim's murder was especially heinous and painful, in part because of the defendant's race:

> One day, one Thanksgiving or one summer at the Starks family reunion, when Phyllis's [the victim's daughter's] baby is a few years older and the eating's done and it's time to sit down in the chair and have grandma read a book, Phyllis's little girl is going to say to her, "Momma, why don't I have a grandma?" And the only thing she's going to be able to do is pat her on the head and say, "Don't cry, baby. It's not so bad. She was killed by a black man."[75]

The Alabama Court of Criminal Appeals rejected the challenge to the propriety of the prosecutor's argument, stating: "We find no plain error in the prosecutor's comments during the closing argument at the penalty phase of the trial."[76]

In most cases, racial bias is covert and operates behind the scenes. One of the most significant forms of such bias is the skewing of jury decision making in capital cases by excluding African Americans from service on the jury. Such exclusion is the product of discrimination at either or both of two stages of the jury selection process. At the very beginning of the process, when a pool of potential venirepersons is assembled, the pool frequently underrepresents eligible African Americans.[77] Dozens of capital defendants have been convicted by juries in cases in which African Americans and other racial minorities have been illegally excluded from even being summoned for jury service.[78] In several Alabama counties, over a quarter of the African American population is illegally underrepresented on the list of prospective jurors.[79]

At the later stage of selection of the jury for a trial, racial discrimination resurfaces in the form of prosecutors' use of peremptory challenges to remove African Americans from the jury. Although the Supreme Court outlawed this practice in Batson v. Kentucky,[80] prosecutors continue to use a variety of tactics to attempt to evade the protections established by Batson. In the past several years, two dozen Alabama death row prisoners have had their convictions and death sentences declared unconstitutional because of prosecutors' racially discriminatory jury selection practices.[81]

Given the reluctance of appellate courts to overturn criminal convictions—and the host of procedural mechanisms an appellate court can invoke to avoid overturning a conviction despite a Batson violation or some other constitutional defect[82]—one can reasonably assume that the cases in which a *Batson* violation was found and relief granted are merely the tip of the iceberg.[83] The question then arises: Why is racial bias in jury selection so prevalent? The ineluctable answer is that prosecutors frequently rely on racial stereotypes and racially coded presumptions of guilt to achieve convictions and increase the likelihood that the death penalty will be imposed.[84]

There have been 23 executions in the state of Alabama between 1975, when the death penalty was reinstated, and 2000. In 21 out of 23 cases—91 percent—African Americans were significantly underrepresented in the juries that condemned the accused to death.[85] In over a third of these cases (35%), the jury was all white although the population in each county was between 33 and 47 percent African American. In 61 percent of the cases in which prisoners have been executed in Alabama since resumption of the use of capital punishment, the juries were either all white or had only one black juror.

On April 14, 2000, Robert Lee Tarver was executed by the state of Alabama even though one of his trial prosecutors had come forward a month before the scheduled execution and admitted that virtually every black person qualified for jury service was intentionally excluded by means of racially discriminatory conduct on the part of state prosecutors.[86] Mr. Tarver was tried by a jury of 11 white individuals and one African American in Russell County, Alabama, which is nearly 40 percent black. He was executed after the Alabama appellate courts refused to address the issue of illegal racial discrimination because his trial counsel failed to adequately object to the biased jury selection procedures.

In one case in Chambers County, Alabama, the prosecutor used peremptory strikes to remove all 26 African Americans qualified for jury service. Prior to trial, the prosecutor segregated potential jurors into four separate groups. The groups were labeled "Strong," "Medium," "Weak," and "Black." At trial, the prosecutor made comments about the race of various witnesses and made thinly veiled racist arguments to the all-white panel about why the African American defendant should be executed for the killing of a white man.[87]

All of these race issues are evaluated by decision makers who are almost exclusively white. Although black people constitute 26 percent of the Alabama population, there are no African American appellate court judges in the entire state, and fewer than 2 percent of the prosecutors and 4 percent of the criminal court judges are black. African Americans make up 63 percent of the prison population. Broad problems of racial bias in the administration of the criminal justice system—including disparate sentencing for noncapital offenses, racial profiling, drug prosecutions that are targeted on minority communities—go uncorrected.[88] Politicians perceive no advantage in pursuing reforms of these long-standing problems, especially since Alabama's practice of permanently disenfranchising anyone with a criminal conviction has resulted in the permanent denial of the right to vote for 31 percent of the black male population.[89]

AMERICA'S DELIBERATE INDIFFERENCE

The underrepresentation of racial minorities among judges, prosecutors, policy makers, and the people who establish rules, procedures, and outcomes within the criminal justice system is not unique to Alabama. Varying degrees of the problem exist in every jurisdiction in the United States where the death penalty is authorized.

However, the indifference with which most decision makers consider issues of racial bias in the administration of criminal justice is especially troubling in the death penalty context. The death penalty occupies an insidious place in the sociohistorical framework that shapes criminal justice debate and policy. Social order rhetoric structures and fuels the enactment of criminal laws and the enforcement of certain punishments.[90] In the south, lynchings and legally sanctioned executions have historically played a primary role in sustaining racial subordination and hierarchy.[91] Imposition of extreme and lethal violence against the poor and African Americans is inexorably linked to the legacy of racial apartheid in the United States.[92] The tolerance of racial bias in the modern death penalty era, placed within the context of this troubling history, represents a serious threat to anti-discrimination reforms and equal justice in America.[93]

David Garland, who has studied the sociology of the death penalty, recently observed:

[T]he struggles over capital punishment in America have been fought from trenches that were dug in other, fateful conflicts in the nation's history—conflicts about slavery, about Southern culture, about state and federal powers, about race relations, and about the cultural values that defined American identity at the beginning of the twentieth century. As a penal measure or social ritual, capital punishment has become inessential. But it lives on as a symbol of cultural identity, a sign of political affiliations, and as part of the psychic make-up of the groups that lend it their support.[94]

When American policy makers, politicians, judges, and other decision makers accept the racially discriminatory imposition of the death penalty, they necessarily undermine the effort to confront the legacy of slavery and the continuing struggle to achieve racial equality. The African American experience of criminal justice administration in the United States has resulted in distrust and bitterness for over two hundred years. Every act, or perceived act, of discrimination and racial injustice sustains and perpetuates this history. Because the death penalty *appears* to be infected by racial bias, one could reasonably support its abolition as a principled gesture of anti-racism in the shadow of America's troubled past. Instead, most policy makers and political leaders take the opposite view: They treat the criminal who offends as not worthy of any consideration or protection in the struggle to overcome race discrimination in America. Even some racial minorities have abandoned those who have offended as exempt from the quest for civil rights and equality. However, it is precisely in the administration of the death penalty, where we deal with some of the most despised, hated, and reviled people in America, that the clearest evidence of our willingness to confront conscious and unconscious racial bias must be measured.

The laws that make it clear that we cannot, as a constitutional matter, accept a death penalty infected with racial bias in the United States have previously required a retreat from capital punishment.[95] A similar retreat is necessary now.

THE CONFLUENCE OF RACE AND POVERTY IN
CAPITAL CASES

Racial minorities face unacceptable, illegitimate discrimination and bias in America's criminal justice system. Racial minorities in the United States are also disproportionately poor. Poverty and economic disadvantage among people of color increase the risk of wrongful or unfair treatment in the criminal justice system and compound the problem of race in death penalty cases. The inability of the poor to obtain adequate legal assistance has been apparent for years to those familiar with the realities of the capital punishment system.[96] Even two Justices of the United States Supreme Court have publicly commented on the pervasive inadequacy of appointed counsel in capital cases.[97]

In Alabama there is no state-funded public defender system. Indigent defendants are represented at trial and on appeal by appointed attorneys who are subject to severe compensation limitations. Until 1999, Alabama's cap on compensation in capital cases was the lowest in the nation. Alabama's hourly rate of compensation was $20 per hour for out-of-court work and $40 per hour for in-court activity. Compensation for out-of-court work was capped at $1,000 per phase of a capital trial.[98] The exceptionally low rate of compensation for representation of capital defendants has frequently meant that lawyers neglect to spend the time necessary to effectively assist a capital defendant. Over 80 percent of those currently under sentence of death were tried, convicted and sentenced to death with defense attorneys whose compensation was capped at $1,000.

In 1997, I represented a death row prisoner on appeal whose appointed trial attorney did not call a single witness or present any evidence whatsoever on behalf of his client at either the guilt or penalty phases of his trial. The evidentiary portion of the penalty phase occupies less than a single page of the court's transcript.[99] In a 2000 Dothan, Alabama, case, the trial lasted only seven hours—including closing statements and jury instructions—before an indigent accused was convicted of capital murder.[100] After the state's presentation of evidence, the defense presented no witnesses and the jury began deliberating at 3:15 P.M. on the same day that the trial had started.[101] After being convicted of capital murder, this defendant was sentenced to death.

Inadequate funding of defense services to capital defendants is a national problem, as is detailed elsewhere in this book. However, for racial minorities, bias against the poor exacerbates the already intolerable risk of unjust treatment and increases the unacceptable risk of wrongful conviction. There are too many capital cases in the United States in which indigent defendants were represented by attorneys who were asleep during trial proceedings, under the influence of drugs and alcohol, or otherwise engaged in unprofessional conduct as counsel for the capitally accused. Poor and minority defendants have been sexually abused by defense attorneys, subjected to racial slurs and bigotry by their counsel in open court, and undermined by the very advocate assigned to defend them. One attorney, by his own admission, defended a capital client with mysticism, prophecy,[102] clairvoyance,[103] and his alleged ability to communicate with the jury by means of telepathy.[104]

These problems go uncorrected in post-conviction proceedings, in which the United States Supreme Court has declared that there is no right to counsel, even for death row prisoners, who want to challenge a wrongful conviction or death sentence in collateral appeals. As is documented in studies showing the high reversal rate of capital convictions and death sentences across the country, post-conviction proceedings are often the only juncture at which evidence of reversible error may be presented. An extraordinary number of capital cases have been reversed by state or federal courts that determined the conviction and/or sentence of death was unconstitutionally imposed.[105] Without access to collateral proceedings, death row prisoners cannot obtain essential state and federal review of their convictions and sentences.[106]

Yet there are hundreds of death row prisoners in America who are currently without legal representation. Many are literally dying for legal assistance.[107] The consequence of all of these factors is that capital punishment really does mean that "them without the capital gets the punishment." Poverty has become a defining feature of America's death penalty system. Support for capital punishment necessarily means accepting a punishment that is applied unequally and that largely condemns poor and disfavored defendants who are unable to obtain adequate legal assistance.

THE IMMORAL CHARACTER OF CAPITAL PUNISHMENT CREATES NEW MORAL ISSUES

As unrepresented death row prisoners are scheduled for execution because they have failed to obtain legal representation in time to meet state and federal appeal deadlines, capital punishment in America takes on defining characteristics that raise a completely different set of moral questions. Can people who are committed to confronting racial bias and economic discrimination accept the execution of prisoners whose death sentences are a product of unequal and unjust application of the law against the poor and people of color? I believe that they cannot and that they must seek an end to capital punishment.

Beyond the abstract debate itself, the racial and economic features of the modern death penalty present moral questions about the death penalty that cannot be adequately answered. Race and poverty bias create results in death penalty cases that are unreliable and unfair. Judges are required to either accept the unfairness or order new trials. The frustration, delay, and angst over accepting a conviction or sentence that is unfair prompt judges and most politicians to relax the law's requirements for fairness so that executions can take place expeditiously. However, this cannot be a morally acceptable approach to capital punishment. As Ronald Dworkin has stated, tolerance of an unfair or unjust administration of the death penalty creates its own immorality:

> If Americans insist on the death penalty, they must accept the moral consequences of their choice. Judges must listen, with painstaking and patient attention, to every argument for life that is not plainly frivolous. If they find any actual mistake in the process that has condemned a human being to death, they must repeat that process and give him another chance for life. These are inescapable moral demands.

What if we cannot meet these demands? What if we cannot tolerate all the stays and appeals and retrials that a decent respect for human life requires without making the law seem foolish and without subverting the point of a death sentence? Then we must abandon capital punishment, even if we think it right in principle, because then we cannot have it, even if it is right, without cheating.[108]

Ultimately, the moral question surrounding capital punishment in America has less to do with whether those convicted of violent crime deserve to die than with whether state and federal governments deserve to kill those whom it has imprisoned. The legacy of racial apartheid, racial bias, and ethnic discrimination is unavoidably evident in the administration of capital punishment in America. Death sentences are imposed in a criminal justice system that treats you better if you are rich and guilty than if you are poor and innocent. Embracing a certain quotient of racial bias and discrimination against the poor is an inexorable aspect of supporting capital punishment. This is an immoral condition that makes rejecting the death penalty on moral grounds not only defensible but necessary for those who refuse to accept unequal or unjust administration of punishment.

In the twenty-first century, human rights around the globe looms large as one of the defining issues of our time. Terrorism, religious and ethnic conflict, and protection of human rights in the face of new fears, tensions, and wars make the commitment to fair and just application of the law essential. Without such a commitment, there is no principled distinction between those who kill out of anger to avenge the death of another and those who seek to end killing. The death penalty is not disconnected from this struggle but core to it. As Albert Camus wrote:

A punishment that penalizes without forestalling is indeed called revenge. It is a quasi-arithmetical reply made by society to whoever breaks its primordial law. That reply is as old as man; it is called the law of retaliation. Whoever has done me harm must suffer harm; whoever has put out my eye must lose an eye; and whoever has killed must die. This is an emotion, and a particularly violent one, not a principle. Retaliation is related to nature and instinct, not to

At a conference on wrongful convictions held in Chicago in 1998, I spoke to innocent men and women who had been exonerated and released from death row in the U.S., some of whom narrowly escaped execution, including two people our office represented. (Photo courtesy of Northwestern University School of Law.)

law. Law, by definition, cannot obey the same rules as nature. If murder is in the nature of man, the law is not intended to imitate or reproduce that nature. It is intended to correct it. Now, retaliation does no more than ratify and confer the status of a law on a pure impulse of nature.[109]

As has been frequently stated, we measure the civility of society—the commitment of a nation to equal justice—not by how it treats the wealthy, the privileged, or the esteemed but rather how it treats the poor, the disadvantaged, and the disfavored. Death row prisoners are the most despised, rejected, and hated people in American society. It is easy to ignore evidence of bias or unfair application of law in the cases that control their fate. However, in the face of such pervasive evidence, one cannot support capital punishment without retreating from a meaningful commitment to combating racial bias and economic inequality or giving into vengeful rage that blinds us to problems of unfairness. Either position is morally indefensible in a nation that is committed to the rule of law, human rights, and equal justice.

CONCLUSION

Sooner or later, capital punishment will be abolished in the United States. The problems with the death penalty are too significant and too overt for this practice to survive. The death penalty is dis-enabling to a nation still struggling to overcome the legacy of slavery and racial apartheid because it operates in a manner that reveals insidious race consciousness. The death penalty presents the wealth-dependent character of the American criminal justice system in a light that raises fundamental questions about our dedication to equal justice under law.

No one can dispute that the death penalty is a punishment that leaves no room for error. It requires completely reliable procedures that leave no question of fairness or injustice unanswered. Yet, capital punishment is administered in court systems that are frequently unreliable and that are replete with errors, misjudgments, and questionable outcomes.

If courage and understanding overcome fear and anger, the changing debate about the death penalty in the United States will evolve into a discussion about how and when capital punishment must be abolished, not whether it should be abolished. Until that time, those who are close to the administration of capital punishment in America must reflect conscientiously about all the moral requirements of equal justice under the law. I am convinced that informed reflection will lead to an end to the use of the death penalty and a commitment to fair and just application of the law, even for the condemned who occupy death rows across America.

NOTES

1. In 1985, I joined the Southern Center for Human Rights (SCHR) in Atlanta, Georgia, as a staff attorney. I was involved in capital trials and death penalty appeals across the south, primarily in Georgia, Alabama, Louisiana, and Mississippi. In 1989, I became the Executive Director of the Alabama Capital Representation Resource Center in Montgomery, Alabama, where I supervised capital litigation for death row prisoners, recruited counsel for indigent inmates, and provided legal aid to capital defendants and condemned prisoners across the United States. In 1995, I founded the Equal Justice Initiative of Alabama (EJI), a private nonprofit organization that provides legal assistance to the poor. I have represented capital defendants and death row prisoners at all levels of the trial, appellate, and post-conviction processes.

2. Concerns about the fairness and propriety of capital punishment can evolve with direct experience in America's criminal justice system, even for those who are not in the defense function. George Ryan, the Illinois Republican governor who campaigned in support of the death penalty in 1998, provides the most dramatic example. After witnessing a steady procession of innocent people exonerated and released from death row in Illinois, Governor Ryan ended his term by commuting every death sentence and calling for an end to capital punishment. Donald Cabana, who was the prison warden at Parchment Prison, Mississippi, where he carried out executions, has now written about his changed view of the death penalty. Former Texas Death Row minister Carroll Pickett has similarly written: "At one point, I did support capital punishment. I was wrong." CAROLL PICKETT WITH CAROL STOWERS, WITHIN THESE WALLS: MEMOIRS OF A DEATH HOUSE CHAPLAIN (2002).

Another example is Supreme Court Justice Harry A. Blackmun, who began at one end of the spectrum by voting to uphold the death penalty in 1972 (*Furman v. Georgia*, 408 U.S. 238, 405–14 (1972) (Blackmun, J., dissenting)) and again in 1976 (*Gregg v. Georgia*, 428 U.S. 153, 227 (1976) (Blackmun, J., concurring in the judgment)) but eventually declared in 1994 that he felt "morally and intellectually obligated simply to concede that the death penalty experiment has failed" and that it was "virtually self-evident to [him] now that no combination of procedural rules or substantive regulations ever can save the death penalty from its inherent constitutional deficiencies" (*Callins v. Collins*, 510 U.S. 1141, 1143–45 (1994) (Blackmun, J., dissenting from denial of *certiorari*)). Former Florida Supreme Court Chief Justice and ex-prosecutor Gerald Kogan is now an outspoken opponent of capital punishment based on his years reviewing death penalty cases. Justice Paul Pfeifer of the Ohio Supreme Court, one of the authors of the state's death penalty law, has recently stated that he now wants to distance himself from capital punishment. "Knowing what I know now, my name wouldn't have been on it" (*Akron Beacon Journal* Web site, 2/18/99). Upon retirement, former Chief Justice Moses Harrison of the Illinois Supreme Court wrote: "Despite the courts' efforts to fashion a death penalty scheme that is just, fair and reliable, the system is not working" (AP, Sept. 5, 2002). Robert F. Utter, a former chief justice of the Washington Supreme Court, began his legal career as a prosecutor in Seattle, where he "assisted on a trial where the death penalty was sought," but "came to believe . . . that our proceduralist approach to regulating capital punishment has perpetuated arbitrariness, unreason, and injustice" and that the death penalty "squanders the legal and moral resources of our nation, in the futile effort to accommodate fundamental tensions that make any civilized administration of the death penalty impossible." Robert F. Utter, *Unjust Laws*, 19 CARDOZO L. REV. 1035, 1036, 1037, 1039 (1997).

3. This may change as critics of capital punishment become increasingly vocal about the enormous financial costs of imposing the death penalty. *See* Ronald J. Tabak, *How Empirical Studies Can Affect Positively the Politics of the Death Penalty*, 83 CORNELL L. REV. 1431, 1439–40 (1998). *See also* PHILIP J. COOK & DONNA B. SLAWSON, THE COSTS OF PROCESSING MURDER CASES IN NORTH CAROLINA, 97–100 (1993) (estimating that the extra cost of processing a capital case, rather than a noncapital one, was more than two million dollars for each death sentence likely to be executed); Christy Hoppe, *Executions Cost Texas Millions*, DALLAS MORNING NEWS, March 8, 1992, at 1A, 12A; Christy Hoppe, *$2.3 Million to Burn: Is This Justice?*, CHI. TRIB., March 24, 1992, at 8 (estimating that in 1992 the processing of each capital case cost Texas an average of $2.3 million, while imprisoning a person for 40 years in a maximum-security cell cost about $750,000).

4. A number of states now permit family members of the victim to sit at counsel table with the prosecution during a capital trial. *See, e.g., State v. Dickens*, 1999 WL 1847333 (Del. Com. Pl. Mar. 18, 1999) (defendant's argument that alleged victim was allowed to sit at the prosecutor's table lacks merit); *Miles v. State*, 411 S.E.2d 566 (Ga. App. 1991) (relative of crime victim permitted to sit at counsel table with prosecutor where victim's presence needed for orderly presentation of case and no improper conduct); *State v. Smoot*, 590 P.2d 1001 (Idaho 1978) (trial court did not abuse discretion by permitting the victim to sit at counsel table during one phase of the trial); *Miller v. State*, 648 N.E.2d 1208 (Ind. App. 4th Dist. 1995) (trial court did not err in allowing the victim to sit at counsel's table with the deputy prosecutor throughout trial when the defense had sought an order for separation of witnesses after the victim had testified).

5. The newspaper articles on this topic are far too numerous to cite here. A

particularly noteworthy example is the five-part series on "The Failure of the Death Penalty in Illinois" that appeared in the *Chicago Tribune*, November 14–18, 1999: Ken Armstrong & Steve Mills, *Death Row Justice Derailed: Bias, Errors and Incompetence in Capital Cases Have Turned Illinois? Harshest Punishment into Its Least Credible*, CHI. TRIB., Nov. 14, 1999, at 1; Ken Armstrong & Steve Mills, *Inept Defenses Cloud Verdicts: with Their Lives at Stake, Defendants in Illinois Capital Trials Need the Best Attorneys Available. But They Often Get Some of the Worst*, CHI. TRIB., Nov. 15, 1999, at 1; Steve Mills & Ken Armstrong, *The Inside Informant*, CHI. TRIB., Nov. 16, 1999, at 1; Steve Mills & Ken Armstrong, *A Tortured Path to Death Row*, CHI. TRIB., Nov. 17, 1999, at 1; Steve Mills & Ken Armstrong, *Convicted by a Hair*, CHI. TRIB., Nov. 18, 1999, at 1. *See also infra* note ___ (citing sources that contain compilations of cases of innocent and probably innocent persons who have been sentenced to death).

6. The first part of a major study—James. S. Liebman, Jeffrey Fagan & Valerie West, *A Broken System: Error Rates in Capital Cases, 1973–1995*—was released in June 2000 and can be found on the Web site http://justice.policy.net. *See also* James S. Liebman, Jeffrey Fagan, Valerie West & Jonathan Lloyd, *Capital Attrition Error Rates in Capital Cases, 1973–1995*, 78 TEX. L. REV. 1839 (2000). The second part of the study—James S. Liebman, Jeffrey Fagan, Andrew Gelman, Valerie West, Garth Davies & Alexander Kiss, *A Broken System, Part II: Why There Is So Much Error in Capital Cases, and What Can Be Done About It*—was released in February 2002, and can be found on the Web site http://www.law.columbia.edu/brokensystem2/.

7. *See* Samuel R. Gross & Phoebe C. Ellsworth, *Second Thoughts: Americans' Views on the Death Penalty at the Turn of the Century*, in BEYOND REPAIR (Stephen P. Garvey ed., 2003).

8. There have been 810 executions at the time of this writing and 102 people have been exonerated or released from death row after being wrongly convicted and sentenced to death.

9. *See, e.g.*, James Liebman, Jeff Fagan & Valerie West, *Technical Errors Can Kill*, NAT'L L.J., Sept. 4, 2000 (describing and responding to criticisms of study). *Compare, e.g.*, Adam L. VanGrack, Note, *Serious Error with "Serious Error": Repairing a Broken System of Capital Punishment*, 79 WASH. U. L.Q. 973 (2001) *with* Jeffrey Fagan, James S. Liebman & Valerie West, *Misstatements of Fact in Adam VanGrack's Student Note: A Letter to the Editors of the Washington University Quarterly*, 80 WASH. U. L.Q. 417 (2002) *and with* Adam L. VanGrack, *Elevating Form over Substance: A Reply to Professors James Liebman, Jeffrey Fagan and Valerie West*, 80 WASH. U. L.Q. 427 (2002) *and with* Jeffrey Fagan, James S. Liebman & Valerie West, *VanGrack's Explanations: Treating the Truth as a Mere Matter of "Form,"* 80 Wash. U. L.Q. 439 (2002). *Compare also, e.g.*, Joseph L. Hoffman, *Violence and the Truth*, 76 IND. L.J. 939 (2001) *with* Valerie West, Jeffrey Fagan & James S. Liebman, *Look Who's Extrapolating: A Reply to Hoffman*, 76 IND. L.J. 951 (2001) *and with* Joseph L. Hoffman, *A Brief Response to Liebman, Fagan, and West*, 76 IND. L.J. 957 (2001).

10. At trial Sheriff Tate testified that, at the time of the arrest, Mr. McMillian was not a murder suspect but was solely wanted for the sodomy charge.

11. Mr. McMillian had no prior felony convictions. He had an affair with a young white woman which was made public by the woman's ex-husband during divorce proceedings. Mr. McMillian believed he became a target of police suspicion as a result of this relationship.

12. Mr. McMillian had never met Ralph Myers before his arrest and the sodomy charges were later dismissed.

13. *McMillian v. Johnson*, 878 F. Supp. 1473, 1488 (M.D. Ala. 1995).

14. Mr. McMillian's transfer from county jail to death row was the result of a motion by the state prosecutor seeking Mr. McMillian's transfer to the custody of the state prison system. The trial court judge, Judge Robert E. Lee Key, granted the motion and Mr. McMillian was taken to Holman State Prison. At Holman, Mr. McMillian was given a death row prisoner's orientation, a death row prisoner's manual, placed in a death row cell, and subjected to all of the restrictions imposed on death row prisoners in Alabama—even though he had not been tried or convicted of any offense. In my review of scores of death penalty cases, it is the only time I have ever seen law enforcement officials effectuate this kind of intimidating treatment of a person arrested for a crime.

15. Mr. Myers remained in the Monroe County Jail for seven months until February 1988, when Mr. McMillian was originally scheduled for trial. The trial was continued because Myers refused to testify on the day of trial. Myers was thereupon again returned to death row. Except for a short period of time when Myers was sent to a state mental hospital, he remained on death row until August of 1988 when he once again agreed to testify. After testifying against Mr. McMillian, Myers was again returned to the Monroe County Jail.

16. See *McMillian v. State*, 616 So.2d 933 (Ala. Crim. App. 1993).

17. Myers' testimony was corroborated by two witnesses who falsely claimed to have seen Mr. McMillian's truck at the crime scene. Bill Hooks testified that he drove past the cleaners on the morning that Ronda Morrison was murdered and saw Mr. McMillian's truck parked outside the store. Although Ralph Myers had testified that the truck was some fifty yards away from the cleaners in another parking lot, Hooks's testimony was presented by the state as corroborative evidence. Hooks gave his statement to the police while he was in jail on a burglary charge. Immediately after giving this statement to the police, he was released from jail, fines that he owed the City of Monroeville were dismissed at the request of the District Attorney and law enforcement officials, and Hooks was permitted to avoid payment of fines on subsequent traffic offenses. Hooks was given money by the sheriff before his testimony and ultimately was paid $5,000 in reward money. A week before Mr. McMillian's trial, another alleged witness, a white man named Joe Hightower, was brought to court by the sheriff. Hightower had been threatened with prosecution for drug charges. Hightower testified that he also saw Mr. McMillian's truck in front of the cleaners. Hightower received at least $2,000 in reward money.

Both Hooks and Hightower testified at trial that they knew the truck belonged to Mr. McMillian because it was a "low-rider" or had been modified to sit close to the ground. Although Mr. McMillian owned a low-rider truck at the time of his arrest, his truck was not modified until May of 1987, six months after the crime took place in November 1986.

18. The state prosecutor completed her examination of Ralph Myers by asking him about the woman with whom Mr. McMillian was alleged to have had a romantic affair. After asking Myers to describe the woman, her race and her hair color, the state posed its last question before resting its case: "Was she a girl friend of Mr. McMillian?" The witness affirmed and the state concluded with "Nothing further, your Honor." *McMillian* Trial Record at 379–380. The prosecutor was subsequently elected to the Supreme Court of Alabama and now sits on the state's highest court as an appellate judge.

19. Alabama law permits elected trial judges to override jury verdicts of life imprisonment without parole.

20. *McMillian v. State,* 570 So.2d 1285 (Ala. Crim. App. 1990); *McMillian v. State,* 594 So.2d 1253 (Ala. Crim. App. 1991).

21. Mr. Myers's admission that he testified falsely against Mr. McMillian opened up additional avenues of investigation that also produced evidence of law enforcement officials' misconduct and abuse. For example, we discovered that a month prior to Mr. McMillian's trial, Myers told several state doctors in a court-ordered pre-trial evaluation that he was about to frame an innocent man for murder. Myers told the doctors that he had no knowledge of Mr. McMillian's involvement in the murder of Ronda Morrison and that he was being pressured to testify falsely to help the state with its case. Myers gave statements to at least four state doctors revealing that his testimony against Walter McMillian was false. The reports from these doctors were sent to the prosecutor and to the Circuit Court judge shortly before Mr. McMillian's trial but were never disclosed to the defense or the jury.

22. We were able to confirm that Mr. McMillian's truck was not a low-rider in November of 1986. We gathered evidence showing that Ralph Myers did not even know who Mr. McMillian was in March of 1987, some four months after they allegedly committed this crime together. We discovered that the state arranged for Bill Hooks to be removed from jail so that he could inspect Mr. McMillian's truck before Hooks gave a written statement stating he saw Mr. McMillian's truck at the crime scene. We also found evidence proving that law enforcement officials knowingly concealed information which would have helped establish Mr. McMillian's innocence prior to trial.

23. *McMillian v. State,* 616 So.2d 933 (Ala. Crim. App. 1993).

24. NAACP Legal Defense and Education Fund, Inc. Death Row U.S.A. (Winter 2003).

25. *Id.* By the end of 2002, 820 executions had taken place in the United States since 1976. All but 92 of these executions took place in the former slave-holding and Jim Crow states of Texas, Virginia, Florida, Georgia, Alabama, Mississippi, Missouri, Tennessee, North Carolina, Oklahoma, South Carolina, Delaware, Louisiana, Kentucky, and Maryland.

26. A recent exoneration of a prisoner in Michigan, convicted of murder and rape

in 1985, was the 110th exoneration in the last several years based on DNA evidence, some of which were capital cases. *See* Jodi Wilgoren, *Man Freed after DNA Clears Him of Murder*, N.Y. TIMES, Aug. 27, 2002, at A10. A compilation of "Recent Cases of Innocence and Possible Innocence," prepared by the Death Penalty Information Center (DPIC), is available at http://www.essential.org/dpic/dpicrecinnoc.html. For earlier compilations of such cases, see, *e.g.*, MICHAEL L. RADELET, HUGO A. BEDAU & CONSTANCE E. PUTNAM, IN SPITE OF INNOCENCE: ERRONEOUS CONVICTIONS IN CAPITAL CASES (1992); Hugo Adam Bedau & Michael L. Radelet, *Miscarriages of Justice in Potentially Capital Cases*, 40 STAN. L. REV. 21 (1987). *See also* JIM DWYER, PETER NEUFELD & BARRY SCHECK, ACTUAL INNOCENCE: FIVE DAYS TO EXECUTION AND OTHER DISPATCHES FROM THE WRONGLY CONVICTED (2000); Samuel R. Gross, *Lost Lives: Miscarriages of Justice in Capital Cases*, 61 LAW & CONTEMPORARY PROBLEMS 125 (Autumn 1998); Samuel R. Gross, *The Risks of Death: Why Erroneous Convictions Are Common in Capital Cases*, 44 Buff. L. REV. 469 (1996); Michael L. Radelet & Hugo Adam Bedau, *The Execution of the Innocent*, 61 LAW & CONTEMPORARY PROBLEMS 105 (Autumn 1998).

27. *See, e.g., United States ex rel. Madej v. Schomig*, No. 98 C 1866, 2002 WL 31386480 (N.D. Ill. Oct. 22, 2002) (holding that Vienna Convention creates individually enforceable rights, noting that operation of certain procedural default rules violates Vienna Convention, and granting habeas corpus relief on ineffective assistance of counsel claim where petitioner was not informed of consular right and thus deprived of effective counsel that would have been provided by Polish consulate); *Valdez v. State*, 46 P.3d 703 (Okla. Crim. App. 2002) (finding Vienna Convention claim procedurally barred despite *LaGrand* but granting relief to correct miscarriage of justice where Mexican consulate discovered significant mitigating evidence which made clear that trial counsel was ineffective); LaGrand Case (*Germany v. United States*), 2001 I.C.J. 104 (June 27, 2001) (United States violated Vienna Convention by permitting Arizona execution of two German nationals who were not informed in a timely manner of their individual right to seek assistance from the German consulate and denied review of consular rights claim on procedural default grounds); *Garza v. Lappin*, 253 F.3d 918 (7th Cir. 2001) (holding that Inter-American Commission on Human Rights' decision that federal prisoner's death sentence was violation of international human rights norms was nonbinding and did not give prisoner judicially cognizable right to stay of execution but acknowledging that decisions of Inter-American Court of Human Rights could be binding if United States ratifies American Convention on Human Rights). *See also* Ginger Thompson, *An Execution in Texas Strains Ties with Mexico and Others*, N.Y. TIMES, Aug. 15, 2002 (President Vicente Fox of Mexico canceled meeting with President George W. Bush at his Texas ranch to protest Texas execution of Javier Suárez Medina, joining 16 other nations in protesting United States' failure to inform Medina of his right to help from his government; noting that many nations, including 15 members of European Union, South Africa, and Canada, have refused to extradite suspects to the United States without assurances that suspects will not face

death penalty, and that Spain and France have refused to cooperate in death penalty cases against suspected terrorists).

28. In 1989, when presented with the question of whether the Eighth Amendment categorically prohibits the execution of mentally retarded persons, the Supreme Court declined to find such a prohibition in the Eighth Amendment, stating that insufficient objective evidence existed of a national consensus against execution of the mentally retarded. *Penry v. Lynaugh*, 492 U.S. 302, 340 (1989). As a result, the United States was, until recently, one of only a handful of nations of the world that permitted the execution of mentally retarded persons. *See* Brief for Petitioner at 43 n.46, *Atkins v. Virginia*, 122 S. Ct. 2242 (2002) (identifying United States, Japan, and Kyrgyzstan as sole countries that reportedly permit execution of mentally retarded persons and explaining that questions had arisen concerning the permissibility of the practice in Kyrgyzstan). In June 2002, in a 6–3 decision, the Supreme Court held that the "consensus" of opinion that has emerged in the 13 years since *Penry* compels the conclusion that "death is not a suitable punishment for a mentally retarded criminal" and that the Eighth Amendment therefore prohibits its use in such cases. *Atkins v. Virginia*, 122 S. Ct. 2242, 2252 (2002). Although *Atkins* would seem to have closed the book on this disgraceful chapter of the United States' experience with the death penalty, the story is hardly over. In the wake of *Atkins*, we are already seeing evidence of the capital punishment process adjusting to diminish the impact of the decision and to continue the abuses of the past. For example, in capital cases in which all parties had—until the issuance of the *Atkins* decision—viewed the defendant as self-evidently mentally retarded, prosecutors now are seeking to prevent the application of *Atkins* to the case by arguing that the defendant is not, in fact, mentally retarded.

29. In *Thompson v. Oklahoma*, 487 U.S. 815 (1988), a plurality of the Court, joined by Justice O'Connor in a concurring opinion, held that defendants under the age of 16 at the time of the crime cannot be executed under a statute that sets no minimum age for eligibility for the death penalty. Thereafter, in *Stanford v. Kentucky*, 492 U.S. 361 (1989), a different plurality of the Court, again joined by Justice O'Connor in concurrence, rejected an Eighth Amendment challenge to the execution of individuals who were 16 or 17 years old at the time of the crime. The United States' condoning of the execution of individuals who were below 18 at the time of the crime places this country in a small group of nations—including Iran, Nigeria, Pakistan, and Saudi Arabia—that tolerate this practice. For discussion of the international norms and conventions condemning the use of the death penalty for individuals who were minors at the time of the crime, see Victor L. Streib, Death Penalty for Juveniles (1987); Victor L. Streib, *American Death Penalty for Juveniles: An International Embarrassment*, 5 Geo. J. on Fighting Poverty 219 (1998); Victor L. Streib, *Emerging Issues in Juvenile Death Penalty Law*, 26 Ohio N.U. L. Rev. 725 (2000); Victor L. Streib, *Moratorium on the Death Penalty for Juveniles*, 61 Law & Contemp. Problems 55 (Autumn 1998).

30. NAACP Legal Defense and Education Fund, Inc., Death Row U.S.A., Summer 2002.

31. *See, e.g.*, David Cole, No Equal Justice: Race and Class in the American

CRIMINAL JUSTICE SYSTEM (1999); MARC MAUER, RACE TO INCARCERATE 118–61 (1999); MARC MAUER & TRACY HULING, YOUNG BLACK AMERICANS AND THE CRIMINAL JUSTICE SYSTEM: FIVE YEARS LATER (October 1995); JEROME MILLER, SEARCH AND DESTROY: AFRICAN-AMERICAN MALES IN THE CRIMINAL JUSTICE SYSTEM (1996); THE REAL WAR ON CRIME: THE REPORT OF THE NATIONAL CRIMINAL JUSTICE COMMISSION 99–121 (Steven R. Donziger, ed., 1996).

32. *Id.*

33. *See* Sherrilyn A. Ifill, *Judging the Judges: Racial Diversity, Impartiality and Representation on State Trial Courts*, 39 B.C. L. REV. 95, 95 & nn. 2–3 (1997) ("Only 3.8 % of all state court judges are African American. Among state trial court judges, only 4.1 % are African American"); Roscoe C. Howard, *Changing the System from Within: An Essay Calling on More African Americans to Consider Being Prosecutors*, 6 WIDENER L. SYMP. J. 139, 167 (Fall 2000) ("The number of minorities for the government in the criminal justice system are very low. Blacks make up only 4% of the attorneys in the criminal justice system, while only 3% are Hispanic"); C. J. Chivers, *For Black Officers, Diversity Has Its Limits*, N.Y. TIMES, April 2, 2001, at A1 (although New York City is 25 percent African American according to the 2000 census, the police force is 9.2 percent African American, the "proportion of male black supervisors has declined since 1990," and "five prestigious commands . . . are almost all white"); Jodi Wilgoren & Michael Cooper, *Police Trailing Other Cities in Diversity*, N.Y. TIMES, March 8, 1999, at B5 (chart showing racial composition of police forces of New York City, Chicago, Los Angeles, and Philadelphia in 1998 and 1999).

34. *See, e.g.*, Eileen Poe-Yamagata & Michael A. Jones, "And Justice for Some" (April 25, 2000), *available at* http://www.buildingblocksforyouth.org/justiceforsome/jfs.html (demonstrating, in the context of the juvenile justice system, sequential process in which youth of color receive harsher treatment than white youth at each of the stages of the process: arrest, referral to juvenile court, pre-trial detention, charging, transfer to adult court, disposition, placement in secure facilities, and incarceration in adult facilities). *See also* Donald C. Nugent, *Judicial Bias*, 42 CLEV. ST. L. REV. 1, 48 (1994) (author, an Ohio appellate judge and former trial court judge, reviews statistical evidence on gender and racial bias in the court systems and then states that these statistics should alert judges to "the absolute necessity . . . to recognize the possibility that gender, race, or ethnicity may influence their judicial decision-making").

35. *See* R. J. Sampson & J. L. Laurisen, *Racial and Ethnic Disparities in Crime and Criminal Justice in the United States, in* ETHNICITY, CRIME AND IMMIGRATION (Michel Tonry, ed., 1997).

36. The Sentencing Project, "Frug Policy and the Criminal Justice System," updated 2001. Available at *www.sentencingproject.org*, Sept. 1, 2001.

37. 408 U.S. 280 (1976).

38. *See id.* at 257 (Douglas, J., concurring) (condemning existing death penalty statutes as "pregnant with discrimination," and citing studies documenting racially discriminatory application of death penalty); *id.* at 364 (Marshall, J., concurring) (citing data showing that blacks had been "executed far more often than whites in proportion

to their percentage of the population" and showing that 405 of the 455 people executed for rape were African American). *See also id.* at 310 (Stewart, J., concurring) ("[m]y concurring Brothers have demonstrated that, if any basis can be discerned for the selection of these few to be sentenced to die, it is the constitutionally impermissible basis of race"); *id.* at 289 n.12 (Burger, C. J., dissenting) (acknowledging that statistics "suggest, at least as a historical matter, that Negroes have been sentenced to death with greater frequency than whites in several States, particularly for the crime of interracial rape").

39. 428 U.S. 153 (1976).

40. 481 U.S. 279 (1987).

41. The raw data from a study of murder cases in Georgia by Professor David Baldus of the University of Iowa constituted the statistical evidence in the case. *See* DAVID C. BALDUS ET AL., EQUAL JUSTICE AND THE DEATH PENALTY 306–93 (1990). The Baldus study revealed that an accused is 8.3 times more likely to receive the death penalty for crimes committed against whites than crimes committed against blacks. *Id.* at 314. If the accused is black, he or she is 21 times more likely to be sentenced to death if the victim is white, as opposed to black. *See id.* at 315 (table 50). Even after controlling for the effects of other variables influencing sentencing decisions in Georgia, a person accused of murdering someone white is 4.3 times more likely to be sentenced to death than someone accused of murdering a black person. *Id.* at 316.

42. *McCleskey,* 481 U.S. at 312.

43. The majority reasoned that "if we accepted McCleskey's claim that racial bias has impermissibly tainted the capital sentencing decision, we could soon be faced with similar claims as to other types of penalty." *Id.* at 315–16. In his dissent, Justice Brennan observed that "such a statement seems to suggest a fear of too much justice." *Id.* at 339.

44. *Id.* at 319 (quoting *Gregg v. Georgia,* 428 U.S. at 199 n.50). *See also McCleskey,* 481 U.S. at 297 ("[b]ecause discretion is essential to the criminal justice process, we would demand exceptionally clear proof before we would infer that the discretion has been abused"); *id.* at 313 ("Where discretion that is fundamental to our criminal justice process is involved, we decline to assume that what is *unexplained* is invidious. In the light of the safeguards designed to minimize racial bias in the process, the fundamental value of jury trial in our criminal justice system, and the benefits that discretion provides to criminal defendants, we hold that the Baldus study does not demonstrate a constitutionally significant risk of racial bias affecting the Georgia capital sentencing process").

45. For further discussion and critique of the *McCleskey* decision, see, *e.g.,* ANTHONY G. AMSTERDAM & JEROME BRUNER, MINDING THE LAW 194–216 (2000); SAMUEL R. GROSS & ROBERT MAURO, DEATH AND DISCRIMINATION 159–227 (1989); Anthony G. Amsterdam, *Race and the Death Penalty,* 7 CRIMINAL JUSTICE ETHICS 2 (1988). Even the author of the *McCleksey* decision, Justice Lewis F. Powell, Jr., was later critical of the opinion. After Justice Powell's retirement from the Court, he was asked by his biographer "whether he would change his vote in any case," whereupon Justice Powell

replied: " 'Yes, *McCleskey v. Kemp.*' " JOHN C. JEFFRIES, JR., JUSTICE LEWIS F. POWELL, JR. 451 (1994).

46. UNITED STATES GENERAL ACCOUNTING OFFICE, DEATH PENALTY SENTENCING: RESEARCH INDICATES PATTERN OF RACIAL DISPARITIES (Report to Senate and House Committees on the Judiciary) 5 (February 1990).

47. David C. Baldus, George Woodworth, David Zuckerman, Neil Alan Weiner & Barbara Broffitt, *Racial Discrimination and the Death Penalty in the Post-*Furman *Era: An Empirical and Legal Overview, with Recent Findings from Philadephia,* 83 CORNELL L. REV. 1638, 1742–45 (1998). These disparities persist even when researchers control for a wide range of variables including the relationship between the offender and the victim and whether the victim was a stranger or known to the accused.

48. The study revealed that from 1995 to 2000, 80 percent of all federal cases submitted by U.S. attorneys seeking the death penalty involved minority defendants. Even after review by the Attorney General, 73 percent of the cases approved for death penalty prosecution involved minority defendants. As of July 2000, 79 percent of the defendants under a federal death sentence were members of minority groups. U.S. DEP'T OF JUSTICE, SURVEY OF THE FEDERAL DEATH PENALTY SYSTEM 27, 34 (Sept. 12, 2000).

49. President Clinton stayed the execution of Juan Raul Garza for six months to allow the Justice Department time to gather and analyze more information about racial and geographic disparities in the federal death penalty system. Edward Walsh, *Clinton Stays Killer's Execution: Delay Prompted by Need to Complete Study on Disparities,* WASH. POST, Dec. 8, 2000, at A12.

50. The Department of Justice issued a supplementary report in response to President Clinton's and Attorney General Reno's requests for more information. The report stated that racial disparities in federal death cases are "not the result of any form of bias" but can be largely explained by the fact that federal prosecutions target drug-related crimes and in the districts where they do so, most "organized drug trafficking is largely carried out by gangs whose membership is drawn from minority groups." U.S. DEP'T OF JUSTICE, THE FEDERAL DEATH PENALTY SYSTEM: SUPPLEMENTARY DATA, ANALYSIS AND REVISED PROTOCOLS FOR CAPITAL CASE REVIEW 1 (June 6, 2001).

51. Dan Eggen, *U.S. Death Penalty System Not Biased, Ashcroft Declares: Study Finds Disparities in Prosecution,* WASH. POST, June 7, 2001, at A29. *See also* David Stout, *Attorney General Says Report Shows No Racial and Ethnic Bias in Federal Death Sentences,* N.Y. TIMES, June 7, 2001; *Mr. Ashcroft's Skimpy Report,* N.Y. TIMES, June 10, 2001 (editorial observing that although Ashcroft promised during confirmation hearings to continue more searching study by National Institute of Justice and outside experts on racial and geographic disparities in the death penalty, he reversed himself, saying it would take too long to complete and might not provide definitive answers). Since the time Ashcroft became Attorney General, the Justice Department has been three times more likely to seek death for black defendants accused of killing whites than for blacks alleged to have killed nonwhites. Minorities account for four of every five federal capital defendants. Dan Eggen, *Ashcroft Aggressively Pursues Death Penalty,* WASH. POST, July 1, 2002, at A1.

52. *Saldano v. Texas*, 530 U.S. 1212 (2000) (vacating judgment and remanding case to Court of Criminal Appeals of Texas for further consideration in light of state's confession of error).

53. *Saldano v. State*, 70 S.W.3d 873, 875 (Tex. Crim. App. 2002).

54. *Id.* at 885.

55. *Id.*

56. *Id.* at 891.

57. *Peek v. Florida*, 488 So.2d 52, 56 (Fla. 1986).

58. *Id.* at 56.

59. *Dobbs v. Zant*, 720 F. Supp. 1566, 1578 (N.D. Ga. 1989), *aff'd*, 963 F.2d 1403 (11th Cir. 1991), *rev'd on other grounds*, 506 U.S. 357 (1993).

60. *Id.*

61. *Id.* at 1575–77.

62. *Dobbs v. Zant*, 506 U.S. 357 (1993).

63. *See* Jay Reeves, *Per Capita, Alabama's Death Row Tops South*, HUNTSVILLE TIMES, July 6, 1999, at A1.

64. House Bill 159 (proposing death sentence for aggravated rape or sodomy), Senate Bill 115 (same) (Alabama Regular Session 2001); House Bill 29 (proposing mandatory death for nonhomicide acts of terrorism), Senate Bill 63 (death for terrorism or "intent to intimidate or coerce civilian population" or "influence the policy of a unit of government") (Alabama Fourth Special Session 2001); House Bill 38 (death for terrorism), HB209 (death for rape or sodomy), SB80 (death for terrorism), SB256 (same), SB357 (death for child abuse) (Alabama Regular Session 2002).

65. The Alabama statute provides that the judge, not the jury, is the final sentencer. *See* ALA. CODE § 13A-5-47(e) (jury's verdict is not binding on the sentencing court). Alabama's statue is unique in its "refusal to constrain its judges' power to condemn defendants over contrary jury verdicts." *Harris v. Alabama*, 513 U.S. 504, 524 (1995) (Stevens, J., dissenting). In Florida, which also has a judicial override system but one that includes some degree of appellate oversight of judicial overrides, the state supreme court has reversed a staggeringly high percentage of the judicial overrides of jury life recommendations. *See* Scott E. Erlich, Comment, *The Jury Override: A Blend of Politics and Death*, 45 AM. U. L. REV. 1403, 1432 & nn.213–17 (1996) ("Data indicates that between two-thirds to three-fourths of all Florida life-to-death overrides have been reversed or remanded on appeal."). In *Ring v. Arizona*, 122 S. Ct. 2428 (2002), the Court held that "capital defendants . . . are entitled to a jury determination of any fact on which the legislature conditions an increase in their maximum punishment." *Id.* at 2432. The Court's ruling may invalidate critical aspects of Alabama's capital sentencing scheme.

66. EJI Case Tracking Project. For discussion of the systemic distortions caused by elected judges' shaping their behavior on the bench to fit the perceived wishes of the electorate, *see* Stephen B. Bright, *Elected Judges and the Death Penalty in Texas: Why Full Habeas Corpus Review by Independent Federal Judges Is Indispensable to Protecting Constitutional Rights*, 78 TEX. L. REV. 1805 (2000); Stephen B. Bright, *Political Attacks*

on the Judiciary: Can Justice Be Done Amid Efforts to Intimidate and Remove Judges from Office for Unpopular Decisions?, 72 N.Y.U. L. REV. 308, 312–26 (1997); Stephen B. Bright & Patrick J. Keenan, *Judging and the Politics of Death: Deciding Between the Bill of Rights and the Next Election in Capital Cases*, 75 B.U. L. REV. 759, 776–813 (1995). *See also Harris v. Alabama*, 513 U.S. at 512 (Stevens, J., dissenting) ("The 'higher authority' to whom present-day capital judges may be 'too responsive' is a political climate in which judges who covet higher office—or who merely wish to remain judges—must constantly profess their fealty to the death penalty. . . . The danger that they will bend to political pressures when pronouncing sentence in highly publicized capital cases is the same danger confronted by judges beholden to King George III"); John Paul Stevens, *Opening Assembly Address, American Bar Association Annual Meeting, Orlando, Florida, August 3, 1996*, 12 ST. JOHN'S J. LEGAL COMMENT 21, 31 (1996) ("making the retention of judicial office dependent on the popularity of the judge inevitably affects the decisional process in high visibility cases, no matter how competent and how conscientious the judge may be").

67. *See* NAACP LEGAL DEFENSE FUND, DEATH ROW USA (Summer 2002).

68. ALABAMA CRIMINAL JUSTICE INFORMATION CENTER, CRIME IN ALABAMA 1999–2001.

69. EQUAL JUSTICE INITIATIVE TRACKING PROJECT (Summer 2002).

70. Trial Tr. at 28, *State v. Richardson*, CC-77-318 (Houston Co. Cir. Ct. 1978).

71. *Ivery v. State*, 686 So. 2d 495, 506 (Ala. Crim. App. 1996).

72. *Id.* at 504.

73. *Id.* at 505–06 (comment was insufficiently prejudicial to amount to plain error). Further appeals were not possible because Mr. Ivery committed suicide in his death row cell shortly after his conviction and death sentence were affirmed. *Ivery v. State*, 686 So. 2d 520 (Ala. Crim. App. 1996) (affirming sentence after remand), *reh'g denied* (Oct. 11, 1996), *cert. dismissed* (Jan. 2, 1997).

74. *Ivery*, 686 So.2d at 505–06.

75. *Frazier v. State*, 758 So.2d 577, 604 (Ala. Crim. App. 1999).

76. *Id.* At trial, the judge's and even defense counsel's willingness to overlook racially discriminatory conduct ultimately resulted in an outburst from the defendant, who shouted at the jury: "Shut the fuck up. That jury right there is racist, man. That jury is racist, man, look at them. That guy looking at me, man. That jury is racist, man. Look at them. Look at that jury, man, 10 mother-fucking white jurors up there. Fuck that." *Frazier*, 758 So. 2d at 593.

77. EQUAL JUSTICE INITIATIVE, RACE AND JURY SELECTION (1999).

78. It is a violation of the Sixth and Fourteenth Amendments to underrepresent cognizable groups from the jury pool from which jurors are selected. *Duren v. Missouri*, 439 U.S. 357 (1979); *Castenada v. Partida*, 430 U.S. 482 (1976); *Taylor v. Louisiana*, 419 U.S. 522 (1975).

79. EQUAL JUSTICE INITIATIVE, RACE AND JURY SELECTION.

80. 476 U.S. 79 (1986). Two decades before *Batson*, the Court had held in *Swain v. Alabama*, 380 U.S. 202 (1965) that a criminal defendant cannot sustain an equal

protection challenge by showing that the prosecutor used peremptory challenges in a discriminatory fashion in the defendant's own trial, but rather must prove discrimination over a prolonged period of time. *See Swain*, 380 U.S. at 223–24. By requiring defendants to look outside their own cases for proof of bias, the Court imposed a burden that was essentially insurmountable. During the two decades that followed *Swain*'s issuance, not a single defendant prevailed on a *Swain* challenge in state or federal court. In 1986, in *Batson*, the Court overruled *Swain* and held that a defendant *can* challenge the prosecutor's use of peremptory challenges in his or her own case. *Batson*, 476 U.S. at 92–93. The *Batson* doctrine has resulted in the reversal of a significant number of convictions in cases in which prosecutors used their peremptory challenges in a discriminatory fashion.

81. *See Bui v. Haley*, 279 F.3d 1327 (11th Cir. 2002); Yancey v. State, 813 So. 2d 1 (Ala. Crim. App. 2001); *Pace v. State*, 714 So. 2d 320 (Ala. Crim. App. 1996), *rev'd in part*, 714 So. 2d 332 (Ala. 1997) (plurality opinion), *remanded to* 714 So. 2d 340 (Ala. Crim. App. 1998); *Morrison v. Jones*, 952 F. Supp. 729 (M.D. Ala. 1996); *Cochran v. Herring*, 43 F.3d 1404 (11th Cir. 1995); *Freeman v. State*, 651 So. 2d 576 (Ala. Crim. App. 1994); *Kynard v. State*, 631 So. 2d 257 (Ala. Crim. App. 1993); Ex Parte Bankhead, 625 So. 2d 1146 (Ala. 1993); *Williams v. State*, 620 So. 2d 82 (Ala. Crim. App. 1992); *Walker v. State*, 611 So. 2d 1133 (Ala. Crim. App. 1992); *Neal v. State*, 612 So. 2d 1347 (Ala. Crim. App. 1992); *Duncan v. State*, 612 So. 2d 1304 (Ala. Crim. App. 1992); *Guthrie v. State*, 598 So. 2d 1013 (Ala. Crim. App. 1991); Ex Parte Floyd, 571 So. 2d 1234 (Ala. 1989); *Powell v. State*, 548 So. 2d 590 (Ala. Crim. App. 1988); *Turner v. State*, 521 So. 2d 93 (Ala. Crim. App. 1987); *Madison v. State*, 545 So. 2d 94 (Ala. Crim. App. 1987); *Owens v. State*, 531 So. 2d 22 (Ala. Crim. App. 1987); *Jackson v. State*, 516 So. 2d 774 (Ala. Crim. App. 1987); *Raines v. State*, 515 So. 2d 82 (Ala. Crim. App. 1987); *Henderson v. State*, 549 So. 2d 105 (Ala. Crim. App. 1987); *Acres v. State*, 548 So. 2d 459 (Ala. Crim. App. 1987); Ex Parte Godbolt, 546 So. 2d 991 (Ala. 1987).

82. For example, a defendant's failure to raise the claim in the proper manner can result in a state court's finding of waiver and a subsequent ruling in federal habeas corpus review that the procedural default doctrine bars federal habeas corpus relief. *See* HERTZ & LIEBMAN, RANDY HERTZ & JAMES LIEBMAN, FEDERAL CORPUS PRACTICE AND PROCEDURE (4th ed. 2001), Chapters 22, 26. Or, for example, a state appellate court or a federal court may determine that a constitutional violation has occurred but that the error was insufficiently "prejudicial" to require reversal. *See id.*, Chapter 31. Or, for example, a federal court may determine that there was a prejudicial constitutional error but that relief nonetheless is barred by the restrictive standard of federal court review established by Congress in 1996 in the Antiterrorism and Effective Death Penalty Act (AEDPA). *See id.*, Chapter 32.

83. A review of Alabama case law reveals cases in which apparently meritorious *Batson* claims were deemed to be waived because of defense counsel's failure to adequately preserve the claim for appellate review. *See, e.g., Lindsey v. Smith*, 820 F.2d 1137, 1142–45 (11th Cir. 1987). An appellate court disinclined to overturn a conviction on *Batson* grounds also can, of course, deny relief on the merits by refusing to find

that a violation occurred notwithstanding overwhelming evidence of discrimination. Thus, for example, in one Alabama case, the appellate court ruled that the defense had failed to make out a prima facie case of discrimination even though the district attorney (who had previously been censured by the Alabama Supreme Court for *Batson* violations) had used more than three-fourths of her peremptory challenges to exclude African American venirepersons. *See Harris v. State,* 632 So. 2d 503, 512–13 (Ala. Crim. App. 1992), *aff'd, Ex parte* Harris, 632 So. 2d 543 (Ala. 1993). In another Alabama case, the appellate court found that the prosecutor had adequately shown the nondiscriminatory basis of his use of all ten of his peremptory strikes to remove all ten African Americans from the venire by asserting, *inter alia,* that he needed to remove one venireperson because he looked "dumb as a fencepost" and needed to remove another because he resembled the defendant. *See Gamble v. State,* 357 S.E.2d 792, 795 (Ga. 1987). Even in cases in which the state all but admitted removing jurors on the basis of race, the reviewing appellate courts have refused to grant relief. For example, in one case the appellate courts treated as "racially neutral" the prosecutor's ostensible rationale of striking potential jurors because they were affiliated with Alabama State University—a predominantly black institution. *See Scott v. State,* 599 So. 2d 1222, 1227–28 (Ala. Crim. App.), *cert. denied,* 599 So. 2d 1229 (Ala. 1992).

84. There is a growing body of case law that establishes that jurors are acting on the racially inflamed messages they receive during jury trials. Juror misconduct claims that are rooted in racial bias rarely result in relief for death-sentenced prisoners but nonetheless reveal disturbing evidence of race conscious decision making. *See, e.g., Bacon v. Lee,* 225 F.3d 470, 472, 485 (4th Cir. 2000), *cert. denied,* 532 U.S. 950 (2001) (declining, in capital case, to consider jurors' evidence that during deliberations, jurors referred to African American defendant's race and his interracial relationship, and made racial jokes); *United States v. Roach,* 164 F.3d 403, 407, 412–13 (8th Cir. 1998) (holding inadmissible, in Native American's federal direct criminal appeal, Native American juror's affidavit alleging, among other things, that other jurors pressured her, referred to her race, and told her it was ten white people versus one Indian); *United States v. Brito,* 136 F.3d 397, 402, 414 (5th Cir.1998) (holding inadmissible, in federal direct criminal appeal, juror's affidavit asserting, among other things, that other jurors coerced her vote through threats and insults).

85. The prosecutors' drive to obtain an all-white jury is particularly evident in Alabama because the state employs a "struck" jury system and therefore a good deal of effort is required for a prosecutor to secure an all or predominantly white jury. Alabama lawyers "strike down" to a jury: They work from the entire venire list and eliminate every member until they are left with 12 names for the jury and two alternates. For example, in the case of Jesse Morrison, the goal of producing an all or predominantly white jury required the prosecutor's removal of 20 of the 21 black individuals who had qualified for jury service (Transcript of Postconviction Rec. at 122c, *Morrison v. State,* CC-78-10014 (Barbour County Cir. Ct. 1988), *aff'd,* 551 So. 2d 435 (Ala. Crim. App. 1989)); 12 of 13 African American venire members were eliminated from Darrell Watkins' capital trial (*Watkins v. State,* 632 So. 2d 555, 558 n.1 (Ala. Crim.

App. 1992)); all 16 African American venire members were removed by the state in Earl McGahee's case (*McGahee v. State,* 554 So. 2d 454, 459–62 (Ala. Crim. App.), *aff'd, Ex parte* McGahee, 554 So. 2d 473 (Ala. 1989).

86. After Mr. Tarver's execution was scheduled in 2000, the assistant prosecutor contacted me and revealed that black prospective jurors had been intentionally excluded from jury service on the basis of race. Mr. Tarver, who is black, had previously argued in his initial habeas corpus petition that the prosecutor used peremptory strikes in a racially discriminatory manner in violation of *Batson v. Kentucky,* 476 U.S. 79 (1986). The state prosecutor used 13 out of 16 peremptory strikes (81%) to exclude almost all of the qualified black veniremembers from jury service at Mr. Tarver's trial. Thirteen of the 14 qualified black jurors (93%) selected for jury service were excluded by the state prosecutor on the basis of race. Even though Russell County is almost 40 percent African American, Mr. Tarver was tried by a jury with 11 white jurors and only one black juror. The circuit court found that "the State was unable to rebut the prima facie case of a *Batson* violation." Russell County Circuit Court Order on Remand, 10/20/92. However, Mr. Tarver's trial counsel failed to preserve this issue at trial and on appeal. The court found that the "[d]efendant's claim is well-founded except for the procedural bar." *Id.* When presented with the claim in a successive state petition on the eve of execution, the Alabama Court of Criminal Appeals denied the petition on procedural grounds and denied a stay of execution (*see Tarver v. State,* 769 So.2d 338 (Ala. Crim. App. 2000), and the Alabama Supreme Court denied *certiorari.*

87. *See* Trial Tr. at 164, *State v. Jefferson,* CC-81-77 (Chambers County Cir. Ct. 1984) (prosecutor urges jury in burglary-murder case to impose death to "stop them" from raping and shooting and "to show them we mean business").

88. INVISIBLE PUNISHMENT: THE COLLATERAL CONSEQUENCES OF MASS IMPRISONMENT (Marc Mauer & Chesney-Lund, eds., 2002); MARC MAUER, DIMINISHING RETURNS: CRIME AND INCARCERATION IN THE 1990S (2000); MARC MAUER, INTENDED AND UNINTENDED CONSEQUENCES: STATE RACIAL DISPARITIES IN IMPRISONMENT (1997).

89. HUMAN RIGHTS WATCH AND THE SENTENCING PROJECT, LOSING THE VOTE: THE IMPACT OF FELONY DISENFRANCHISEMENT LAWS IN THE UNITED STATES (1998).

90. *See* David Garland, *Punishment and Culture: The Symbolic Dimensions of Criminal Justice,* 11 STUD. L. POL. & SOC'Y 191 (1991); Austin Sarat, *Capital Punishment as a Legal, Political, and Cultural Fact: An Introduction, in* THE KILLING STATE: CAPITAL PUNISHMENT IN LAW, POLITICS AND CULTURE 3 (Austin Sarat, ed., 1999); Austin Sarat, *The Cultural Life of Capital Punishment: Responsibility and Representation in* Dead Man Walking *and* Last Dance, 11 YALE J.L. & HUMAN. 153 (Winter 1999).

91. "In the first decades of the twentieth century, when death penalty opponents were securing abolitionist legislation in the North, the southern states were lynching and executing blacks at a higher rate than ever. Below the Mason-Dixon line, campaigns for the abolition of capital punishment encountered the same implacable resistance that had greeted earlier demands for the abolition of slavery." David Garland, *Judicial Lightning,* THE TIMES LITERARY SUPPLEMENT, Oct. 25, 2002.

92. STUART BANNER, THE DEATH PENALTY: AN AMERICAN HISTORY (2002).

93. *See* Loic Wacquant, *From Slavery to Mass Incarceration: Rethinking the "Race Question" in the US*, 13 NEW LEFT REV. 41 (2002).

94. Garland, *supra* note 91.

95. *See Furman v. Georgia*, 408 U.S. 238 (1972).

96. *See, e.g.*, Stephen B. Bright, *The Death Sentence Not for the Worst Crime but for the Worst Lawyer*, 103 YALE L.J. 1835 (1994); Stephen B. Bright, *In Defense of Life: Enforcing the Bill of Rights on Behalf of Poor, Minority and Disadvantaged Persons Facing the Death Penalty*, 57 MO. L. REV. 849 (1992); Stephen B. Bright, *Neither Equal nor Just: The Rationing and Denial of Legal Services to the Poor When Life and Liberty Are at Stake*, 1997 ANN. SURV. AM. L. 783; Ruth E. Friedman & Bryan A. Stevenson, *Solving Alabama's Capital Defense Problems: It's a Dollars and Sense Thing*, 44 ALA. L. REV. 1 (1992); Anthony Paduano & Clive A. Stafford Smith, *The Unconscionability of Sub-Minimum Wages Paid Appointed Counsel in Capital Cases*, 43 RUTGERS L. REV. 281 (1991).

97. *See* Charles Lane, *O'Connor Expresses Death Penalty Doubt; Justice Says Innocent May Be Killed*, WASH. POST, July 4, 2001, at A1 (quoting Justice Sandra Day O'Connor's statement, at speech to Minnesota Women Lawyers in Minneapolis, that "[p]erhaps it's time to look at minimum standards for appointed counsel in death cases and adequate compensation for appointed counsel when they're used" and Justice Ruth Bader Ginsburg's statement in April 9 speech in Washington that she had "yet to see a death case, among the dozens coming to the Supreme Court on the eve of execution petitions, in which the defendant was well represented at trial"). While on the bench, Supreme Court Justice Harry A. Blackmun expressed similar sentiments. *See McFarland v. Scott*, 512 U.S. 1256, 1257 (1994) (Blackmun, J., dissenting from denial of *certiorari*) ("The unique, bifurcated nature of capital trials and the special investigation into a defendant's personal history and background that may be required, the complexity and fluidity of the law, and the high, emotional stakes involved all make capital cases more costly and difficult to litigate than ordinary criminal trials. Yet, the attorneys assigned to represent indigent capital defendants at times are less qualified than those appointed in ordinary criminal cases.").

98. Compensation was improved in 1999, when the hourly rates were increased and the compensation caps for capital cases were lifted. However, of the 190 inmates currently on death row, 161 inmates (89%) were tried before the capital compensation scheme was altered. ALA. CODE §15-21-12 (1975).

99. *James v. State*, CC-95-4747 (trial record).

100. Kendall Clinton, *Henry County Man Convicted of Murder in 1998 Stabbing Death*, DOTHAN EAGLE, August 23, 2000 ("Hocker's trial was relatively short for a capital murder case").

101. *Id.*

102. Cindy West, *Mysticism Focus of Neelley Case*, GADSDEN TIMES, Jan. 9, 1991.

103. *Neelley v. State*, 642 So. 2d 494, 498 (Ala. Crim. App. 1993) (citing trial judge's order).

104. *Neelley v. State*, Postconviction record, at 308–322.

105. The Liebman-Fagan-West study, cited *supra* note __, concluded that nationally, over the entire period from 1973 to 1995, the overall error-rate in our capital punishment system was 68 percent. In Alabama, the error rate is even higher. The Liebman-Fagan-West study concludes that 55 percent of capital cases were reversed in direct appeals. Of those that were not reversed in direct appeal, another 9 percent were reversed in state post-conviction. Finally, of those capital cases that were considered on federal habeas corpus review, 45 percent were reversed. Alabama's overall rate of error, including state post-conviction, from 1973 to 1995 was 75 percent. The Liebman-Fagan-West study revealed that an astonishing 82 percent of the cases that were reversed in state post-conviction (247 of 301) were replaced on retrial with a sentence of less than death, or no sentence at all. Seven percent of these reversals (22/301) resulted in a determination on retrial that the defendant was not guilty of the capital offense. *See* Liebman, Fagan & West.

106. When Jesse Morrison's case was reviewed in federal habeas corpus proceedings, the court concluded that his trial was marred by racial discrimination. As noted, the prosecutor removed 20 of the 21 qualified African American jurors and obtained a capital conviction and death sentence against Mr. Morrison with a nearly all-white jury in a county that is over 45 percent black. *Morrison v. Jones*, 952 F. Supp. 729 (M.D. Ala. 1996).

Bo Cochran would have been executed but for a federal court's determination that his capital murder and death sentence were unreliable, given the district attorney's informal policy of removing African Americans from the jury venire, and the removal of seven of the nine qualified African American veniremembers from Mr. Cochran's jury panel. *Cochran v. Herring*, 42 F.3d 1404, 1412 (11th Cir. 1995). Mr. Cochran was subsequently released from prison after more reliable proceedings were conducted at the trial court and he was found not guilty of capital murder.

The Eleventh Circuit determined that federal habeas corpus relief was warranted for Quang Bui, whose capital conviction and death sentence were obtained in a proceeding in which the district attorney used his peremptory strikes in a discriminatory manner to remove nine of the eleven qualified African American veniremembers. *Bui v. Haley*, No. 00-15445 (11th Cir. January 25, 2002).

107. Alabama has no state-funded agency, center, or defender organization to manage services for death row prisoners. Finding volunteer counsel to represent death row prisoners in Alabama has proven to be a difficult task. Attorneys appointed to handle these cases are still subject to a cap on compensation of $1,000 per case. The $1,000 fee cap for appointed counsel in state post-conviction proceedings was increased from $600, effective June 10, 1999. ALA. CODE § 15-12-23(1975), as amended by Act 99-427 (1999). Currently there are approximately 40 individuals on death row in Alabama who have neither legal representation nor the ability to recruit volunteer counsel.

108. Ronald Dworkin, *The Court's Impatience to Execute*, L.A. TIMES, July 11, 1999.

109. Albert Camus, *Reflections on the Guillotine, in* RESISTANCE, REBELLION, AND DEATH 197–98 (1960).

5

Truth and Consequences: The Penalty of Death

Joshua K. Marquis

I come to the debate over capital punishment with a very different background from my learned colleagues in this book. I am neither a scholar, a jurist, nor a crusader for the wrongly accused. I have spent most of the last 20 years as a prosecutor; in the last decade I've served as an elected district attorney who answers to the voters every four years, and I've made very personal decisions about capital punishment. In the previous decade, I was the chief deputy—the number two person—in two other prosecutors' offices. In both jobs I was assigned, or later assigned to myself, the job of handling all murder cases, including the worst of them: capital cases, or what in many states is called "aggravated murder."

The average size of a prosecutor's office in the United States is nine employees, three of whom are lawyers. My office has six lawyers and ten support staff. We handle about 900 misdemeanors and 400 felonies per year, including, on average, one murder. In much larger offices the top prosecutor often impanels a committee of assistants to advise on which murder cases should be elevated to death penalty status. But large office or small, in each of the 38 states where the death penalty is a possibility, it falls to the district attorney to decide which cases fit the special criteria for capital murder.

Prosecutors often feel isolated and besieged by larger groups of defense attorneys and judges who suffer us at best. As prosecutors have become more professionalized over the last couple of decades, and as lawyers commit to making prosecution a career and not merely a stepping-stone, there is more communication among us nationwide. I often rely on that community of prosecutors to provide a sounding board to confirm or disabuse myself of thoughts on a particular case. But for the great part, my community remains within Oregon, both because I regularly associate with these colleagues and because the laws and customs vary so much from state to state. My office overlooks the state of Washington, a few miles across the mouth of the Columbia River, and I've never discussed a capital case with my Washington counterpart.

One reason there is such diversity on how and when capital cases are pursued is because "death is different," as the Supreme Court remarked and is oft repeated. Each case must be examined on its own merits. Each killer is different, as is the constellation of horrors made by the killer. What is easily a death penalty case in Texas might not be considered as such in Oregon. Baltimore, Maryland, offers a good example of how elected prosecutors reflect their constituency. The city district attorney almost never seeks death sentences, while the suburban county prosecutor, just next door, frequently does. Both women are following their conscience and beliefs—and those of their respective constituencies.

Now, it's a common myth that prosecutors seek the death penalty because a mob, metaphorical or real, gathers below their office window to demand it. Only in the movies. And it's often easier for a prosecutor to plea bargain a capital case—because juries are most likely *not* to impose the death penalty, because the costs of the cases are astronomical, and because the odds are so high of a conviction or sentence being reversed. But some prosecutors believe it unethical even to consider offering or taking a plea when the death penalty is sought, reasoning that it is the jury and not the prosecutor who should decide the defendant's sentence. I've never asked for the death penalty except when I was prepared sincerely to urge 12 individuals to vote for death. By

the same token, I've agreed to seek a life sentence without parole because of the sheer costs—emotional for the victims and financial for
the system—of a capital case.

For me, death is not an abstract concept but a gritty reality that I
must face when I visit the scene of a particularly horrible murder just
after it's discovered. Who deserves the possibility of the ultimate penalty? I grapple with that decision while reviewing the evidence, while
talking with the victim's family, and often while sitting a couple feet
away from the very real human being whom I might later urge a jury
to sentence to death. No intelligent person should approach so onerous
a decision without ambivalence. Zealots may be welcome in the fight
against capital punishment, but like Judge Alex Kozinski of the Ninth
U.S. Circuit Court of Appeals, who wrote of his sleepless nights after
deciding whether to stay a death sentence,[1] those of us who would
administer capital justice are always asking ourselves questions. I have
yet to meet a prosecutor from any part of the United States who does
not take such decisions with gravity. Opposition to the death penalty
is highly organized and well funded, and most prosecutors often feel
as if they are playing defense. Therefore the conventional wisdom becomes a reality that must be addressed in the debate over capital
punishment.

The debate about issues like race and the death penalty are no less
personal for me. As a prosecutor in an overwhelmingly white state, I
have faced the prospect of seeking the death penalty against a black
man for the rape and murder of a white woman in a community with
almost no minority population. Joel Fort was a drifter who rode the
freight trains that passed through Bend, in the high desert of central
Oregon. His victim, Lynn Oliverio, was a young woman who, on November 9, 1989, took a shortcut to work by crossing the railroad tracks.
Fort claims he was just trying to rob her, but after grabbing her purse
he raped Lynn, beat her to death, and hopped a freight headed for
California. He was caught 2,000 miles away after investigators tracked
down a piece of Lynn's jewelry Fort had hocked at a pawn shop in
Klamath Falls, a hundred miles down-track from the scene of the
crime.

After being appointed chief deputy district attorney in Deschutes
County (where Bend is the county seat) in 1990, one of my first major

tasks was the prosecution of Mr. Fort. I could not help but consider the racist past of American jurisprudence. In a struggle that I suspect is echoed hundreds of times across America by other prosecutors charged with the same responsibility, I considered the possibility that this man might more likely be sentenced to death partly because of his race. I didn't think those who would serve on the jury were racists, but the possibilities gnawed at me. Ultimately I offered a plea that precluded the imposition of a death sentence. Did race play a part in my decision? Yes, in just the way capital punishment should be decided: each case on its own, within its own context, using the specific facts of the case, considering the community where the crime occurred and the background of the defendant.

The murder that is horrible enough to merit death in Georgia may not be terrible enough to be deemed capital in New Hampshire (a state with capital punishment as an option that has gone unused for more than half a century). Opponents of the death penalty often cite the concept of "evolving moral standards" as a justification for abolition. Does that mean Oregonians who voted to abolish capital punishment in 1964 morally devolved when, 24 years later, they voted to reestablish the penalty?

Popular culture all too often describes a barbaric American legal system that regularly hurls innocent people onto death row for no reason other than the fickle whims of an ambitious prosecutor. I choose to challenge this urban legend, accepted as dogma by media and academics anxious to verify their own, often deeply felt and sincere objections to the death penalty. These images are reinforced in television dramas like *The Practice* and television magazines such as *60 Minutes* or *Frontline*; in movies like *The Hurricane* that claim to be "true stories"; and in popular fiction (*The Green Mile*). The myths arise from the examination in headlines and sound bites of an altogether serious and complex subject. The breathless claim "Another Innocent Freed!" rarely tells the whole story and, as I will point out, may not be at all accurate. Each case must be examined from beginning to middle to end. And it's critical to know "the rest of the story."

It's much easier to be forgiving if someone you love hasn't been butchered by some sociopath. But since very few murder victims come from the upper strata of our society, murder rarely hits home with society's elite. Most murder victims, like their killers, come from the margins of our society. (One notable exception is the actress Dominque Dunne, daughter of noted author Dominick Dunne. Her murder and the resulting injustice transformed Dunne into one of the most articulate voices speaking out for victims' rights.) Despite the fevered efforts of death penalty opponents, many states have passed laws giving prosecutors the ability to tell jurors something about the victims. African Americans are victimized by murder at a rate disproportionate to their number in the general population. Yet their killers go to death row less frequently than murderers of white people, all other factors being equal. What is ignored in this analysis are the types of murders that white murderers inflict on their almost invariably white victims. As white men on death row are far more likely to be serial killers or sexual predators than are African Americans, is it that surprising that juries send these particularly horrendous white killers to death row at a higher rate than killers who are people of color?

Opponents of the death penalty often refer to it as "state-sanctioned murder," a phrase that betrays how little they know. In criminal murder there is no solemnity, no opportunity to make peace with your maker or say your last good-byes. There was no dignity in the way Karla Fay Tucker's victims, Deborah Thornton and Jerry Dean, died. A Texas woman who pickaxed Thornton and Dean to death, Tucker found religion in prison and became a *cause célèbre* of the religious right, who urged then-Texas Governor George W. Bush to spare her life.[2] David Marshall, Tucker's brother, has a memorial web site in which he recalls his sister's execution:

> When Karla had only a few minutes left to live on this earth, even though she was very weak from fasting, she cheered up the guards and chaplains and witnessed to them as they assisted and comforted her. With her last words, she expressed her sorrow to her victim's family, and her love for all who had been "so good" to her. Then, smiling, she went to be "face to face with Jesus."

Rod and Lois Houser had no such opportunity. Rod, a retired labor relations expert, achieved a lifelong dream when he and Lois moved to a home in the high desert of Terrebone, in central Oregon. He and

Lois had raised two girls who lived nearby, and Rod was in a second career he had long dreamed of, as a firefighter with the U.S. Forest Service, in nearby Redmond.

The doorbell at Rod and Lois Houser's home rang about three o'clock in the dark morning hours of June 29, 1987. When Rod answered the door, three young men pushed their way in, armed with a semi-automatic rifle, a revolver, and a knife. The trio was led by 18-year-old Randy Guzek, an honors student at Redmond High School who was a favorite of teachers and many of the girls at school. By day a promising student, Guzek led a double life: He sexually abused his younger sister, and at night he led a pack of robbers and thieves who, armed with guns and police scanners, burglarized dozens of homes. Sometimes Guzek would pretend to convert to different religious faiths in order to gain entry into parishioners' homes, to which he would later return to plunder.

On this dark morning, at Guzek's command Mark Wilson trained the rifle on Rod Houser, firing more than 20 rounds. Lois Houser, who had come downstairs to see who was at the door in the middle of night, tried to run back up the stairs. Randy Guzek shot her with the revolver. Wounded, Lois tried to crawl into a linen closet. Guzek pursued her, shooting her twice more. As she lay dying, he ripped her wedding ring off her finger.

Guzek's gang looted the house after they murdered the couple. They stabbed Lois Houser's lifeless body and planted the knife in her dead husband's hand. Later the killers told police they were trying to make it look like a cult killing. Then they shut the door and left the house so they could meet up with Guzek's father to divide with him the spoils of the evening.

The Housers' two adult daughters were accustomed to regular contact with their parents. Susan and Maryann initially attributed their parents' failure to answer the phone to a downed phone line to their remote home on top of a mesa. They went to the house and discovered the bodies of their murdered parents. Those daughters and their families have spent the last 15 years sitting through three separate trials of Randy Guzek, who has been three times sentenced to death by three different juries. The Oregon Supreme Court has overturned each of the death sentences, not on the issues of guilt but only on the sentence, and is expected to force the Houser family to sit through yet a fourth trial.

Randy Guzek has spent more than 10 years swimming in due process. Millions of dollars have been spent on his defense by Oregon taxpayers. I have twice stood before juries, first in 1991 and again in 1997, and asked them to impose the ultimate penalty for Guzek's act of ultimate evil. Yet, can I claim absolute faith in the total righteousness of my belief that the death penalty is justified? Absolutely not. Human fallibility requires everyone in the multisegmented American justice system to examine his or her own heart and mind when making such important decisions. In many ways it would be much easier simply to believe that executions are always wrong. But even those who are ambivalent about capital punishment tend to agree that convicted child murderers or those convicted of rape, torture, and murder—to say nothing of those who would kill scores, even thousands, in a terrorist act—deserve nothing less than death.

New urban myths have been created by those who zealously seek the abolition of capital punishment. After having largely lost the argument with most Americans[3] (and also with most Europeans, for that matter[4]) that the death penalty is morally wrong in any case, opponents have tacked into the wind and come up with a new troika of arguments: (1) innocents crowd America's death rows; (2) the death penalty is irretrievably racist; and (3) defendants facing capital punishment are afforded poor legal representation against massive government resources. Their conventional wisdom also claims that Americans have had a major change of heart on the death penalty. Although a 2000 Gallup Poll claimed that support for the death penalty had slipped from 77 percent to 63 percent, that number rose to 73 percent in May of 2002. Another poll, commissioned by *Parade* magazine in summer 2001 (before September 11) and using more than 2,000 respondents, showed that 82 percent of Americans supported capital punishment *in some cases*. It's all in how the question is asked.

Is it more civilized to turn from great evil and claim that a truly evolved society has no need to respond with any institutional force or violence? Is the logical extension of a progressive society that it moves to the point where no one is punished? Or is the more reasonable extension a society that is ever more discriminating in its use and extent of punishment? Discrimination, in the truest sense of that word, is what must be sought.

Abolitionists cite one of America's founding fathers, Benjamin Rush, as the political forebear of their movement. Rush was one of only two signers of the Declaration of Independence who opposed the death penalty. But latter-day abolitionists ignore the context of Rush's day, which included a legal system that barely recognized the defendant's rights, had few of the procedures that we take for granted today, and exhibited a zeal to punish by death an enormous list of crimes. Some colonies were more sparing about when a criminal would face the noose, but New York instituted the so-called Duke's Laws of 1665. These directed the death penalty for denial of the true God, premeditated murder, killing someone who had no weapon of defense, killing by lying in wait or by poisoning, sodomy, buggery, kidnapping, perjury in a capital trial, traitorous denial of the king's rights or raising arms to resist his authority, conspiracy to invade towns or forts in the colony, and striking one's mother or father (upon complaint of both).[5]

Equating capital punishment for striking your mother in colonial New York to current-day practice makes no more sense than calling the surgeons of that era sadistic butchers for what we now know to be bad medicine; yet that is what abolitionists who cite Rush as their moral authority would do.

Context, like language, matters.

AMERICA: ROGUE OR RIGHT?

By the same token, the charge that America "stands alone among the civilized world" in maintaining capital punishment ignores several important realities. Opponents of capital punishment are fond of pointing to largely homogenous societies with low murder rates that also have banned capital punishment. They highlight countries like China and Saudi Arabia but ignore nations like Japan and India, which continue to impose capital punishment. Other authors of this book would have the reader believe that if America allows the execution of anyone, it is a barbaric state on a par with Iran, China, or Malaysia, implying that our New Testament Christian values of forgiveness are at the most evolved end of the moral spectrum. What gives that particular strain of morality superiority over all other cultures in the world? Is America the most "evolved" place on earth in every sense of the word? Is the "moral authority" of the United States some sort of legal manifest destiny?

Again, context is essential. The nations that first foreswore capital punishment were Germany and Italy, whose very recent history was rife with state-sanctioned murder and even genocide. Add to that legal systems where defendants were and sometimes are presumed guilty, the absence of a comprehensive jury system, and a recent legal history of judicial corruption and you would likely find the staunchest of American death penalty supporters understanding why the European Union requires any nation seeking admission to renounce capital punishment.

After the execution of Oklahoma bombing mass murderer Timothy McVeigh, one leader of Germany's chapter of Amnesty International remarked that the difference between Europe and America was that "in Europe the leaders are ahead of the people, while in America it is the other way around."[6] He couldn't have been more correct. In the more republican European parliaments, the leaders make decisions that in America are left to its citizens. The elites of America (religious, political, academic, and artistic) have traditionally opposed the death penalty while general public opinion in America has swung back and forth as long as polls have measured feelings on the subject. Since the 1970s, support for capital punishment has ranged from 60 to 80 percent. What is almost unknown is that the populations of many western European nations share similar sentiments. Anthony Blinken, senior adviser to President Clinton for European affairs, noted in a December 2001 essay in *Time* magazine that "across the Atlantic it turns out that Europeans support capital punishment in numbers similar to Americans . . . [but] their voice will be ignored because the European Union requires aspiring members to prohibit capital punishment."[7]

The usual response from abolitionists is that mere majority opinion should not dictate public morality. That may be true if the majority opinion conflicts with basic concepts of decency such as prohibition of slavery or, more recently, segregation; but our legal codes are replete with laws reflecting evolving moral sentiment. One need only look at what would be considered pornographic 50 or even 25 years ago. Abolitionists will point to states like Maine, with low murder rates and without the death penalty, but ignore jurisdictions like Michigan or the District of Columbia (with the highest per capita murder rate in the nation by far), neither of which have the death penalty but do have very high murder rates. Could it be that states where there is more violent crime are more likely to express popular support for the death penalty? States with relatively high murder rates, like Louisiana and Texas, aggressively practice capital punishment while states with low murder rates—Vermont and North Dakota—have forsworn the death penalty.

Fundamentally, Americans live in a republic that holds its democratic principles dear. Each state makes the decision of whether to allow death as a penalty. The residents of twelve states and the District of Columbia have decided against capital punishment. New Hampshire has neither asked for nor imposed the death penalty in almost 70 years, yet its residents hold out the possibility that some murder will be so bad as to deserve the capital sentence held in reserve on New Hampshire's laws. Beyond that, each jury impaneled in the 37 other states must make the decision to impose a death sentence.

The causality between abolition and the murder rate is complex, and the debate about whether Americans really support capital punishment or whether America is a rogue nation misses the real point that many abolitionists wish to avoid by misdirection: whether it is ever right for the state to sanction the taking of a life. In his argument in this book Stephen Bright points to the fact that Harris County, Texas, hands down more death sentences than 36 of the 38 states that allow capital punishment. What goes unsaid is that in the last 20 years the murder rate in that jurisdiction has dropped more than 70 percent.

Almost everyone would agree that when necessity demands it, there is moral justification for the use of deadly force: in self-defense, by members of the police or military under certain conditions, or to save the life of another. What if the preservation of an innocent's life can be guaranteed only by taking the life of someone who has been shown to have no regard for the life of others? A recent Emory University study of more than 20 years of data suggests that for every execution in America, 18 murders are prevented, plus or minus almost nine lives.[8]

If this study is to be believed (or two others issued by two separate research groups at the University of Houston[9] and the University of Colorado[10]), the death penalty has saved thousands of people from becoming victims of murder. The author of one of these studies, an economist, felt compelled to comment that while his research clearly showed that murders were deterred by the death penalty, he still personally opposes capital punishment because of what he perceives to be racial inequities.

WHAT CONSTITUTES "INNOCENCE"?

The most persuasive argument offered by abolitionists is the dark shadow that looms largest in the minds of people who have conflicting thoughts about the existence of capital punishment: the execution of an innocent person. But the death penalty as imposed in late twentieth- and early twenty-first-century America is very different from the bleak picture painted by my esteemed colleagues from Georgia and Alabama. When we debated in June 2001 in New York City, Steven Bright repeatedly hurled examples from his own state's past as typical of capital cases. He cited cases involving trials that took place 15 to 25 years ago to stand for the proposition that the death penalty as it is constituted today is fundamentally unfair. He cited the horrors of the electric chair, when almost every state has adopted lethal injection.

DNA testing has become the holy grail of many abolitionists. It has the power to establish factual guilt or innocence beyond virtually all doubt—in certain cases.

Despite the fevered opposition of criminal defense attorneys in the 1980s, America's prosecutors managed to get DNA evidence accepted as scientific evidence in courts across the country. Barry Scheck, who gained fame by ridiculing the DNA evidence in the O. J. Simpson case, established a program called The Innocence Project. In the vast majority of murders the presence or absence of a particular individual's DNA answers no real question about guilt; Scheck's program painstakingly selects that tiny number of convictions in which some real doubt remains after a conviction, and in which DNA will tell whether the defendant "did it."

Scheck and others have used DNA to free a handful of people from death row, and more from long prison sentences. Of course, any criminal defense lawyer who relied for income on innocent clients would go bankrupt within a couple of months. And for every case in which DNA exonerates, there are hundreds in which it inculpates. Those stories rarely make the news, and when they do, they end up in what are called the "airplane pages" (B-16, C-4, etc.). Even one of Scheck's supposedly exonerated clients, Keri Kotler, was convicted on the strength of DNA for a rape committed just after he had collected a huge settlement for a claim of false imprisonment.[11]

Rick McGinn's photo is reprinted 12 times on the June 12, 2000, cover of *Newsweek,* an issue titled "Rethinking the Death Penalty." McGinn, who sat on Texas's death row, won a reprieve from then-governor George W. Bush after his appellate lawyers, led by Barry Scheck, argued that a cutting-edge DNA test not available at the time of his original trial might cast doubt on whether he had raped, as opposed to merely murdering, his 12-year-old stepdaughter, Stephanie Rae Flanary. DNA tests done for his trial had showed that blood splattered throughout McGinn's truck belonged to Stephanie. Scheck's team pointed to a stain on Stephanie's underwear that DNA testing then available had been unable to match. Since merely chopping Stephanie to death with an axe was insufficient under Texas law to merit the death penalty, the prosecution had been made to prove at trial that she was raped as well. Scheck hoped that if the stain on the underwear turned out *not* to belong to his client, the rape charge would be called into question, thereby making McGinn ineligible for a death sentence.

McGinn got his new tests—and they reaffirmed his guilt for the rape as well as the murder. But that story dropped off the media radar.

The same thing happened a few months later, when Derek Barnabei's death sentence garnered international attention. Barnabei, a young white man of Italian ancestry, was convicted of the rape and murder of Sarah Wisnosky, a college student whose body was found dumped in the river. He claimed that the physical evidence that linked him to the crime scene was the result of a consensual sexual encounter and that he had left Sarah uninjured. His appellate lawyers said new DNA testing of fingernail scrapings would show the wrong man was on Virginia's death row. A dramatic last-minute stay was granted. The scrapings were tested. The *Washington Post*, covering the story locally, reported that the tests confirmed Barnabei's guilt, but few other papers told the end of the story.[12]

Most murder cases do not involve DNA, and so those looking for innocents on death row now resort to verbal gymnastics when pointing to a person who supposedly never should have been in prison. A decision by Oregon's Supreme Court gives a vivid example of "guilty man walking." In 1989, two-year-old Kristina Hornych was raped and murdered. A man who was using drugs in the child's home quickly became a suspect. Evidence of his guilt mounted, and during a polygraph test Scott Dean Harberts allowed that he might well have murdered the child. Since lie detector tests are banned as evidence in Oregon courts, the prosecution sought to use the admission without reference to the polygraph test. The trial judge refused to allow the statement in evidence. The prosecution appealed, and after years in the appellate courts, the evidence was ruled to be admissible. Faced with admitting the damning evidence, the trial judge again refused to allow its introduction before a jury. Again the state appealed.

By this time four years had passed since the arrest, and after filing a second appeal, prosecutors changed their minds, dropped the appeal, and took their chances of trying the case without the confession. Even without that statement, Harberts was convicted and sentenced to die in 1994. The same trial judge denied Harberts's claim that he had been denied a speedy trial. Because he was sentenced to death, Harberts's case was directly and automatically appealed to the Oregon Supreme Court. Six years after his conviction and years after the appellate briefs had been filed, the state Supreme Court ruled that the prosecutor's delay of seven months in launching the second appeal constituted such a gross violation of his rights under the state constitution that Harberts should be freed. Going further, the state court held that Harberts should not only get a new trial, but that his case should be dismissed with prejudice, meaning he never again could be tried for the rape and murder. The court made pains to decide the case under the state and not the federal constitution, so the prosecution had no opportunity to appeal to the federal courts.[13] By the definition bandied about in mainstream media, Scott Dean Harberts had been "exonerated," but by any reasonable interpretation he is not an "innocent man." Harberts is the only man in modern times to be freed from death row in Oregon, and his freedom has nothing to do with his "innocence."

So, what does "innocent" actually mean? The word has been stretched to the point of being tortured. Most people assume "innocent" means that the person *did not do it*. Did not kill anyone or help someone else commit a murder. Wasn't there. Didn't know a thing about the crime.

Northwestern University sponsored a conference which literally heralded a group of people it claimed were innocents on death row. One of the men on the stage was Dr. Jay Smith, made infamous by Joseph Wambaugh's book *Echoes in the Darkness*. Smith is even featured as one of Amnesty International's 87 men who have been "freed from death row." Smith was convicted of the murder of Susan Reinert and her two children. A jury concluded that he and a high school teacher who worked at Smith's school had conspired to murder Reinert, a fellow teacher, and her children were collateral damage of the murder scheme, killed because they might have given witness to their mother's murder. Reinert's body was recovered, but the children's bodies have never been found.

A state appellate court held that state prosecutors failed to disclose the existence on the victim's body of two grains of sand that might possibly have supported Smith's claim of innocence. Smith's conviction was set aside, he was freed from a life sentence in prison, and the state was forbidden from retrying him. Emboldened by his newfound freedom (and despite his undisturbed convictions for theft by deception, receiving stolen property, possession of a firearm without a license, and possession of marijuana), Smith filed lawsuits against the state of Pennsylvania, the officer who arrested him, and virtually everyone connected with his prosecution.

There was only one problem: Smith was not innocent. In its final decision throwing Smith's case out of court in 2000, the United States Circuit Court of Appeals for the Third Circuit concluded: "Our confidence in Smith's convictions for the murder of Susan Reinert and her two children is not the least bit diminished by consideration of the suppressed lifters and quartz particles, and Smith has therefore not established that he is entitled to compensation for the unethical conduct of some of those involved in the prosecution."[14] Yet Smith is on

Amnesty International's list of those exonerated from death row and was feted by the Innocence Project at Northwestern University in 1998.

Two of the most famous cases of innocents on death row involve men who were in fact innocent of the crimes for which they were condemned—Earl Washington of Virginia and Anthony Porter of Illinois. What doesn't make the stock footage of their release from prison is how they got there. Porter was committing an armed robbery in the same park where a drug murder occurred simultaneously. He ran, gun in hand, from the park, in full view of witnesses who identified Porter to police. Porter denied not only the murder but even being in the park, a lie he maintained until long after his convictions were affirmed. When students from Northwestern's Journalism School, operating without any of the strictures or restraints of traditional investigators, discovered the true killer, Porter was exonerated and freed from prison.

Earl Washington had burglarized and beaten an elderly woman, a crime to which he rightfully confessed and was convicted and sentenced to a lengthy prison term. When a similar crime resulted in a murder, Washington wrongfully confessed. After being cleared of the murder, Washington still owed Virginia time for the crime, which never gets mentioned when his stirring tale of innocence is told.

Do either of these mistakes justify a wrongful death sentence? Of course not. But, as *Chicago Tribune* columnist Eric Zorn, a death penalty opponent, pointed out to supporters of Mumia Abu-Jamal, convicted of the 1981 murder of Philadelphia Police Officer Daniel Faulkner, be careful of whom you call "innocent" if you expect the public to accept that argument for the abolition of capital punishment.[15] Jamal, who has been named an honorary citizen of Paris, has been conceded by many death penalty opponents to almost certainly be factually guilty of his crime.[16]

In an important article in the 2000 *Annual Review of Sociology*, noted abolitionist Michael Radelet urged a new definition of innocence. He cited the case of Ernest Dobbert, executed in 1984 for beating his daughter to death. Radelet points to Justice Thurgood Marshall's dissent in the case, which argues that maybe there wasn't sufficient premeditation to constitute the first-degree murder charge that resulted in a capital sentence. Radelet goes on to make the startling statement, "If Justice Marshall's assessment was correct, then Dobbert was not guilty of a capital offense and—in this qualified sense—Florida executed an innocent man." Radelet concedes that "death row inmates have indeed killed someone," but perhaps a more perfect system would not have sentenced them to death.

Professor Hugo Bedau, the academic godfather of the modern abolitionist movement, in collaboration with Radelet issued a study in 1985[17] in which they named 23 people they say were innocent but who had been executed. This number is accepted as gospel by most media. In a closer look at those same cases five years later, then-professor (now U.S. District Court Judge) Paul Cassell and Michigan Supreme Court Justice Steve Markman found that a thorough review failed to establish a single case of documented innocence.[18] Yet this number "23" has taken on talismanic proportions and is frequently quoted in advertisements run by the ACLU.

THE WRONGFULLY FREED

Does the existence of people who did not commit the crime for which they sit on death row vindicate the claims of abolitionists? No more so than the thousands of Americans who die each year because of honest mistakes by pharmacists. America has executed fewer than eight hundred people since 1976. More people die in America each year because of design errors in household appliances. Should we ban toaster ovens? To claim that there isn't a risk/benefit calculation in all human affairs is to deny reality. Automobile manufacturers know that a certain number of their customers will die because of certain design deficiencies in automobiles. They could build an absolutely safe car, but it would cost more than $100,000 and find few buyers. If we remained locked in our homes 24 hours a day we would be unable to avoid a far greater risk of death than of wrongful conviction. Calculate that against the absolute certainty that hundreds if not thousands of Americans judged innocent by *any* standard would die if the justice system failed to immobilize or execute the man who will eventually kill them.

Many opponents of capital punishment offer life imprisonment without possibility of parole as a palatable alternative to the death penalty. This penultimate punishment is seen by many as the perfect solution for indisputably guilty killers on the theory that they won't be able to prey on general society again. Unfortunately, experience with the American correctional system teaches otherwise. To understand why "life in prison" rings hollow with many who spend their life in the justice system we need only review a few stark examples:

- Kenneth McDuff of Texas was convicted and sentenced to die for killing three teenagers in 1966. Despite conviction and a death sentence (and no claim of actual innocence), courts later overturned the penalty portion of his sentence and he ended up on parole. After release he murdered at least six innocent women.[19]
- Richard Marquette of Oregon went to prison in the late 1950s for meeting, killing, and dismembering women. He did well in prison. No women there to bother him. He got paroled (as did almost all murderers in Oregon serving "life" sentences). After his release, parts of young women killed by Marquette started appearing around Oregon. He ended up in 1961 on the FBI's Ten Most Wanted list before being returned to a prison in a state where the death penalty was abolished by popular vote in 1964.
- In 1981, author Norman Mailer and many other New York literati embraced convicted killer Jack Henry Abbott (who had murdered a fellow prison inmate) and succeeded in having him released early from a Utah prison. On July 18, 1981, six weeks after his release, Abbott stabbed actor Richard Adan to death in New York. He was convicted of manslaughter and received a 15-year-to-life sentence.
- Robert Lee Massie, whose execution in 2001 was memorialized by abolitionists like TV actor Mike Farrell, was originally sentenced to death for the robbery and murder of Mildred Weiss after robbing her in her home in San Gabriel, California. But in 1972, he, along with more than one hundred other men on California's death row, were granted a permanent reprieve by the decision of the United States Supreme Court. Because Massie behaved well in prison, he was paroled in 1979. Within a

few months of his release he robbed and murdered San Francisco liquor store owner Boris Naumoff and wounded store
clerk Charles Harris. Not surprisingly, Massie received a death
sentence for the crime.

All were convicted killers whose guilt was never at issue, yet the
legal system released them—to the eternal sorrow of those people who
lost family members to the legally freed killers. Although abolitionists
claim that "real" life without parole (LWOP) would prevent more killings by killers, they fail to take into account possible changes in the
law or societal trends. And they fail to acknowledge that a system that
makes mistakes even under the rigorous review given to a death penalty case is even more disposed to make mistakes that result in the
early release of the guilty and dangerous. More disingenuously they offer
alternatives such as the so-called SuperMax prisons or SHUs—Security
Housing Units—that in other contexts are just as widely denounced
by many of the same activists who would have the public think there
are safe alternatives for the worst of killers short of their execution

A frequently repeated maxim is that it is better for ten guilty men
to go free so that an innocent man is spared. Most of us are willing
to agree that it is even acceptable for 1,000 guilty men to go free to
spare the innocent. But what if that number becomes 100,000 and the
consequence is not merely injustice but the very real death of a victim
who but for the absence of the death penalty would never have been
murdered.

If those of us who support the death penalty are willing to admit
that mistakes can and have been made, that such mistakes are unacceptable, and that we are willing to make the reforms necessary to
insure that only the guilty enter death row, will abolitionists concede
that capital punishment may save a far greater number of truly innocent than the number of truly guilty the United States has executed
in modern legal history?

No other society provides criminal suspects with as many rights or
bars the government from gathering evidence in ways set down by law
and precedent as the United States. Still, our justice system is less than
perfect. Does that deprive us of the moral authority to make final
decisions, whether that is the one out of a thousand murderers who

are executed, or the thousands who serve life without possibility of parole? Ultimately, abolitionists argue that unless the justice system is not merely fair, not merely equitable, race-blind, and proportional, but unless it is *perfect*, then capital punishment must be abolished, whether gradually—through a "moratorium"—or by outright abolition.

THE RACE CARD

Having failed to convince either the public or their legislatures that death row is packed with the innocent, abolitionists often turn to what worked so well for O.J. Simpson. They play the race card.

The statistical debate about race rarely touches on the gross over-representation of racial minorities as the victims of serious crime, particularly murder. The U.S. Department of Justice's Bureau of Justice Statistics (BJS) measured murder trends by race over a quarter century, from 1975 to 1999.[20] The BJS study showed that a black person was six times more likely to be murdered than a white. It showed that, contrary to the myth of cross-racial murder, 86 percent of white victims are killed by whites and 94 percent of black victims are killed by blacks. Certain types of murder seem to be concentrated in identifiable ethnic groups. Serial killers and those who commit sex-related murders and workplace murders are far more likely to be white than black. Drug-related murders are more likely to be committed by black defendants. In that 25-year period from 1975 to 1999, 51.2 percent of homicide victims were white and 46.6 percent were black; 46.5 percent of those convicted of homicide were white and 51.5 percent were black.

It would be folly to deny the existence of racism in American society and thus necessarily in the justice system. Not only African Americans, but Asian Americans, Hispanics, Native Americans, and almost any group of people with a non-Western European heritage have historically been treated as second-class citizens both in general society and in the legal system. This prejudice is codified in our founding documents, which allocated African Americans (except those who had been specifically designated "free men") the status of a fraction of a human being. Against this history it should come as no surprise that a disproportionate number of members of the two largest minority populations, African American and Hispanic, end up being overly represented in the justice system. But it takes a huge leap to assume this is solely, or even primarily, due to racism in law enforcement and the courts. For whatever reasons, young men of all races, but particularly African Americans, commit a greater proportion of crime than other groups, a fact that many leaders of the African American community have acknowledged. Jesse Jackson made headlines when he confessed that if he encountered a group of young black men walking down a city street he would cross the street out of a fear, real or imagined, that they posed a greater risk than some other group of youths of another ethnicity.

Bryan Stevenson has pointed to the racial disparities in his home state of Alabama as evidence of the inherent racism of capital punishment. Yet in my state of Oregon only one of the 26 men on death row is African American although several of the *victims* of the white men on Oregon's death row were people of color. There is considerable risk in using the experience of any one state to explain why so many young black men are in prison. The good news is that the justice system has changed enormously in two decades and continues to evolve. The horror stories of racial bias, most notably the injustice wreaked on the so-called Scottsboro boys, contain shameful truths of our history but fail to represent modern reality. To paraphrase Robert Frost, we have "miles to go before we sleep," and much can be done to further reduce the legacy of racism as it affects the legal system. But to claim that the death penalty is racist because of the proportion of minorities on death rows is to ignore the fact that statistically a white man on death row is more likely to be executed than a black man, and in considerably less time.

The other authors in this book rely heavily on the studies of Professor David Baldus to reinforce their claim of racial bias. They fail to mention that Baldus's work has been heavily criticized. Citizen activist Dudley Sharp, who has accumulated the most extensive site supporting capital punishment on the web, noted, "The most thorough evaluation of this subject was presented in *McCleskey v. Georgia* (Zant/Kemp), wherein Federal District Judge Owen Forester accurately found that 'the best models which (McCleskey expert) Baldus was able to devise . . . produce no statistically significant evidence that race (of the victim or of the defendant) plays a part in either (the prosecution's or the jury's capital decisions)' " (580 Federal Supplement 338, p 368, 2/1/84). This hasn't stopped Professor Baldus from continuing to publish and argue that his statistics support his proposition, but there can be no doubt about his own particular bias on the subject.

There has been a sea change in the professionalism of American law enforcement. Women and minorities have far greater representation in all aspects of the justice system, as police officers, lawyers, and judges. Juries, which even 20 years ago would rarely show anything but white faces, are today far more representative of their communities. These changes are the result of a national consciousness about the effects of racism, affirmative action, and specific decisions of the Supreme Court—such as the Batson 14 case,[21] which forbids excluding jurors solely because of race, ethnicity, or gender. Recent decisions of the United States Supreme Court have emphasized the absolute prohibition of using race as any basis for excluding jurors. Several of my co-authors of this book would have Americans believe that such decisions show the system is "fatally flawed," yet it would make equally as much sense to argue that such a level of scrutiny only underlines the "super due process" capital sentences receive in twenty-first-century America.

Therefore, to compare the capital punishment system of 1975 to that of the twenty-first century is akin to comparing the safety features of a 1975 Chrysler to the safety technology present in a new Honda Accord.

The year both sides involved in this debate mark as the current era of capital punishment in American law is 1976, when the U.S. Supreme Court reauthorized execution in its decision in *Gregg vs. Georgia*, which established guidelines to prevent unfair and capricious capital sentences. Since then there have been almost half a million homicides in America. About 7,000 have resulted in death sentences, although only about 3,700 of those convicted remain on death row. The disparity between the condemned and the executed can be attributed to the extraordinary level of scrutiny and appellate review to which capital cases are subjected—not, as abolitionists claim, to a massive number of near-fatal legal errors. (This claim is often attributed to a study conducted by James Liebman,[22] a defense lawyer who also teaches at Columbia University. Liebman's study was completed in 1995 after being commissioned by Senator Joseph Biden in 1988 when Biden was chair of the U.S. Senate Judiciary Committee. But many scholars have challenged Leibman's claim that more than two-thirds of capital convictions are overturned due to "serious errors."[23])

As of mid-2001, just over 3,600 men and 54 women sat on America's death rows. Almost 1,700 were white (the BJS classifies Hispanics as white), 1,600 were black, 29 were Native American, and 27 were Asian.[24] Those numbers show that certain ethnic groups are both under- and overrepresented on death row. Statistics generated by abolitionists[25] agree that despite the numbers on death row, the race of those actually executed is markedly different. Of the slightly more than seven hundred people actually executed since 1976, 55 percent were white and 36 percent were black.

THE FEDERAL EXPERIENCE

In response to concerns about racial injustice in capital punishment as it exists today—not 20 years ago—a major study was launched by Attorney General Janet Reno during the Clinton administration.[26] Released June 6, 2001 (preliminary results were reported in September 2000), the study undertook a systemic review of the elaborate procedures required when the federal government seeks the death penalty. Federal prosecutors must send prospective death penalty cases to Washington, D.C., where a committee at the Justice Department examines the facts of the specific case and makes a recommendation to the attorney general. Federal prosecutions of capital cases represent a relatively small proportion of total death penalty cases, but the study is illuminating because it was a comprehensive and precise examination of that subset of murders for which the defendant might be eligible for a death sentence.

The attorney general approved the death penalty in 38 percent of cases with white defendants, 25 percent with black defendants, and 20 percent with Hispanic defendants. This federal study mirrors the national trend which—contrary to the conventional wisdom—shows that, all other things being equal, a white murderer is about twice as likely to be executed as a black murderer.

In a nongovernment study released in 1998, in the journal *Law and Contemporary Problems*,[27] Professor John McAdams of Marquette University debunked many of the commonly held beliefs that form the foundation for the claim that the death penalty system is inherently racist. He noted that "in a considerable display of chutzpah, the opponents of capital punishment who first adopted an offender-based concept of justice (when it was convenient to argue that too many blacks were being executed) simply turned on a dime and adopted a victim-centered concept of justice (when the data in fact showed that too many whites are being executed)." McAdams' review of statistics from one southern state known for a large number of death sentences, Florida, confirms that "the data [are] striking. White suspects are treated more harshly than black suspects, [a fact that] is especially true under non-felony circumstances." Even death penalty skeptic Jonathan Alter, in his cover story in *Newsweek* magazine during the apex of a death penalty debate fueled by the 2000 Bush–Gore presidential race, conceded that "the role of race and the death penalty is often misunderstood."[28]

A more recent study commissioned by the Virginia General Assembly concluded that suburban Virginia prosecutors were more likely to seek a death sentence than their urban counterparts—in part, no doubt, because (as the Baltimore example showed) prosecutors reflect the values of their constituency. The study also found that while blacks make up only 20 percent of the state's population and 51 percent of the people on death row in Virginia were black, prosecutors were much more likely to seek the death penalty for white defendants than for their black counterparts.[29]

THE MYTH OF THE SLEEPING LAWYER

The last of the abolitionist's trifecta is the claim that people on trial for their lives consistently receive substandard representation. Lawyers are indeed human, and no amount of money or screening or number of qualifying panels can ever absolutely guarantee the premium level of counsel that most thoughtful people would expect in capital cases. Abolitionists delight in pointing to a Texas case where a defendant's lawyer was perceived to be sleeping during the trial. The appellate courts, while never convinced that the attorney had been asleep, refused to overturn the conviction on that basis alone. The hue and cry that followed pushed the state to require, quite sensibly, the assignment of two lawyers to each capital defense.

There is a maxim in criminal law that a defendant first tries his case to a jury, then he tries the prosecutor to the appellate court, then the trial judge to the Supreme Court. If all else fails, he tries his own lawyer in a post-conviction *habeas corpus* proceeding. Habeas corpus means literally "bring me the person," but it's really an escape clause that can grant a defendant a new trial, or even freedom, if a fundamental constitutional right was violated in a way that profoundly affected the result in the case. Habeas practice is a subset of appellate criminal law and one in which co-author Brian Stevenson specializes. Habeas proceedings can take a very long time, granting decades of life to condemned murderers.

Oklahoma City bomber Timothy McVeigh offers an interesting example.

In what was the highest profile capital case ever undertaken by federal authorities, the courts made sure that McVeigh had more than merely adequate counsel. Lead attorney Steven Jones had established an eminent reputation as a litigator when he was chosen to represent McVeigh. The federal court system spent more than six million dollars on McVeigh's defense. The defense team sent investigators to Eastern Europe and the Middle East to follow up bizarre conspiracy theories. No effort and certainly no taxpayer money was spared in researching every hare-brained scenario that the most fevered defense conspiracy theorist could concoct. (Unlike most state capital prosecutors, the federal prosecutors certainly had massive resources as well, and in this sense McVeigh was an atypical case.) Yet even with this level of indigent defense, it was no surprise to capital prosecutors when McVeigh filed claims of ineffective assistance of counsel. A murder defendant, condemned to death or otherwise, will always eventually come to claim his trial lawyers did a lousy job. McVeigh recognized, sooner than most, the improbability of winning any of his claims, and chose to waive further appeals. Like the only two people executed on Oregon's death row in 40 years, McVeigh hastened his execution when he instructed his attorneys to abandon all appeals. McVeigh was not alone in believing that a humane death, the likes of which many terminal cancer patients would envy, might be a less cruel fate than a life behind bars without hope of release.

THE OREGON EXPERIENCE

Given the widely differing resources, values, and culture of our states, most prosecutors believe a detailed national standard for handling death penalty cases, beyond those established by volumes of court rulings, is not feasible. Nonetheless, my home state of Oregon provides a general view of how death penalty cases are tried in the twenty-first century. Oregon's experience is far closer to the norm than states such as Texas, which receive great publicity.

Oregon is similar to many states in that a government-funded agency, the Indigent Defense Board, contracts with lawyers for all court-appointed capital cases. The trial judges technically approve requests for funds, requests that are conducted *ex parte* (in secret) to prevent prosecutors from learning defense strategies; and lower court judges are reluctant to say no to a request when a future appellate court might deem this reversible error.

Oregon taxpayers spent almost seventy-five million dollars in 2001 to fund indigent defense. By comparison, the total budget of all prosecutorial offices was just under fifty million dollars. Nowhere but in capital cases were the differences more vivid. A person with no visible means of support or assets who is charged with aggravated (capital) murder in Oregon will receive a defense that would do the "Dream Team" proud.

In case after case in the 1990s, Oregon capital defendants received hundreds of thousands of dollars of indigent defense funding. In one case,[30] defense counsel secured the services of cultural anthropologists whose job it was to explain why their client, a Mexican national, would shoot Oregon State Trooper Bret Clodfelter in the back after being given a ride when his car broke down. They endeavored to convince the jury that a man from a nation where the police were more often than not corrupt and brutal would assume the same of a North American policeman. The same fund paid for a number of the defendant's relatives to fly up from Mexico to provide "moral support" for the defendant. Hernandez was convicted of the murder but one juror voted against a death sentence, sparing his life. Oregon taxpayers shelled out more than a million dollars to spare Francisco Manzo-Hernandez from death row.

Randy Guzek, who so brutally murdered Rod and Lois Houser in the summer of 1987, never testified at any of his three murder trials, but taxpayers paid tens of thousands of dollars for psychologists to probe his psyche. In his 1997 trial, the indigent defense fund paid $1,500 to fly in an English pen pal of the convicted killer, apparently so she could provide moral support from the front row of the courtroom. Witnesses were excluded, as they are in most cases, and the young Briton never testified, but she was able to wave hello to her new-found pal.[31] Under normal circumstances no one would ever have learned of these expenditures because they are kept sealed not only during the trial but for the life of the capital case, which in Oregon has been virtually forever. In this instance the local newspaper uncovered the expenditures.

"Mitigation specialists" whose job, distinct from defense investigators, is to dig up any scrap of positive information about someone facing a possible death sentence, round out defense teams that often include two or three lawyers and as many support staff. Any Oregon prosecutor could only dream of such resources.

THE BATTLE OF 2000

As part of his sincere desire to abolish capital punishment, Richard Dieter, founder and director of the neutral-sounding Death Penalty Information Center (financed by Roderick MacArthur and his series of foundations), helped orchestrate what has been made to appear a major shift in public opinion about the death penalty over the past 20 years.[32] The strategy was to shift the debate from whether it is morally

correct ever to execute murderers to calling into question the fundamental fairness of the death penalty. To accomplish this misdirection
it was necessary to seek out those few cases in which an obvious injustice had occurred. Along with Scheck's Innocence Project, Centurion
Ministries and Professor David Protess of Northwestern University
have succeeded in publicizing a spate of cases they hold out not as
aberrations but as typical of capital cases. The *Chicago Tribune* (in a
massive but ultimately unsuccessful effort to win a Pulitzer Prize) ush-
ered in the new century with a slashing series of articles[33] questioning
a series of dubious convictions arising from the early 1980s in Chicago.
The series ended with articles that essentially accused prosecutors
across America of consistent misconduct, implying that innocent men
and women were routinely wrongly convicted of murder. To paint this
picture it was necessary to show that crooked cops, overreaching prosecutors, and incompetent defense lawyers were commonplace in America. It was no accident that the Republican candidate for president that
year was the governor of the state with America's largest death row—
Texas. Cases from Texas took center stage, and stories abounded of
sleeping lawyers and cases allegedly tried with just a few hundred dollars for defense expenses.

The *Tribune* series itself was fatally flawed.[34] Like so many articles
written by reporters who allow their own sympaties to rise to the
surface, the conclusions relied on anecdotal evidence and war stories
of the criminal defense bar, ever anxious to cast themselves as heroes
and prosecutors as villains. Although far from uniform, and in many
cases still unsatisfactory, most capital states had already instituted reforms concerning indigent counsel. Even the *Tribune* had to admit
grudgingly that the public defender system in Cook County delivered
consistently competent and skilled counsel. The strange legal glamor
that accompanies some capital cases has convinced dozens of silk-
stocking law firms in major cities to assign platoons of lawyers *pro
bono*, all seeking their elusive prize: the innocent man on death row.
Contrast this with the usually meager resources under which most state
prosecutors labor, and the picture is often quite different from the one
portrayed by the media or popular culture.

THE POLITICS OF CAPITAL PUNISHMENT AND
THE REPENTANT CONSERVATIVES

The debate over capital punishment has never broken down along strictly partisan lines. As a lifelong Democrat I find myself joined by Senator Diane Feinstein, New Hampshire Governor Jeanne Shaheen, and a host of other "progressives" who support capital punishment, while death penalty skeptics include conservative commentators George Will and Pat Robertson, founder of the Christian Coalition. It should really be no surprise that a classic conservative, who thinks government has little place in a citizen's life, would take the position that the government has no right to take that same life away.

In 2000 the political currents in Illinois brought that state's one-term Governor George Ryan, who was elected on a pro-death penalty platform, to the forefront of the "moratorium movement" in 2000. After enduring a series of exposés by the *Chicago Tribune* unrelated to capital punishment, Ryan reacted to a series of highly publicized failures of the Illinois justice system by waiting until after the execution of a particularly reprehensible killer and then declaring that he would permit no more executions until the state's system was perfect.

A retiring justice of the Illinois Supreme Court publicly questioned what authority the governor legally possessed to halt executions through a moratorium, pointing out that under the separation of powers so critical to our legal system, the judiciary could grant stays or overturn sentences based on a legal appeal, the legislature could enact or abolish the death penalty, and the governor could commute a sentence of death. Nonetheless, in 2000 Ryan declared the Illinois death penalty to be under a "moratorium." The phrase took hold and many in the abolition movement who realized that wholesale repeal was out of reach, thought maybe a "moratorium" was a palatable alternative. Senator Russ Feingold, a long-time opponent of capital punishment and a Democrat from Wisconsin (a state without the death penalty) goes so far as to push for a national "moratorium," although many question what authority the United States Senate would have for such an action.

In the spring of 2002, the Illinois Death Penalty Commission (IDPC) issued a series of 85 proposed reforms. Any sensible person would agree that the system can be improved, so the question is whether the reforms are really improvements or just an excuse to block executions. The prosecutors and courts in Illinois had already instituted more than 25 of these recommendations by early 2003 and in the spring of that year the Illinois legislature adopted virtually all the rest. Suggestions that included better training for lawyers on both sides of the capital bar were met with almost universal agreement. But requirements that *all* interrogations be videotaped caused many in law enforcement to ask just how early a suspect's statements need be captured on video. Defendants and their lawyers will inevitably claim that any police misconduct took place just before the tape was turned on. The only solution would seem to be face-mounted cameras recording every interaction police have with anyone—a good example of a "reform" that sounds reasonable until you look at its practical implications.

Other "reforms" included requiring outside panels to review the decision to seek death, a move most prosecutors view as inimical to the accountability and separation of powers that balances our justice system. The IDPC was handicapped in that only one of its 14 members was a sitting prosecutor, who dissented from many of the group's "findings." Many of the panel were avowed foes of capital punishment, a belief that calls into question many of their suggestions. The panel's chief demanded that Illinois "reform or repeal" capital punishment. One recommendation was to provide a sort of "civilian review board" to oversee prosecutors' decisions in capital cases. Given that the vast majority of state prosecutors are elected and our actions are thoroughly scrutinized by the courts, the press, the defense bar, and ultimately our constituents, what better transparency could there be? ABC television's program *Nightline* profiled several different prosecutors and the way in which they selected capital cases. This ranged from a committee that reviewed and made recommendations to the chief prosecutor to the process in which I must engage when making such an important decision. In jurisdictions like my own where capital cases are rare, such decisions are the subject of intense interest and discussion. Prosecutors operate in a far more accountable environment than any other component of the criminal justice system.

Ryan stunned the nation when after making promises that he would carefully examine each case, he granted blanket clemency to all 171 residents of Illinois's death row. After spending weeks meeting with convicted killers' lawyers, their families, and supporters, and after refusing to grant any such similar meeting with his state's prosecutors, Ryan engaged in exactly the sort of arbitrary and capricious action that so often is cited as a reason to abolish capital punishment. Ryan waited until the last months of his scandal-plagued administration to call his state's clemency board to review all those on Illinois's death row. The hearings turned public opinion in Illinois against most of the condemned, as one after another of the friends and families of the 250 murdered victims spoke to why the sentence imposed by jurors and affirmed by appellate courts should be carried out. Ryan then chose to ignore the recommendations of the board, whose members angrily revealed that they had recommended clemency in only 10 cases and pardons in none (Ryan granted four pardons—which unlike clemency did not merely reduce the sentence but wiped the record of conviction away entirely). Ryan had spent the last two years of his administration dodging questions about his own role in a license-for-bribes scandal that was implicated in the vehicular crash deaths of the six children of the Reverend Scott Willis. Instead Ryan found that he was received with open arms at many college campuses and the meetings of death penalty opponents who hailed Ryan as a hero and nominated him for a Nobel Peace Prize. In his long, meandering speech printed in this book, delivered to an adoring crowd at Northwestern University, whose conduct was more appropriate to a football rally than a serious speech, Ryan borrowed quotes from Gandhi, President Vicente Fox of Mexico, and President Lincoln to justify his unprecedented action. Ryan made a political "Hail Mary pass" he hopes will wipe the memory of his other actions as a politician from the history books. Clearly impressed with his new-found celebrity, Ryan described how he had received a telephone call from former South African president Nelson Mandela urging him to grant clemency to all those within his power. Ryan's abuse of this power resulted in action by the Illinois legislature—after he left office—which voted by a huge margin to rein in the plenary power of clemency previously vested in the office of governor in Illinois. Many, even in the anti-death penalty community and including the normally supportive *Chicago Tribune*, voiced profound concerns about what the legacy will be of Ryan's actions. He made no distinction between killers such as Fedell Caffey and Jacqueline William (they stabbed a pregnant woman, cut the full-term fetus from her body and then slaughtered the dying woman's ten- and six-year-old children to eliminate witnesses) and other inmates whose guilt was less certain. All are now off death row and it is a virtual statistical certainty that some of those Ryan spared in his self-aggrandizing quest will kill again. Their victims will likely be other inmates or maybe prison staff. One spared inmate was on death row for having murdered the prison warden. Another, Henry Brisbon, was *not* on death row for the murder of 29-year-old Betty Lou Harmon, whom Brisbon robbed, stripped, and then shot; nor was he there for his subsequent murder of an engaged couple, whom he robbed and then shot to death, telling them to "kiss your last kiss" before slaughtering them with a shotgun. Brisbon was on death row for his fourth murder—of another inmate—after he had been given a life sentence.

Ryan declared that he simply didn't like the law or the way it was carried out, and in an act more arbitrary and capricious than any flawed death penalty trial, Ryan abused the power of his office.

Just before leaving office, Maryland's Democratic governor Parris Glendening announced a moratorium—not to seek out innocents on death row but to await another study about whether that state's death sentences were race motivated. Like Ryan, Glendening left the fate of his state's death row prisoners for his successor. That governor's race became something of a referendum on the moratorium, supported by the Democratic gubernatorial candidate, Kathleen Kennedy-Townsend, who lost, many political observers believed, *because* of her support of the moratorium. In 2003 a sniper killed several citizens in both Maryland and Virginia. The case against John Lee Malvo ended up going to Virginia prosecutor Robert Horan, probably because his jurisdiction was most likely to consider the death penalty for this particularly heinous series of murders. Therein lies the biggest problem with so-called moratoriums: Wait until exactly what is established? A system that, as former governor Ryan demanded, is "100 percent perfect?" Such a system will never exist.

THE LAST INNOCENT MAN

The standard popular culture depiction of the legal system has the mentally challenged and utterly innocent defendant arrested by brutal and racist police officers and persecuted by rich, ambitious district attorneys whose careers seem to depend on a certain number of court-room victories. The defense lawyer is threadbare but dedicated and is usually victorious through sheer force of will and a burst of conscience from some government minion who can no longer look at himself in the mirror. It's a plot that describes uncounted movies and is best portrayed on television by ABC's *The Practice*, in which creator David Kelley, trained as a lawyer, populates his alternate universe of Boston lawyers with stereotypes that will someday bring the ridicule that *Reefer Madness* engenders today. The show is so popular with abolitionists that they have awarded its cast various honors and awards.

The true face of evil, as Hannah Arndt explained in a different context, is much more banal. The innocent die anonymously at the hands of murderers who almost never pay for their crime with their own life. Until the advent of the crime victims' rights movement and the United States Supreme Court's decision in *Payne vs. Tennessee*,[35] the victim's voice was stunningly absent from any murder case. While not all murder victims' families support the death penalty, defense attorneys spare no effort to keep the victim's voice from being heard in the courtroom. The victim fades even more quickly into obscurity as the entire capital litigation system focuses solely on the defendant. During one recent capital case I tried, jurors asked during the trial why all they had heard about the murdered woman was a one-minute de-scription by her closest living relative. The law does not allow me to respond that they aren't permitted to know any more than the single photograph of Exhibit Number One and the victim's name and age—37 when murdered, and 37 forever.

I confess that American justice is a work in progress.

Innocent men have been sent to death row, and while there is no conclusive evidence affirming that an innocent person has been exe-cuted in the last quarter century, the possibility requires constant im-provements in our system. Anyone facing death, or even a long prison term, deserves not merely average counsel but lawyers capable and experienced in criminal defense.

When asked why I support the death penalty, I respond that I remain cautious about such a serious decision but believe that there are some crimes so heinous, some criminals so evil, that no other sentence can satisfy justice. Many "reformers," claiming to seek a middle ground in the debate, concede that life without parole is merely a first step in an attack on what they consider an inhumane system[36] and that it will be their next target if the death penalty is abolished. Life without parole might be a palatable alternative to the death penalty if we could trust the correctional system actually to keep killers in prison forever. But, as psychologists say, the best predictor of future behavior is the past. And based on past performance there seems little assurance of future protection.

Many of the apocryphal stories that have become the bread and butter of the movement to abolish the death penalty crumble under the weight of the truth. Learn the actual crimes of the residents of death row celebrated by the infamous Benetton advertising campaign of 2000. These poster boys for abolition had tortured, raped, and mutilated their victims in ways terrible to describe. They are the worst of the worst.

Most of the people freed from death row are anything but innocent, and police and prosecutors almost always do get the right person. We do not live in the legal world popularized by the television program *Perry Mason*, in which the police invariably arrest the wrong person for murder and the prosecutor invariably prosecutes an innocent person, only to have the true murderer exposed in a dramatic courtroom incident. There are indeed stories of people wrongfully sent to prison and even death row, but they are so few and the situations so easily remedied that they are hardly the basis for abolishing the ultimate punishment for the worst of murderers.

There is a parable about a rabbi who chooses to disguise himself as a peasant. He travels by train to address the congregation at a neighboring town and is treated poorly by passengers, who think him not worthy of their respect. When his identity is revealed at the end of his trip, the same passengers who are members of the congregation he came to address beg his forgiveness. He tells them he cannot grant such a pardon and such amnesty can be granted only by the man whom they slighted—the peasant on the train who no longer exists. Who can grant forgiveness on behalf of the dead?[37]

The vast majority of murderers do not deserve a death sentence and only one in a thousand actually receives such a penalty. It may well be that some states in America need to become much more discriminating about whom they put on death row. Professor Robert Blecker argues[38] that we should execute only a fraction of those currently condemned and do so much more quickly than the current average wait of 10 to 12 years from conviction. Count me among those like Professor Blecker and Judge Kozinski who believe that only the worst of the worst belong on death row.

Americans are generally a compassionate people. Their support for the possibility of a death sentence in the most egregious cases is not a paradox. It is a sign that life is so precious that it should be taken only with the greatest of care.

NOTES

1. Alex Kozinski, "Tinkering with Death," *The New Yorker*, February 10, 1997.

2. *Texas vs. Karla Faye Tucker*, 180th Judicial District of Texas, 1998.

3. The Gallup Organization, Death Penalty Polls, March 2, 2001; May 2002.

4. Joshua Micah Marshall, "Death in Venice," *The New Republic*, July 31, 2000.

5. Phillip English Mackey, *Voices Against Death: American Opposition to Capital Punishment, 1787–1975*, New York: Burt Franklin & Co., 1976.

6. C-SPAN, "Deutsche Welle," May 2001.

7. *Time* Europe, December 16, 2001.

8. Hashem Dezhbakhsh, Paul Rubin, & Joanna Sheperd, "Deterrence and the Death Penalty," Emory University, January 2002.

9. Dale O. Cloninger and Roberto Marchesini, "Execution Moratorium Is No Holiday for Homicides," *Applied Economics*, vol. 33, no. 5, April, 2001.

10. H. Noci Mocan and R. Kaj Gittings, "Pardons, Executions and Homicide," National Bureau of Economic Research, Working Paper 8639, December 2001.

11. Peter J. Boyer, "DNA on Trial," *The New Yorker*, January 17, 2000.

12. Brooke Masters, "DNA Tests Don't Clear Inmate, Gilmore Says," Washington *Post*, September 12, 2000.

13. *State vs. Harberts*, 331 OR 72 (2000).

14. *Jay C. Smith vs. John Holtz et al.*, United States Court of Appeals for the Third Circuit, 2000.

15. Eric Zorn, "Mumia Is No Poster Boy," *Chicago Tribune*, July 31, 2000.

16. Stuart Taylor, Jr., "Guilty and Framed," *The American Lawyer*, December 1995.

17. Michael L. Radelet, Hugo A. Bedau, and Constance Putnam, *In Spite of Innocence: Erroneous Convictions in Capital Cases*, Northeastern University Press, 1992.

18. Paul G. Cassell and Stephen J. Markman, "Protecting the Innocent: A Response to the Bedau-Radelet Study," 41 *Stanford Law Review* 121, 1988.

19. "Free to Kill", *48 Hours*, CBS News, aired April 28, 1993.

20. United States Department of Justice (USDOJ), Bureau of Justice Statistics (BJS), "Homicide Trends in the US," 2001.

21. *Batson vs. Kentucky*, 476 US 579 (1986).

22. James Liebman, *A Broken System: Error Rates in Capital Cases*, Columbia University, 1995.

23. *Death Penalty "Error" Study Has Errors of Its Own*, Criminal Justice Legal Foundation, June 19, 2000.

24. USDOJ, BJS, "Death Penalty" (as of July 1, 2001).

25. Death Penalty Information Center, "Death Row Statistics," 2001.

26. USDOJ, "The Federal Death Penalty System," June 2001.

27. Professor John McAdams, "Race and the Death Penalty," *Law and Contemporary Problems*, vol. 61, no. 4, 1998.

28. *Newsweek*, June 12, 2000.

29. Brooke Masters, "Death Penalty, Location Are Linked in Va. Study," *Washington Post*, December 11, 2001.

30. *State vs. Manzo Hernandez*, Klamath County, Oregon, 1993.

31. Steve Lundgren, "Guzek Penpal Flown In," *Bend Bulletin*, October 29, 1997.

32. Byron York, "The Death of Death," *American Spectator*, April 2000.

33. "Trial and Error" (series), *Chicago Tribune*, January 2000.

34. Michael Miner, *Chicago Reader*, June 9, 2000.

35. *Payne vs. Tennessee*, 111 Sup. Ct. 2597 (1991).

36. Nadine Strossen, *Justice Talking* debate in August 2001.

37. Ann Michael, *Fugitive Pieces*, New York: Random House, 1998.

38. Robert Blecker, *Who Deserves to Die*, New York: Basic Books, 2003.

6

Why the United States Will Join
the Rest of the World in
Abandoning Capital Punishment

Stephen B. Bright

The United States will inevitably join other industrialized nations in abandoning the death penalty, just as it has abandoned whipping, the stocks, branding, cutting off appendages, maiming, and other primitive forms of punishment. It remains to be seen how long it will be until the use of the death penalty becomes so infrequent as to be pointless, and it is eventually abandoned. In the meantime, capital punishment is arbitrarily and unfairly imposed, undermines the standing and moral authority of the United States in the community of nations, and diminishes the credibility and legitimacy of the courts within the United States.

Although death may intuitively seem to be an appropriate punishment for a person who kills another person and polls show strong support for the death penalty, most Americans know little about realities of capital punishment, past and present. As Bryan Stevenson describes in another chapter, the death penalty is a direct descendant of the darkest aspects of American history—slavery, lynching, racial oppression, and perfunctory capital trials known as "legal lynchings"— and racial discrimination remains a prominent feature of capital punishment. The death penalty is not imposed to avenge every killing and—as some contend—to bring "closure" to the family of every victim, but is inflicted in less than 1 percent of all murder cases. Of more than 20,000 murders in the United States annually, an average of fewer than 300 people are sentenced to death, and only 55 are executed each year.[1] Only 19 states actually carried out executions between 1976, when the U.S. Supreme Court authorized the resumption of capital punishment after declaring it unconstitutional in 1972, and the end of 2002. Eighty-six percent of those executions were in the South. Just two states—Texas and Virginia—carried out 45 percent of them.

Any assessment of the death penalty must not be based on abstract theories about how it should work in practice or the experiences of states like Oregon, which seldom impose the death penalty and carry it out even less. To understand the realities of the death penalty, one must look to the states that sentence people to death by the hundreds and have carried out scores of executions. In those states, innocent people have been sentenced to die based on such things as mistaken eyewitness identifications, false confessions, the testimony of partisan experts who render opinions that are not supported by science, failure of police and prosecutors to turn over evidence of innocence, and testimony of prisoners who get their own charges dismissed by testifying that the accused admitted the crime to them. Even the guilty are sentenced to death as opposed to life imprisonment without the possibility of parole not because they committed the worst crimes but because of where they happen to be prosecuted, the incompetence of their court-appointed lawyers, their race, or the race of their victim.

Former Illinois Governor George Ryan is a prominent example of a supporter of capital punishment who, upon close examination of the system, found that it "is haunted by the demon of error—error in determining guilt, and error in determining who among the guilty deserves to die." As a member of the legislature in 1977, Ryan voted to adopt Illinois's death penalty law and he described himself as a "staunch supporter" of capital punishment until as governor 23 years later, he saw that during that period the state had carried out 12 executions and released from its death row 13 people who had been exonerated. In 2003, Governor Ryan pardoned four people who had been tortured by police until they confessed to crimes they did not commit and commuted the sentences of the remaining 167 people on Illinois's death row for reasons that he eloquently sets out elsewhere in this book.

Many other supporters of capital punishment, after years of struggling to make the system work, have had sober second thoughts about the fairness with which the death penalty is imposed. Justice Sandra Day O'Connor, who joined the United States Supreme Court in 1981 and has regularly voted to uphold death sentences, has acknowledged that "serious questions are being raised about whether the death penalty is being fairly administered in this country" and that "the system may well be allowing some innocent defendants to be executed."[2] Justices Lewis Powell and Harry Blackmun also voted to uphold death sentences as members of the court, but eventually they came to the conclusion, as Justice Blackmun put it, that "the death penalty experiment has failed."[3]

Further experimentation with lethal punishment after centuries of failure has no place in a conservative society that is wary of too much government power and skeptical of the government's ability to do things well. Further experimentation might be justified if it served some purpose. But capital punishment is not needed to protect society or to punish offenders, as shown by over 100 countries around the world that do not have the death penalty and states such as Michigan and Wisconsin, neither of which have had the death penalty since the mid-1800s.[4] It can be argued that capital punishment was necessary when America was a frontier society and had no prisons. But today the United States has not only maximum security prisons, but "super maximum" prisons where serial killers, mass murderers, and sadistic murderers can be severely punished and completely isolated from guards and other inmates.

Nor is crime deterred by the executions in fewer than half the states of an arbitrarily selected 1 percent of those who commit murders, many of whom are mentally ill or have limited intellectual functioning. The South, which has carried out 85 percent of the nation's executions since 1976, has the highest murder rate of any region of the country. The Northeast, which has the fewest executions by far—only 3 executions between 1976 and the end of 2002—has the lowest murder rate.

The United States does not need to keep this relic of the past to show its abhorrence of murder. As previously noted, 99 percent of the murders in the United States are not punished by death. Even at war crimes trials in The Hague, genocide and other crimes against humanity are not punished with the death penalty. The societies that do not have capital punishment surely abhor murder as much as any other, but they do not find it necessary to engage in killing in order to punish, protect, or show their abhorrence with killing.

Finally, capital punishment has no place in a decent society that places some practices, such as torture, off limits—not because some individuals have not done things so bad that they arguably deserved to be tortured, but because a civilized society simply does not engage in such acts. It can be argued that rapists deserve to be raped, that mutilators deserve to be mutilated. Most societies, however, refrain from responding in this way because the punishment is not only degrading to those on whom it is imposed, but it is also degrading to the society that engages in the same behavior as the criminals. When death sentences are carried out, small groups of people gather in execution chambers and watch as a human being is tied down and put down. Some make no effort to suppress their glee when the sentence is carried out and celebrations occur inside and outside the prison. These celebrations of death reflect the dark side of the human spirit— an arrogant, vengeful, unforgiving, uncaring side that either does not admit the possibility of innocence or redemption or is willing to kill people despite those possibilities.

A HUMAN RIGHTS VIOLATION THAT UNDERMINES THE STANDING AND MORAL AUTHORITY OF THE UNITED STATES

If people were asked 50 years ago which one of the following three countries—Russia, South Africa, or the United States—would be most likely to have the death penalty at the turn of the century, few people would have answered the United States. And yet, the United States was one of four countries that accounted for 90 percent of all the executions in the world in 2001 (the others were China, Iran, and Saudi Arabia), while Russia and South Africa are among the nations that no longer practice capital punishment.[5] Since 1985, over 40 countries have abandoned capital punishment whereas only four countries that did not have it have adopted it.[6] One of those, Nepal, has since abolished it. Turkey abolished the death penalty in 2001 in its efforts to join the European Union, leaving the United States the only NATO country that still has the death penalty.[7]

The United States is also part of a very small minority of nations that allow the execution of children. Twenty-two of the 38 states with death penalty statutes allow the execution of people who were under 18 at the time of their crimes. Between 1990 and the end of 2001, these states put 15 children to death, with Texas carrying out over 60 percent of those executions. The only other countries that executed children during this time were the Congo, Iran, Nigeria, Pakistan, Saudi Arabia, and Yemen.[8] The United States and Somalia are the only two countries that have not ratified the International Covenant on the Rights of the Child, which, among other things, prohibits the execution of people who were children at the time of their crimes.

Being among the world leaders in executions and the leader in execution of children is incompatible with asserting leadership on human rights issues in the world. As Frederick Douglass said over a century ago, "Life is the great primary and most precious and comprehensive of all human rights—[and] whether it be coupled with virtue, honor, and happiness, or with sin, disgrace and misery, . . . [it is not] to be deliberately or voluntarily destroyed, either by individuals separately, or combined in what is called Government."[9]

The retention of capital punishment in the United States draws harsh criticism from throughout the world. It is suggested elsewhere in this book that the democracies in European countries function so poorly that the elite have prevented the use of the death penalty in them for decades; however, Felix G. Rohatyn, who saw the people of Europe firsthand during four years as U.S. Ambassador to France, found that "no single issue evoked as much passion and as much protest as executions in the United States."

Capital punishment also affects the United States's relations with other countries in other ways. Canada and Mexico have repeatedly protested when their nationals are executed by the United States, as have other countries. Canada, Mexico, and most European countries will not extradite suspects to the United States if they are subject to capital punishment and will not assist in the prosecution of people facing the death penalty. Just as the United States could not assert moral leadership in the world as long as it allowed segregation, it will not be a leader on human rights as long as it allows capital punishment.

ARBITRARY AND UNFAIR INFLICTION

Regardless of the practices of the rest of the world or the morality of capital punishment, the process leading to a death sentence is so unfair and influenced by so many improper factors and the infliction of death sentences is so inconsistent that this punishment should be abandoned.

The exoneration of many people who spent years of their lives in prisons for crimes they did not commit—many of them on death rows—has dramatically brought to light defects in the criminal justice system that have surprised and appalled people who do not observe the system every day and assumed that it was working properly. The average person has little or no contact with the criminal courts, which deal primarily with crimes committed against and by poor people and members of racial minorities. It is a system that is overworked and underfunded, and particularly underfunded when it comes to protecting the rights of those accused.

Law enforcement officers, usually overworked and often under tremendous public pressure to solve terrible crimes, make mistakes, fail to pursue all lines of investigation, and, on occasion, overreach or take shortcuts in pursuing arrests. Prosecutors exercise vast and unchecked discretion in deciding which cases are to be prosecuted as capital cases. The race of the victim and the defendant, political considerations, and other extraneous factors influence whether prosecutors seek the death penalty and whether juries or judges impose it.

A person facing the death penalty usually cannot afford to hire an attorney and is at the mercy of the system to provide a court-appointed lawyer. While many receive adequate representation (and often are not sentenced to death as a result), many others are assigned lawyers who lack the knowledge, skill, resources—and sometimes even the inclination—to handle a serious criminal case. People who would not be sentenced to death if properly represented are sentenced to death because of incompetent court-appointed lawyers. In many communities, racial minorities are still excluded from participation as jurors, judges, prosecutors, and lawyers in the system. In too many cases, defendants are convicted on flimsy evidence, such as eyewitness identifications, which are notoriously unreliable but are seen as very credible by juries; the testimony of convicts who, in exchange for lenient treatment in their own cases, testify that the accused admitted to them that he or she committed the crime; and confessions obtained from people of limited intellect through lengthy and overbearing interrogations.

Judge Cassell dismisses concerns about the unfair application of the death penalty as mere "administrative objections" that are ill-founded or easily cured. But these are not minor, isolated incidents; they are long-standing, pervasive, systemic deficiencies in the criminal justice system that are not being corrected and, in some places, are even becoming worse. There is tremendous resistance to change, as shown by the unwillingness of the Illinois legislature to adopt many of the recommendations of Governor Ryan's commission to reduce the likelihood of wrongful convictions in capital cases. Law enforcement agencies have been unwilling to videotape interrogations and use identification procedures that are more reliable than those presently employed. People who support capital punishment as a concept are unwilling to spend millions of tax dollars to provide competent legal representation for those accused of crimes. And courts have yet to find ways to overcome centuries of racial discrimination that often influence, consciously or subconsciously, the decisions of prosecutors, judges, and juries.

A Warning That Something Is Terribly Wrong: Innocent People Condemned to Death

Over 100 people condemned to death in the last 30 years have been exonerated and released after new evidence established their innocence or cast such doubt on their guilt that they could not be convicted.[10] The 100th of those people, Ray Krone, was convicted and sentenced to death in Arizona based on the testimony of an expert witness that his teeth matched bite marks on the victim. During the ten years that Krone spent on death row, scientists developed the ability to compare biological evidence recovered at crime scenes with the DNA of suspects. DNA testing established that Krone was innocent.[11] On Krone's release, the prosecutor said, "[Krone] deserves an apology from us, that's for sure. A mistake was made here. . . . What do you say to him? An injustice was done and we will try to do better. And we're sorry." Although unfortunate to be wrongfully convicted, Krone was very fortunate that there was DNA evidence in his case. In most cases, there is no biological evidence for DNA testing.

Other defendants had their death sentences commuted to life imprisonment without the possibility of parole because of questions about their innocence. For example, in 1994, the governor of Virginia commuted the death sentence of a mentally retarded man, Earl Washington, to life imprisonment without parole because of questions regarding his guilt. Washington, an easily persuaded, somewhat childlike special-education dropout, had been convicted of murder and rape based on a confession he gave to police, even though it was full of inconsistencies. For example, at one point in the confession Washington said that the victim was white and at another that the victim was black. Six years later, DNA evidence—not available at the time of Washington's trial or the commutation—established that Washington was innocent and he was released.

Although DNA testing has been available only in cases where there was biological evidence and the evidence has been preserved, it has established the innocence of many people who were not sentenced to death—more than 100 by the end of 2002. A Michigan judge in 1984 lamented the fact that the state did not have the death penalty, saying that life imprisonment was inadequate for Eddie Joe Lloyd for the rape and murder of a 16-year-old girl. Police had obtained a confession from Lloyd while he was in a mental hospital. Seventeen years later, DNA evidence established that Lloyd did not commit the crime. On his release, Lloyd commented, "If Michigan had the death penalty, I would have been through, the angels would have sung a long time ago."[12]

Sometimes evidence of innocence has surfaced only at the last minute. Anthony Porter, sentenced to death in Illinois, went through all the appeals and review that are available for one so sentenced. Every court upheld his conviction and sentence. As Illinois prepared to put him to death, a question arose as to whether Porter, who was brain damaged and mentally retarded, understood what was happening to him. A person who lacks the mental ability to understand that he is being put to death in punishment for a crime cannot be executed unless he is treated and becomes capable of understanding why he is being executed. Just two days before Porter was to be executed, a court stayed his execution in order to examine his mental condition. After the stay was granted, a journalism class at Northwestern University and a private investigator examined the case and proved that Anthony Porter was innocent. They obtained a confession from the person who committed the crime.[13] Anthony Porter was released, becoming the third person released from Illinois's death row after being proven innocent by a journalism class at Northwestern.[14]

Some people have been executed despite questions of their innocence. Gary Graham was sentenced to death in Texas based on the identification of a witness who said she saw a murder from 40 feet away. Studies have demonstrated that such identifications are often unreliable. But Graham had the misfortune to be assigned a notoriously incompetent lawyer, Ron Mock, who had so many clients sentenced to death that some refer to the "Mock Wing" of death row. Mock failed to seriously contest the state's case, conduct an independent investigation, and present witnesses at the scene who would have testified that Graham was not the person who committed the crime and that the perpetrator was much shorter than Graham. Although it was apparent that Graham did not receive a fair trial and adequate legal representation, he was executed by Texas in 2000. Whether Graham was innocent or guilty will never be resolved because in his case, like most others, there was no DNA evidence that would conclusively establish guilt or innocence.

Some proponents of capital punishment argue that the exoneration of Porter and others shows that the system works and that no innocent people have been executed. However, someone spending years on death row for a crime he did not commit is not an example of the system working. When journalism students prove that police, prosecutors, judges, defense lawyers, and the entire legal system failed to discover the perpetrator of a crime and instead condemned the wrong person to die, the system is not working. Porter and others were spared, as Chief Justice Moses Harrison of the Illinois Supreme Court observed, "only because of luck and the dedication of the attorneys, reporters, family members and volunteers who labored to win their release. They survived despite the criminal justice system, not because of it. The truth is that left to the devices of the court system, they would probably have all ended up dead at the hands of the state for crimes they did not commit. One must wonder how many others have not been so fortunate."[15]

If there had been no question about Antony Porter's ability to understand why he was to be put to death, his execution would not have been stayed. If his intellectual functioning had been just a little higher and he had had a little less brain damage, he would have been executed. The journalism students would not have investigated his case. Similarly, had it not been for the scientific breakthrough regarding DNA, Ray Krone would have been executed. Had not Governor Douglas Wilder commuted his sentence to life imprisonment, Earl Washington would not have lived until DNA testing proved his innocence. A different governor at a different time might well have denied commutation. Had Porter, Krone, and Washington been put to death, the proponents of capital punishment would still be strenuously arguing— as some do in chapters in this book—that no innocent person has been executed, safe in their ignorance that such fatal mistakes had been made. But for every Anthony Porter, Ray Krone, or Earl Washington whose innocence has been discovered, there are others for whom there is no biological evidence that can be subject to DNA testing, no journalism class, no lawyer, no serendipitous discovery of evidence that exonerates them. And as executions become more "routine," with less attention to each one, they and other innocent people will be put to death.

Other proponents of capital punishment, instead of insisting that the system works when journalism students free people wrongfully sentenced to death, admit that the system is not working. Gerald Kogan, formerly the head of the homicide unit of the prosecutor's office in Miami-Dade County, Florida, asked for the death penalty as a prosecutor and supervised other prosecutors asking for and obtaining the death penalty. He presided over capital cases as a trial judge and reviewed hundreds more as a justice and then chief justice of the Florida Supreme Court. Upon retiring, he stated that capital punishment "does not work at this time and has not worked in the State of Florida for many, many, many years."[16]

Gerald W. Heaney announced, after 30 years of reviewing capital cases as a federal appellate judge, that he was "compelled . . . to conclude that the imposition of the death penalty is arbitrary and capricious." He found that "the decision of who shall live and who shall die for his crime turns less on the nature of the offense and the incorrigibility of the offender and more on inappropriate and indefensible considerations: the political and personal inclinations of prosecutors; the defendant's wealth, race, and intellect; the race and economic status of the victim; the quality of the defendant's counsel; and the resources allocated to defense lawyers."[17]

After declaring a moratorium on executions in Illinois, Governor Ryan appointed a 14-member commission made up of respected judges, prosecutors, defense attorneys, business leaders, an author, and a former U.S. senator to study the criminal justice system in Illinois; the commission made 85 recommendations in 2002 for reforms to minimize the risk of wrongful convictions. The legislature, however, was unwilling to enact reforms such as reducing the number of capital prosecutions so that each one could be handled with appropriate care, and prohibiting death sentences when a defendant is convicted with just a single witness, a jailhouse informant, or an accomplice whose testimony is not corroborated with other evidence. Illinois and other states want the death penalty, but they are unwilling to pay the cost of reducing the risk of error and making the system fairer. And even if every single reform were adopted, it would not eliminate the possibility of executing innocent people. As the Canadian Supreme Court recognized in holding that it would not allow the extradition of people to the United States if the death penalty could be imposed, courts will always be fallible and reversible, while death will always be final and irreversible. [18]

The Two Most Important Decisions—Made by Prosecutors

The two most important decisions in every death penalty case are made not by juries or judges, but by prosecutors. No state or federal law ever requires prosecutors to seek the death penalty or take a capital case to trial. A prosecutor has complete discretion in deciding whether to seek the death penalty and, even if death is sought, whether to offer a sentence less than death in exchange for the defendant's guilty plea. The overwhelming majority of all criminal cases, including capital cases, are resolved not by trials but by plea bargains. Whether death is sought or imposed is based on the discretion and proclivities of the thousands of people who occupy the offices of prosecutor in judicial districts throughout the nation. (Texas, for example, has 155 elected prosecutors, Virginia 120, Missouri 115, Illinois 102, Georgia 49, and Alabama 40.) Some prosecutors seek the death penalty at every opportunity, and others never seek it; some seldom seek it; some frequently seek it. There is no requirement that individual prosecutors—who, in most states, are elected by districts—be consistent in their practices in seeking the death penalty.

As a result of this discretion, there are great geographical disparities in where death is imposed within states. Prosecutors in Houston and Philadelphia have sought the death penalty in virtually every case in which it can be imposed. As a result of aggressive prosecutors and inept court-appointed lawyers, Houston and Philadelphia have each condemned over 100 people to death—more than most states. Harris County, which includes Houston, has had more executions in the last 30 years than any *state* except Texas and Virginia. A case is much more likely to be prosecuted capitally in Houston and Philadelphia than in Dallas, Ft. Worth, or Pittsburgh.

At the other end of the spectrum, Manhattan District Attorney Robert Morgenthau, who opposed the adoption of New York's death penalty law in 1995, and Bronx District Attorney Robert Johnson, an outspoken opponent of the law, have not sought the death penalty in a single case since New York enacted this punishment. Other New York prosecutors in areas that have far lower crime rates than Manhattan and the Bronx have sought and obtained death sentences.

A study conducted in 1999, found that 15 counties in the country account for almost one third of all the nation's death sentences.[19] A small county in Georgia with an average of two murders a year had more people on the state's death row than Fulton County, which includes Atlanta and averages 230 murders a year. Hamilton County, Ohio, which includes Cincinnati, had 50 people under death sentence while Franklin County, which includes Columbus and has twice as many murders a year as Hamilton, had only 11.[20]

Whether death is sought may depend on the side of the county line where the crime was committed. A murder was committed in a parking lot that contained the boundary between Lexington County, South Carolina, which at the time had sentenced 12 people to death, and Richland County, which had sent only one person to death row. The crime was determined to have occurred a few feet on the Lexington County side of the line. The defendant was tried in Lexington County and sentenced to death.[21] Had the crime occurred a few feet in the other direction, the death penalty almost certainly would not have been imposed.

On occasion, prosecutors manipulate the courts to get death sentence. For example, Attorney General John Ashcroft decided to have Virginia conduct the first trials of two people accused of being snipers who killed ten people in the Washington, D.C., metropolitan area because it was more likely that Virginia would give them the death penalty. The suspects could have been tried in Maryland, where most of the shootings occurred, or in the federal system, but Maryland law and federal law prohibit the execution of those who are children at the time of the crime, as was one of the sniper suspects. Beyond that, Virginia with 87 executions is second only to Texas in the number of people it has executed in the last 30 years. And the legal representation provided to poor people who cannot afford lawyers is far worse in Virginia than in Maryland or the federal system.

The policy of a particular office with regard to seeking the death penalty may change when a new prosecutor is elected. For example, an Illinois prosecutor announced that he had decided not to seek the death penalty for Girvies Davis after Davis's case was reversed by the state supreme court. However, while the case was pending, a new prosecutor took office and decided to seek the death penalty. He was successful and Davis was executed in 1995.[22] In several cases in which an innocent person was wrongfully convicted and sentenced to death, prosecutors did not seek the death penalty for the actual culprit when that person was found.

Thus, whether the death sentence is imposed may depend more on the personal predilections and politics of local prosecutors than the heinousness of the crime or the incorrigibility of the defendant.

The Role of Racial Bias

The complete discretion given to prosecutors in deciding whether to seek the death penalty and whether to drop the death penalty in exchange for guilty pleas also contributes to racial disparities in the infliction of the death penalty. In the 38 states that have the death penalty, 97.5 percent of the chief prosecutors are white.[23] In 18 of the states, all of the chief prosecutors are white.[24] Even the most conscientious prosecutors who have had little experience with people of other races may be influenced in their decisions by racial stereotypes and attitudes they have developed over their lives.

But the rest of the criminal justice system is almost as unrepresentative of American's racial diversity as prosecutors' offices. In the South, where the death penalty is most often imposed and carried out, over half the victims of crime are people of color, well over 60 percent of the prison population is made up of people of color, and half of those sentenced of death are members of racial minorities. Yet people of color are seldom involved as judges, jurors, prosecutors, and lawyers in the courts.

For example, there is not one African American or Hispanic judge on the nine-member Texas Court of Criminal Appeals, the court of last resort for all criminal cases in that state even though 43 percent of the population of Texas is nonwhite, over 65 percent of the homicide victims are people of color, and nearly 70 percent of the prison population is black, Hispanic, or other nonwhite. This court handles over 10,000 cases each year, most of them involving the lives and liberty of people of color. In Alabama, no African American sits among the nine members of the Alabama Supreme Court or the five members of the Alabama Court of Criminal Appeals—the two courts that review capital cases—even though 26 percent of the population of Alabama is

African American, 59 percent of the victims of homicide are African American, and over half those on death row are black. In many court-houses, everything looks the same as it did during the period of Jim Crow justice. The judges are white, the prosecutors are white, the law-yers are white and, even in communities with substantial African American populations, the jury may be all white. In many cases, the only person of color who sits in front of the bar in the courtroom is the person on trial. The legal system remains the institution that has been least affected by the civil rights movement.

Although African Americans constitute only 12 percent of the na-tional population, they are victims of half the murders that are com-mitted in the United States. Yet 80 percent of those on death row were convicted of crimes against white people. The discrepancy is even greater in the Death Belt states of the South. In Georgia and Alabama, for example, African Americans are the victims of 65 percent of the homicides, yet 80 percent of those on death rows are there for crimes against white persons. Studies of capital sentencing have consistently revealed such disparities.[25] Practices in Georgia's Chattahoochee Judi-cial Circuit, which includes the city of Columbus and accounts for a disproportionate number of people sent to Georgia's death row, illus-trate how discretionary decisions by prosecutors produce these results. An investigation of all murder cases prosecuted in the circuit from 1973 to 1990 revealed that in cases involving the murder of a white person, prosecutors met with the families and discussed whether to seek the death penalty. If the family wanted the death sentence, the prosecutors sought it. For example, in a case involving the murder of the daughter of a white contractor who the prosecutor knew, the prosecutor asked the contractor if he wanted the death penalty. When the contractor replied in the affirmative, the prosecutor said that was all he needed to know. The practice was very different in the 65 percent of murder cases during this period in which the victims were African American. The prosecutors did not meet with family members to ask what sen-tences they wanted. Many families were not even notified that the cases in which their loved one had been victims had been resolved. As a result, 85 percent of the capital cases in the circuit involved white victims even though African Americans were the victims of 65 percent of the murders.

Study after study has confirmed what lawyers practicing in the criminal courts observe every day: People of color are treated more harshly than white people. A person of color is more likely than a white person to be stopped by the police, to be abused by the police during that stop, to be arrested, to be denied bail when taken to court, to be charged with a serious crime as opposed to a less serious one that could be charged, to be convicted, and to receive a harsher sentence.[26] But a person of color is much *less* likely to be a participant in the criminal justice system as a judge, juror, prosecutor, or lawyer.

It would be quite remarkable if race affected every aspect of the criminal justice system except with regard to the death penalty—the area in which decision makers have the broadest discretion and base their decisions on evidence with tremendous emotional impact. The sad reality is that race continues to influence who is sentenced to death as it has throughout American history.

The Death Sentence for Being Assigned the Worst Lawyer

Capital cases—complex cases with the highest stakes of any in the legal system—should be handled by the most capable lawyers, with the resources to conduct thorough investigations and consult with various experts on everything from the prosecution's scientific evidence to psychologists and psychiatrists to investigate the defendant's mental health. The right to counsel is the most fundamental constitutional right of a person charged with a crime. A person accused of a crime depends on a lawyer to investigate the prosecution's case; to present any facts that may be helpful to the accused and necessary for a fair and reliable determination of guilt or innocence and, if guilty, a proper sentence; and to protect every other right of the accused. However, U.S. Supreme Court Justice Ruth Bader Ginsburg observed in 2001 that she had "yet to see a death case among the dozens coming to the Supreme Court ... in which the defendant was well represented at trial. People who are well-represented at trial do not get the death penalty."[27]

Those receiving the death penalty are not well represented because many states do not provide the structure, resources, independence, and accountability that is required to insure competent representation in an area of such specialization. Many states that have sentenced hundreds of people to death—such as Alabama, Georgia, and Texas— do not have public defender systems. For example, Texas, which has 254 counties, and Georgia, which has 159, leave primary responsibility for providing representation for those who cannot afford lawyers to each county. In some counties, there may be different approaches to providing counsel in different courts. Such a hopelessly fragmented system cannot and does not deliver quality legal representation. In addition, both states for many years left funding entirely to the counties, and now merely provide the counties with a small percentage of the total cost of indigent defense.

In states with no public defender offices, lawyers in private practice are assigned to defend capital cases and paid well below market rates. Lawyers, like many people, are attracted to work that pays well. Few lawyers are willing to take the most difficult and emotionally demanding cases with the highest stakes for wages that are among the lowest in the legal profession. A paralegal who works on a federal bankruptcy case is compensated at a higher hourly rate than a lawyer who defends a capital case in Alabama, Georgia, Mississippi, Virginia, and many other states that send many people to death rows.

Clarence Darrow made an observation in 1924 that is as true today as it was when he made it: "[N]o court ever interferes with a good lawyer's business by calling him in and compelling him to give his time" in defense of a poor person accused of a crime. Instead, judges appoint lawyers willing to take the cases for what the courts pay. In Mississippi, lawyers are paid a flat $1,000 fee plus expenses to defend a death penalty case. In other states the hourly rate may not amount to much more than what it costs to pay a lawyer's overhead expenses. Some capable lawyers take capital cases despite the meager compensation, but not nearly enough lawyers do so to defend the hundreds of people facing capital trials. And some judges refuse to appoint capable lawyers even when they are available. Almost half the trial judges in Texas, responding to a survey, said that an attorney's reputation for moving cases quickly, regardless of the quality of the defense, was a factor that entered into their decisions about what lawyer to appoint. Even when this is not a judge's motivation, court-appointed lawyers may provide less than zealous representation for fear of alienating the judge and losing future business.

In several states where journalists have investigated—Illinois, Kentucky, Tennessee, and Texas—they have found that a fourth to a third of those sentenced to death were represented at their trials by lawyers who were later disbarred, suspended, or convicted of crimes. Four of those exonerated in Illinois were represented at trial by attorneys who were later disbarred or suspended.[28] Dennis Williams, convicted twice of the 1978 murders of a couple from Chicago's south suburbs, was represented at his first trial by an attorney who was later disbarred and at his second trial by a different attorney who was later suspended. Williams was exonerated by DNA evidence. Four other men sentenced to death in Illinois were represented by a convicted felon who was the only lawyer in Illinois history to be disbarred twice. He handled those cases after being disbarred the first time and then reinstated despite concerns about his emotional stability and drinking. The list of lawyers eligible to handle capital cases in Tennessee in 2001, circulated to trial judges by the state Supreme Court, included a lawyer convicted of bank fraud, a lawyer convicted of perjury, and a lawyer whose failure to order a blood test let an innocent man languish in jail for four years on a rape charge.

Many courts continue to operate on the fiction that anyone licensed to practice law—even someone whose practice is mostly real estate or divorce law—is competent to handle capital cases. This is like saying that every doctor is competent to do brain surgery. Gary Drinkard was sentenced to death in Alabama at trial where he was represented by a lawyer who did collections and commercial work, another who handled foreclosures and bankruptcy cases, and a recent law graduate. Drinkard was imprisoned for seven years, five of them on Alabama's death row, before his case was reversed on appeal. He received a new trial at which he was represented by criminal defense lawyers with experience in defending capital cases. After they proved that he was at home on the night the murder was committed with a back injury so severe that it would have been impossible for him to commit the crime, he was acquitted and released.

In Houston, which sentences more people to death than most states, the *Houston Chronicle* described the trial of a capital case as follows:

Seated beside his client—a convicted capital murderer—defense attorney John Benn spent much of Thursday afternoon's trial in apparent deep sleep.

His mouth kept falling open and his head lolled back on his shoulders, and then he awakened just long enough to catch himself and sit upright. Then it happened again. And again. And again.

Every time he opened his eyes, a different prosecution witness was on the stand describing another aspect of the Nov. 19, 1991, arrest of George McFarland in the robbery-killing of grocer Kenneth Kwan.

When state District Judge Doug Shaver finally called a recess, Benn was asked if he truly had fallen asleep during a capital murder trial.

"It's boring," the 72-year-old longtime Houston lawyer explained. ... Court observers said Benn seems to have slept his way through virtually the entire trial.[29]

This sleeping did not violate the right to a lawyer guaranteed by the United States Constitution, the trial judge explained, because, "[t]he Constitution doesn't say the lawyer has to be awake." On appeal, the Texas Court of Criminal Appeals rejected McFarland's claim that he was denied his right to counsel over the dissent of two judges who pointed out that "[a] sleeping counsel is unprepared to present evidence, to cross-examine witnesses, and to present any coordinated effort to evaluate evidence and present a defense."[30]

George McFarland was one of three people sentenced to death in Houston at trials where their lawyers slept. Two others were represented by Joe Frank Cannon, who was appointed by Houston judges for 40 years to represent people accused of crimes in part because of his reputation for hurrying through trials like "greased lightning," and despite his tendency to doze off during the trial.[31] Ten of Cannon's clients were sentenced to death, one of the largest numbers among Texas attorneys. Another notorious lawyer appointed by Houston judges had 14 clients sentenced to death. Their 24 clients totaled more than the number of people on the death rows of 18 states in 2001.

Cannon was the only lawyer appointed to represent Calvin Burdine at his capital trial in Houston. The clerk of the Court later testified that he "was asleep on several occasions on several days over the course of the proceedings," according to the clerk of the court. Cannon's file on the case contained only three pages of notes. The Texas Court of Criminal Appeals upheld Burdine's conviction and sentence.[32] A federal judge, making the unremarkable observation that "sleeping counsel is the equivalent of no counsel at all," granted Burdine a new trial.[33] Texas appealed. While acknowledging that the lawyer slept, the lawyers for Texas argued that a sleeping lawyer was no different from a lawyer under the influence of alcohol or drugs, or suffering from Alzheimer's disease, pointing out that death sentences had been upheld in such instances. The Court of Appeals reversed by a 2–1 vote, reinstating the conviction and death sentence.[34] Although that decision was overruled by the full 14-member Court of Appeals by a 9–5 vote,[35] five judges would have allowed Burdine to be executed even though his lawyer slept during trial. Burdine was returned to Houston for a new trial. The trial judge refused to appoint the lawyer who had represented him for 15 years in post-conviction proceedings and had won the new trial. Instead, the judge appointed a lawyer who had no familiarity with Burdine or his case.

Most people caught sleeping on the job in any line of work are fired. But Houston judges continued to appoint Cannon to capital and other criminal cases. Cannon also slept during the capital trial of Carl Johnson. A law professor who later represented Johnson found in reading the trial transcript that Cannon's "ineptitude . . . jumps off the printed page."[36] Nevertheless, the death sentence was upheld by the Texas and federal courts. Johnson was executed by Texas in 1996.[37]

Of course, most lawyers do not sleep during trial. But Johnson's execution and the bitter division of a federal court of appeals over whether sleeping during a capital trial violates the Constitution sadly demonstrates how little regard the courts have for the quality of representation provided to poor people facing the death penalty. The courts have upheld death sentences in cases in which lawyers were not aware of the governing law, were not sober, and failed to present any evidence regarding either guilt-innocence or penalty. One federal judge, in reluctantly upholding a death sentence, observed that as interpreted by the U.S. Supreme Court, the Constitution "does not require that the accused, even in capital cases, be represented by able or effective counsel."[38]

Capital defender offices in Colorado, Connecticut, and New York have demonstrated what a difference legal representation by competent lawyers makes. Those states have well-staffed offices of lawyers, investigators, and paralegals who specialize in defending capital cases and have the resources to do so. Unlike southern states that have sentenced hundreds to death, none of those states have as many as ten people on death row. Courts in those three states have imposed an average of less than one death sentence a year since the reinstatement of capital punishment in 1976. Colorado has executed only one person, Connecticut and New York have not carried out any executions during this time. In these states, the death penalty exists largely as a statement by the legislature and governor that they are tough on crime, but it is used so seldom that it is inconsequential as a tool of law enforcement. Josh Marquis, a prosecutor, defends the death penalty based in large part on his experiences in Oregon, a state that is not much different. Oregon has carried out only two executions since 1976 and has only 30 people on its death row.

As bad as representation may be at trial, there are later, critical stages of review in which one under death sentence is not even entitled to a lawyer. The U.S. Supreme Court has held that states are required to provide a lawyer for those who cannot afford them only at trial and one appeal. While some states provide lawyers to represent the poor at later stages of review, some do not. Exzavious Gibson, whose I.Q. was found on different tests to be between 76 and 82, stood totally bewildered in front of a judge at his first state post-conviction hearing in Georgia without a lawyer. The case proceeded as follows:

> THE COURT: OK, Mr. Gibson are you ready to proceed?
> MR. GIBSON: I don't have an attorney.
> THE COURT: I understand that.
> MR. GIBSON: I am not waiving my rights.
> THE COURT: I understand that. Do you have any evidence to put up?
> MR. GIBSON: I don't know what to plead.
> THE COURT: Huh?
> MR. GIBSON: I don't know what to plead.[39]

The state of Georgia, which sought to bring about Gibson's execution, was represented by a lawyer who specializes in capital post-conviction cases. After the state's lawyer presented testimony, the judge turned again to Mr. Gibson:

THE COURT: Mr. Gibson, would you like to ask [the witness] any questions?

MR. GIBSON: I don't have counsel.

THE COURT: I understand that, but I am asking, can you tell me yes or no whether you want to ask him any questions or not?

MR. GIBSON: I'm not my own counsel.

THE COURT: I'm sorry, sir, I didn't understand you.

MR. GIBSON: I'm not my own counsel.

THE COURT: I understand, but do you want . . . to ask him anything?

MR. GIBSON: I don't know.

THE COURT: Okay, sir. Okay, thank you, Mr. Mullis, you can go down.[40]

The evidence presented at this hearing was to be used in determining whether Exzavious Gibson would be put to death.

Most states that have the death penalty, unlike Georgia, provide lawyers for later stages of review even though they are not required to do so. But the lawyers provided may be as bad as or worse than those assigned to defend the accused at trial. Texas has executed people who had no review of their cases after one appeal because the lawyers assigned to represent them failed to file pleadings on time or failed to raise any issues. Leonard Rojas, who was executed in December 2002, was the fourth person put to death by Texas with no further review because the appointed lawyer missed a critical filing deadline. The lawyer appointed to defend Rojas had never handled a death penalty appeal and at the time of his appointment was under two probated suspensions handed down by the Texas bar because he ineffectively represented other clients, suffered from a bipolar disorder, and conducted no investigation of the Rojas case.[41] A study found that because of poor representation, those sentenced to death in Texas "face

a one-in-three chance of being executed without having the case properly investigated by a competent attorney or without having any claims
of innocence or unfairness heard."[42]

Justice Hugo Black wrote for the U.S. Supreme Court in 1956 that
"[t]here can be no equal justice where the kind of trial a [person] gets
depends on the amount of money he [or she] has."[43] But today, no
one seriously doubts that the kind of trial, and the kind of justice, a
person receives depends very much on the amount of money he or
she has. The quality of legal representation tolerated by some courts
shocks the conscience of a person of average sensibilities. But poor
representation resulting from lack of funding and structure has been
accepted as the best that can be done with the limited resources available. The commitment of many states to providing lawyers for those
who cannot afford them was aptly described by a Chief Justice of the
Georgia Supreme Court: "[W]e set our sights on the embarrassing
target of mediocrity. I guess that means about halfway. And that raises
a question. Are we willing to put up with halfway justice? To my way
of thinking, one-half justice must mean one-half injustice, and one-
half injustice is no justice at all."[44]

The proponents of capital punishment are always quick to say that
people facing the death penalty *should* receive better legal representation. But they, including those who have contributed chapters to this
book, do not explain how this is going to be accomplished—whether
by a sudden burst of altruism on the part of members of the legal
profession, who are going to suddenly start taking capital cases for a
fraction of what they can make doing other work; a massive infusion
of funding from state legislatures that are searching for revenue for
education, transportation, and other areas that have a constituency; or
some other miracle. The right to competent representation is celebrated in the abstract, but most states—and most supporters of capital
punishment—are unwilling to pay for it. As a result the death penalty
will continue to be imposed not upon those who commit the worst
crimes, but upon those who have the misfortune to be assigned the
worst lawyers.

Death for the Disadvantaged

Capital punishment is inflicted on the weakest and most troubled members of our society such as children, the delusional, the paranoid, the brain-damaged, the chemically imbalanced, those who were abused and neglected as children, and people who endured the most terrible trauma imaginable in military service during war, who came back with post-traumatic stress syndrome, addicted to drugs, with various mental and emotional problems.

Charles Rumbaugh is one of many examples of the execution of the mentally ill. He was only 17 at the time of his crime and suffered from schizophrenia and depression to the point that he repeatedly mutilated himself and attempted suicide. Rumbaugh's parents tried to convince a court not to let him withdraw his appeals. During a hearing, Rumbaugh advanced on a marshal and provoked the marshal to shoot him in the courtroom.[45] He was taken to the hospital while the hearing continued. He was allowed to withdraw his appeals and was executed by Texas.

Another example is Pernell Ford, who was allowed to discharge his lawyers and represent himself at his capital trial in Alabama in 1984. Ford wore only a sheet to the penalty phase of the trial. He tried to call as witnesses people who were no longer alive. After lawyers appealed his conviction to a federal court, Ford wrote to the court and asked that the petition be dismissed. During a hearing, Ford said that he wanted to die because he was a member of the Holy Trinity, he had supernatural powers that would be enhanced when he died, and he would be able to transfer his soul to people outside the prison. He said that when he died, his 400 thousand wives would receive the millions of dollars he had put in Swiss bank accounts. One psychiatrist who evaluated Ford said that these statements were reflective of Ford's religious beliefs—not evidence of mental illness. Another psychiatrist found that Ford suffered from depression and personality disorder but was still capable of making rational choices. A third psychiatrist found that Ford was incapable of thinking rationally. The court concluded that Ford could give up his appeals because he understood the "bottom line" of his legal situation. Like Charles Rumbaugh, he was allowed to withdraw his appeals. Alabama executed him.

Courts found that Claude Eric Maturana, a French citizen suffering from paranoid schizophrenia who was sentenced to death in Arizona in 1992, could not be executed because he did not understand what was happening to him. Some manifestations of his illness were beliefs that the CIA took him from his cell to perform investigations and assassinations; that the jail put a device in him that allowed him to talk to people telepathically; that he was an agent of the "world police" who monitored him through a device in his chest; and that he had frequently visited with his mother who had been dead for over 30 years. Instead of using words, he often spoke in numbers and initials that made no sense such as his assertion that his sentence had been commuted by "Rule 11, Margaret 3." Dr. Jerry Dennis, medical director and chief psychiatrist of Arizona's State Mental Hospital, refused to give Maturana enough medication to make it possible for him to understand his legal situation because it would mean that he would be executed. Dr. Dennis believes this would violate the Hippocratic Oath he took as a physician. He stated, "I'm upholding the ethics of my profession. It's not right to give a patient treatment just so that he can be executed."[46]

At the insistence of prosecutors, Arizona officials conducted a nationwide search for a doctor who would treat Maturana. For a long time the search was unsuccessful, but in January of 2000, Dr. Nelson C. Bennet, the medical director for Georgia inmates came forward, examined Maturana, and pronounced him to be "competent to face death" and not in need of any more medication. Maturana was moved back to death row while the legal battle over whether he should be executed continued.

The execution of such severely mentally ill people and treating mentally ill people so that they can be executed should be beneath the American people. Unfortunately, many mentally ill people are left on their own without support and supervision. Society would be better served by providing some care to insure that they take their medications and receive proper treatment to prevent episodes of violence than by executing people who are out of touch with reality. And once a severely mentally ill person has committed a serious crime, as Rumbaugh, Ford, and Maturana did, the appropriate response is to place them in secure mental health facilities, not in execution chambers.

Corruption of the Courts

Not only are death sentences products of an unfair criminal justice system that does not treat people equally, but the death penalty further corrupts the courts in many ways. Despite the recognition that innocent people are being sentenced to death in a system that is seriously flawed, and the irrevocablity of a death sentence once carried out, carrying out executions has become more important in some states than the fairness and integrity of the process. Justice Moses Harrison of the Illinois Supreme Court noted, based on years of observing the process, "The prognosis for wrongly accused defendants facing capital charges is not improving. To the contrary, legislatures and the courts appear to have abandoned any genuine concern with insuring the fairness and reliability of the system. Achieving 'finality' in death cases, and doing so as expeditiously as possible, have become the dominant goals in death penalty jurisprudence."[47]

One way to achieve finality has been to remove judges from courts who uphold the Constitution instead of expediting executions. In almost all the states that have the death penalty, judges are elected. It has become increasingly clear that by voting to reverse a capital case even when the law clearly requires it, judges may be signing their own political death warrants.

The practice of targeting judges for defeat based on their votes in capital cases started in 1986 in California when the governor announced that he would campaign against justices of that state's supreme court unless they changed their votes on the death penalty.[48] They did not, and he made good on his promise. He was successful in his campaign to have Chief Justice Rose Bird and two of her colleagues voted off the court.[49]

Similar challenges spread to other states, including Texas, Mississippi, and Tennessee. In Texas, Stephen W. Mansfield challenged a conservative judge who had written the opinion reversing the conviction in a particularly notorious capital case, campaigning on promises of greater use of the death penalty and sanctions for attorneys who file "frivolous appeals especially in death penalty cases."[50] Before the election, it came to light that Mansfield had misrepresented his experience and record. Mansfield admitted lying about his birthplace (he claimed to have been born in Texas, but was born in Massachusetts), his political experience (he portrayed himself as a political novice, but he had twice run unsuccessfully for Congress), and the amount of time he had spent in Texas.[51] It was also disclosed that he had been fined for practicing law without a license in Florida,[52] and contrary to his assertions that he had experience in criminal cases and had "written extensively on criminal and civil justice issues," he had virtually no such experience. Nevertheless, Mansfield received 54 percent of the votes in the general election and served as a judge. The *Texas Lawyer*, a legal publication, declared him an "unqualified success."

Justice Penny White was voted off the Tennessee Supreme Court after five members of that court voted to order a resentencing in a death penalty case.[53] Justice White's opponents told the voters that she had overturned the conviction and set free the condemned man.[54] Actually, the conviction was affirmed. The defendant was not released but held for resentencing. (After the election he was again sentenced to death.) Justice White did not write the opinion setting aside the death sentence. Nevertheless, the Republican party and other groups distorted the ruling in the case and her role in it to convince Tennessee voters to remove Justice White from the court.

Abandoning fairness, reliability, the quest for racial equality, the rule of law, and the independence and integrity of the judiciary are enormous prices to pay to bring about executions. Some are willing to sacrifice even more—the lives of innocent people. They argue that we are fighting a "war on crime," and, as in any war, there are going to be some innocent casualties. The American notion of justice was once that it was better for ten guilty people to go free than for an innocent person to be convicted. Now, proponents of the death penalty argue it is acceptable to sacrifice more than a few innocent people to wage a war on crime.

CONCLUSION

Courts should not be war zones, but halls of justice. It is time to reexamine the "war of crime"—a war the United States is fighting against its own people, its own children, and the poorest and the most

powerless people in society. The American people must ask what kind of society they want to have and what kind of people they want to be. Whether they want a hateful, vengeful society that turns its back on its children and then executes them, that denies its mentally ill the treatment and the medicine they need and then puts them to death when their demons are no longer kept at bay, that gives nothing to the survivors of the victims of the crime except a chance to ask for the maximum sentence and watch an execution.

We should have the humility to admit that the legal system is not infallible and that mistakes are made. We should have the honesty to admit that our society is unwilling to pay the price of providing every poor person with competent legal representation, even in capital cases. We should have the courage to acknowledge the role that race plays in the criminal justice system and make a commitment to do something about it instead of pretending that racial prejudice no longer exists. And we should have the compassion and decency to recognize the dignity of every person, even those who have offended us most grievously. The Constitutional Court of South Africa addressed many of these issues in deciding whether the death penalty violated that country's constitution. Despite a staggering crime rate and a long history of racial violence and oppression, the Court unanimously concluded that in a society in transition from hatred to understanding, from vengeance to reconciliation, there was no place for the death penalty.[55] The American people will ultimately reach the same conclusion, deciding that, like slavery and segregation, the death penalty is a relic of another era, and that this society of such vast wealth is capable of more constructive approaches to crime. And the United States will join the rest of the civilized world in abandoning capital punishment.

NOTES

1. Hugo Bedau, chapter 2 this volume.

2. "Justice O'Connor Expresses New Doubts about Fairness of Capital Punishment," *Baltimore Sun*, July 4, 2001, p. 3A.

3. *Callins v. Collins*, 510 U.S. 1141, 1145 (1994) (Blackmun, J., dissenting). See also John C. Jeffries, Jr., Justice Lewis F. Powell, Jr., 451 (1994) (quoting Justice Powell after his retirement saying that the death penalty "reflect[s] discredit on the law").

4. Michigan retained the death penalty for treason, but not for murder or any other crimes.

5. Amnesty International, "Facts and Figures on the Death Penalty," available at http://web.amnesty.org/rmp/dplibrary/nsf (these statistics as of January 10, 2003).

6. Id.

7. Amnesty International, "Death Penalty Developments in 2001," available at http://web.amnesty.org/rmp/dplibrary/nsf (January 10, 2003).

8. Ibid.

9. Resolution Proposed for Anti-Capital Punishment Meeting International Publishers Co. Rochester, N.Y., October 7, 1858, in *The Life and Writings of Frederick Douglass*, p. 418 (P. Foner, ed., 1950).

10. Henry Weinstein, "Florida Man Freed after 16 Years on Death Row," *Los Angeles Times*, Jan. 25, 2003, p. A16 (reporting that Rudolph Holton was the 103d person released from death row after being exonerated). For a list of those exonerated, see www.deathpenaltyinfo.org.

11. Henry Weinstein, "Arizona Convict Freed on DNA Tests Is Said to Be the 100th Known Condemned U.S. Prisoner to Be Exonerated since Executions Resumed," *Los Angeles Times*, April 10, 2002, p. A16.

12. Jodi Wilgoren, "Man Freed after DNA Clears Him of Murder," *New York Times*, August 27, 2002, Section A, p. 10.

13. Pam Belluck, "Class of Sleuths to Rescue on Death Row," *New York Times*, February 5, 1999, p. A14.

14. Jon Jeter, "A New Ending to an Old Story," *Washington Post*, February 17, 1999, p. C1; Don Terry, "DNA Tests and a Confession Set Three on a Path to Freedom in 1978 Murders," *New York Times*, June 15, 1996, p. A6.

15. *People v. Bull*, 705 N.E.2d 824, 847 (Ill. 1998) (Harrison, J., dissenting).

16. Mark D. Killian, "Chief Justice Shares Parting Thoughts with Judges," *Florida Bar News*, July 15, 1996, p. 6.

17. *Singleton v. Norris*, 108 F.3d 872, 874–75 (8th Cir. 1997) (Heaney, J., concurring).

18. United States v. Burns, 2001 SCC 7 (Can.).

19. Richard Willing, "Geography of the Death Penalty," *USA Today*, December 20, 1999, pp. 1A, 6A.

20. Id.

21. Id.

22. See *People v. Davis*, 579 N.E.2d 877 (Ill. 1991).

23. Jeffrey J. Pokorak, "Probing the Capital Prosecutor's Perspective: Race of the Discretionary Actors," 83 *Cornell L. Rev.* 1811, 1817 (1998).

24. Id., pp. 1817–18.

25. See, e.g., David C. Baldus, "Racial Discrimination and the Death Penalty in the Post-Furman Era: An Empirical and Legal Overview, with Recent Findings from Philadelphia," 83 *Cornell L. Rev.* 1638 (1998); U.S. Department of Justice, *The Federal Death Penalty System: A Statistical Survey (1988–2000)* (Sept. 12, 2000); David Baldus, George Woodworth, and Charles Pulaski, "Equal Justice and the Death Penalty: A Legal and

Empirical Analysis" Northeastern University Press, Boston (1990); U.S. General Accounting Office Report No. Ggd-90-57, *Death Penalty Sentencing: Research Indicates Pattern of Racial Disparities*, 5 (1990).

26. See David Cole, "No Equal Justice: Race and Class in American Criminal Justice" New Press, New York (1999); *Los Angeles v. Lyons*, 461 U.S. 95, 116 n.3 (1983) (Marshall, J., dissenting) (noting that although only 9% of residents of Los Angeles are black males, they have accounted for 75% of deaths resulting from chokeholds by police); Charles J. Ogletree, "Does Race Matter in Criminal Prosecutions?" *Champion*, July 1991, pp. 7, 10–12 (describing discriminatory practices by police against racial minorities); Mary Maxwell Thomas, "The African American Male: Communication Gap Converts Justice Into 'Just Us' System," 13 *Harv. BlackLetter J.* 1, 5 (1997); Ian Ayres and Joel Waldfogel, "A Market Test for Race Discrimination in Bail Setting," 46 *Stan. L. Rev.* 987 (1994) (documenting discrimination in the setting of bail rates for African Americans); Bill Rankin, "Unequal Justice: Whites More Apt to Get Probation," *Atlanta Journal and Constitution*, February 8, 1998, p. A1 (reporting that since 1990 white people convicted in Georgia were 30% to 60% more likely than blacks to get probation for various crimes even though prior criminal records were about same among blacks and whites); Keith W. Watters, "Law Without Justice," *Nat'l B. Ass'n Mag.*, March–April 1996, pp. 1, 23 (reporting that whites are more likely to be placed on probation than African Americans, and that African Americans make up only 12% of population and 13% of drug users, but comprise 55% of drug convictions).

27. "Oklahoma Governor Commutes Death Case; Texas Bill Boosts Defense for the Poor," *Chicago Tribune*, April 11, 2001, p. 8N.

28. Ken Armstrong and Steve Mills, "Inept Defense Clouds Verdicts," *Chicago Tribune*, November 15, 1999, p. 1.

29. John Makeig, "Asleep on the Job: Slaying Trial Boring, Lawyer Says," *Houston Chronicle*, August 14, 1992, p. A35.

30. McFarland, 928 S.W.2d at 527 (Baird, J., dissenting).

31. Paul M. Barrett, "Lawyer's Fast Work on Death Cases Raises Doubts about System," *Wall Street Journal*, September 7, 1994, p. A1.

32. Ex parte Burdine, 901 S.W.2d 456 (Tx. Crim. App. 1995).

33. *Burdine v. Johnson*, 66 F. Supp. 2d 854, 866 (S. D. Tex. 1999).

34. *Burdine v. Johnson*, 231 F.3d 950 (5th Cir. 2000).

35. *Burdine v. Johnson*, 262 F.3d 336 (5th Cir. 2001) (en banc)

36. David R. Dow, "The State, The Death Penalty, and Carl Johnson," 37 *Boston College Law Review* 691, 694–95 (1996).

37. Id. at 711.

38. *Riles v. McCotter*, 799 F.2d 947, 955 (5th Cir. 1986) (Rubin, J., concurring).

39. Transcript of Hearing of Sept. 12, at 2–3, *Gibson v. Turpin* (Super. Ct. of Butts Co., Ga.) (No. 95-V-648).

40. Id.

41. Steve Mills, "Texas Judges Attack Decision Leading to Execution," *Chicago Tribune*, February 13, 2003.

42. Texas Defender Service, "Lethal Indifference" (December 2002), available at http://www.texasdefender.org/.

43. *Griffin v. Illinois*, 351 U.S. 12 (1956).

44. Chief Justice Harold G. Clarke, Annual State of the Judiciary Address, reprinted in *Fulton County Daily Reporter*, January 14, 1993, p. 5.

45. *Rumbaugh v. Procunier*, 753 F.2d 395, 397, 405–07 (5th Cir. 1985), cert. denied, 473 U.S. 919 (1985).

46. Lindsay A. Horstman, "Commuting Death Sentences of the Insane: A Solution for a Better, More Compassionate Society," 36 *University San Francisco Law Review* 823 (2002).

47. *People v. Bull*, 705 N.E.2d 834, 847 (Ill. 1998) (Harrison, J., dissenting).

48. Steve Wiegand, "Governor's Warning to 2 Justices," *San Francisco Chronicle*, March 14, 1986, p. 1.

49. Stephen B. Bright and Patrick J. Keenan, "Judges and the Politics of Death: Deciding between the Bill of Rights and the Next Election in Capital Cases," 75 *Boston University Law Review* 759. 760–61 (1995) (describing campaigns against judges in California and other states).

50. Janet Elliott and Richard Connelly, "Mansfield: The Stealth Candidate; His Past Isn't What It Seems," *Texas Lawyer*, October 3, 1994, pp. 1, 32 (reprinting a campaign advertisement of a Texas Court of Criminal Appeals candidate that lists a series of pro-death penalty positions).

51. Janet Elliott, "Unqualified Success: Mansfield's Mandate; Vote Makes a Case for Merit Selection," *Texas Lawyer*, November 14, 1994, p. 1; Janet Elliott and Richard Connelly, "Mansfield: The Stealth Candidate; His Past Isn't What It Seems," *Texas Lawyer*, October 3, 1994, pp. 1, 32; "Q & A with Stephen Mansfield: 'The Greatest Challenge of My Life,' " *Texas Lawyer*, November 21, 1994, p. 8 (a post-election interview with Mansfield in which he retracts a number of statements made before and during the election).

52. John Williams, "Election '94: GOP Gains Majority in State Supreme Court," *Houston Chronicle*, November 10, 1994, p. A29.

53. *State v. Odom*, 928 S.W.2d 18, 33 (Tenn. 1996).

54. For a detailed discussion of the campaign against Justice White see Stephen B. Bright, "Can Judicial Independence Be Attained in the South? Overcoming History, Elections and Misperceptions about the Role of the Judiciary," 14 *Georgia State University Law Review* 817 (1998), and Stephen B. Bright, "Political Attacks on the Judiciary: Can Justice Be Done Amid Efforts to Intimidate and Remove Judges from Office for Unpopular Decisions?" 72 *New York University Law Review* 308 (1997).

55. *State v. Makwanyane*, reprinted in *Human Rights Law Journal*, 16, p. 154 (1995).

7

In Defense of the Death Penalty

Paul G. Cassell[*]

Abolitionist arguments concerning the death penalty, such as the one in the preceding chapters, always seem a bit unsatisfying. Concepts of retribution, deterrence, and just punishment are discussed in the most thoughtful terms, but nowhere do we find a clear discussion of the crimes at issue. In some ways, these discussions are a bit like playing Hamlet without the ghost, reviewing the merits of capital punishment without revealing just what a capital crime is really like and how the victims have been brutalized.[1]

So, enter a ghost . . . or rather, enter one Kenneth Allen McDuff. McDuff raped, tortured, and murdered at least nine women in Texas in the early 1990s, and probably many more. The facts of just one such killing will reveal the horror of his crimes. On December 29, 1991, in Austin, Texas, McDuff and an accomplice manhandled 28-year-old Colleen Reed into the back of a car driven by an accomplice. Reed

---

*U.S. District Court Judge for the District of Utah and professor of law, University of Utah College of Law. This article was substantially completed before Judge Cassell assumed the bench.

Colleen Reed was murdered on December 29, 1991 by Kenneth Allen McDuff, whose execution was commuted by the Supreme Court's temporary abolition of capital punishment in 1972 and who was later paroled.

screamed, "Not me, not me," but McDuff forced her in, and tied her hands behind her back. As the accomplice drove to a remote location, McDuff repeatedly struck and raped Reed in the back seat of the car. Not finished, McDuff then got cigarettes from his accomplice, puffed them into a cherry glow, and inserted them into her vagina. Finally, as Reed pleaded for her life, McDuff killed her by crushing her neck. McDuff would later say that "Killing a woman's like killing a chicken. . . . They both squawk." After *America's Most Wanted* aired a program about him, McDuff was arrested in 1992, convicted, and given two death sentences. He was finally executed in 1998.[2]

McDuff's torture and slaying of Reed and numerous other women are horrific standing alone. But what makes his murders even more tragic is that they were easily preventable. McDuff resembles a ghost in more ways than one. He had previously been a "Dead Man Walking," that is, a prisoner sentenced to die. In August 1966, McDuff and an accomplice had forced a teenage girl and two teenage boys into the trunk of a car. McDuff drove them to a secluded spot, murdering the two boys with gunshots to the head at close range. McDuff and his companion then raped the boys' companion, Edna Sullivan. Not finished, McDuff then tortured Sullivan with a soft drink bottle and a broken broom handle, finally killing her by crushing her neck. A jury convicted McDuff of the crimes, and recommended death. The judge agreed, imposing a capital sentence, which was affirmed by the Texas courts. McDuff narrowly escaped execution three times before the United States Supreme Court acceded to abolitionist pressure and, in its 5–4 decision in *Furman v. Georgia*, invalidated all death penalties in 1972. As a result, McDuff escaped execution and was ultimately released by Texas authorities in 1989, producing the killing spree that left Colleen Reed and many other women dead.

Abolition of the death penalty has its consequences.

As I write this chapter, I remain haunted by these consequences, by the story of Colleen Reed. Perhaps it is photograph I have seen of her in a book—*No Remorse*—which recounts Reed's murder and the manhunt that ultimately apprehended McDuff. Reed looks so young, enthusiastic, energetic—so full of life.

Perhaps it is the young girls in my neighborhood. What will they look like when they are 28 years old? Could something like this happen to them?

Perhaps is the crime victims' volunteers I know in Texas. They were galvanized by Reed's murder and have fought hard, with little recognition, to make sure that victims like Reed and others will never be forgotten. Their moving Web site (*www.murdervictims.com*) contains a seemingly endless string of photographs—similar to Colleen Reed's—of men and women, boys and girls, who all seem full of life before their brutal murders. Behind each photograph lies a story—a tragic story—that one might recount just as well as Reed's. These photographs represent what Judge Alex Kozinsky calls in the first chapter of this book "the tortured voices of the victims crying out . . . for vindication."[3]

Our legal system, of course, has a procedure in place for hearing these voices. A jury of 12 persons, selected for their ability to be impartial in evaluating the facts, reviews all of the evidence—including whatever evidence a defendant might choose to present—before determining whether a defendant has committed an aggravated, capital murder and, if so, whether death is the appropriate penalty. No death penalty is ever imposed unless the jury (or, in some states, a judge) decides that the ultimate penalty is justified by the facts of the case.

Obviously, reasonable people might disagree about what constitutes fair and just punishment in particular cases. Reasonable people might likewise disagree over whether the death penalty ought to even be in the statute books. In a democratic society, disputes about appropriate sentencing are resolved through the legislative process. Today in our country, the great majority of state legislatures and the Congress have authorized the use of a death sentence for aggravated murderers like McDuff.

Those who would abolish the death penalty, of course, see things differently. In this volume, Professor Hugo Bedau decries the "brutality and violence" of the death penalty.[4] Bryan Stevenson contends that the punishment is "rooted in hopelessness and anger."[5] And Stephen Bright maintains that the penalty is "inconsistent with the aspirations of equal justice and fairness which have long been promised in the U.S. Constitution."[6]

These views have not resonated with either the courts or the public. In 1976, the Supreme Court emphatically rejected the constitutional challenge to the death penalty.[7] Similarly, in the court of public opinion, the abolitionists have lost. A Gallup poll in October 2002 found that 70 percent of Americans favor the death penalty while only 25 percent oppose it.[8] These results come from a generic question—"Are you in favor of the death penalty for a person convicted of murder?" Support is even higher when the respondents are asked for their views not in the abstract but in regard to a particular case. For instance, even among those who identify themselves as generally opposing the death penalty, more than half believed Oklahoma City bomber Timothy McVeigh should have been executed.[9] These numbers are especially interesting because they starkly reveal the true public view of the death penalty in the context of an actual case. The strong support for McVeigh's execution suggests (contrary to the assertions of some abolitionists) that more information about the death penalty's application might, at least in some cases, increase public support.

In the face of the public's rejection of their philosophical arguments, abolitionists have recently decided to change tactics. Rather than mounting a frontal assault on capital punishment, today they make a tactical end run by stressing narrower administrative arguments—such as alleged racial disparities in the application of the penalty and deficiencies in appointed counsel. These new arguments seem to have gained some modest traction. Governor Ryan of Illinois, on his way out of office and contrary to previous promises made to victims' families, issued a blanket commutation of death row inmates in his state. As explained in his speech contained in chapter 8, his concern was defects in the way death sentences were determined in Illinois.

These administrative arguments, however, provide no general reason for abolishing the death penalty. And the consequence of abolition, for the Colleen Reeds of the future, may be no less grim.

The aims of this chapter are twofold. The first is to provide a brief overview of the underpinnings of the death penalty. The death penalty is firmly grounded in many traditional rationales for punishment, a fact that may explain why death penalty abolitionists have made so little progress in challenging it head-on. The second is to examine the new wave of administrative challenges to the death penalty. Here again, these claims fail to provide a significant reason for abolishing capital punishment.[10]

JUSTIFICATIONS FOR THE DEATH PENALTY

Incapacitation

Perhaps the most straightforward argument for the death penalty is that it saves innocent lives by preventing convicted murderers from killing again. If the abolitionists had failed to obtain a temporary moratorium on death penalties from 1972 to 1976, for example, McDuff would have been executed and Colleen Reed and at least eight other young women would be alive today.

Some sense of the risk here is conveyed by the fact that of roughly 52,000 state prison inmates serving time for murder, an estimated 810 had previously been convicted of murder and had killed 821 persons following those convictions.[11] Executing each of these inmates after the first murder conviction would have saved the lives of more than 800 persons.

Abolitionists respond to this argument by observing that only a fraction of murderers receive the death penalty. Professor Bedau, for instance, argues that "the only way to [completely] prevent such recidivism would be execute *every* murderer—a policy that is politically unavailable and morally indefensible."[12] This response is unsatisfying. It is no indictment of death penalty procedures to learn that they do not single-mindedly pursue the goal of incapacitating murderers. Instead, the American death penalty responds to a variety of concerns— including not only incapacitation but also the possibility of rehabilitation and mercy. No other criminal justice sanction makes the prevention of recidivism its exclusive goal. Society sends most criminals to prison for a term of years, rather than for life, reserving the life sentence for the worst of the worst. Yet no one would argue that recidivism is somehow inappropriately pursued with life imprisonment merely because such sentences are reserved for the circumstances where, in light of all relevant factors, they are most appropriate.

While the abolitionist response to incapacitation concern is unsatisfying, it does contain an important implicit concession whose implications are worth considering. The abolitionists argue that the death penalty for some murderers fails to prevent recidivism by other murderers, implicitly conceding that the penalty at least prevents some recidivism. In plain words, *some innocent people will die if we abolish the death penalty*. For example, we know that Colleen Reed would be alive today but for the temporary suspension of the death penalty in 1972. The only point open to debate is how many others like her were killed during those years. Moreover, the group of the murderers sentenced to death are no doubt much more dangerous than the "average" murderer. The jury that first considered the risks posed by McDuff reached the conclusion that he deserved to die for his crimes, presumably because of the serious potential that he might repeat them. Unfortunately, that jury's conclusion was not respected, with fatal consequences for Colleen Reed and other women.

Deterrence

The death penalty's incapacitative benefits come from preventing the individual murderers who are apprehended and executed from killing again. This effect is what criminologists refer to as *specific* deterrence. More significant benefits come from the death penalty's restraining effect on the much larger pool of persons who are potential murderers—what criminologists refer to as *general* deterrence. Evidence for capital punishment's general deterrent effect comes from three sources: logic, firsthand reports, and social science research.

LOGICAL SUPPORT FOR DETERRENCE

Logic supports the conclusion that the death penalty is the most effective deterrent for some kinds of murders—those that require reflection and forethought by persons of reasonable intelligence and unimpaired mental faculties. Such an assumption is uncontroversial in other contexts. As Professor James Q. Wilson has explained: "People are governed in their daily lives by rewards and penalties of every sort. We shop for bargain prices, praise our children for good behavior and scold them for bad, expect lower interest rates to stimulate home building and fear that higher ones will depress it, and conduct ourselves in public in ways that lead our friends and neighbors to form good opinions of us. To assert that 'deterrence doesn't work' is tantamount to either denying the plainest facts of everyday life or claiming that would-be criminals are utterly different from the rest of us."[13]

Whenever society faces a problem with a burgeoning number of crimes—be it kidnappings in the 1930s, aircraft hijackings in the 1970s, domestic violence in the 1980s, or political terrorism in the 2000s—the public response is almost invariably to increase the criminal penalties associated with those crimes. We take it as uncontroversial that these increased penalties will deter at least some prospective criminals, which makes the increased penalty worthwhile. Our entire criminal

justice system is premised on the belief that increasing penalties increases deterrence.

The logic of deterrence applies to aggravated homicides no less than
to other crimes. As the Supreme Court observed in *Gregg v. Georgia*,
"There are carefully contemplated murders, such as the murder for
hire, where the possible penalty of death may well enter into the cold
calculus that precedes the decision to act."[14] Of course, as the Supreme
Court suggests, the death penalty applies only to "carefully contemplated" first-degree murders—that is, murders committed with premeditation and malice. It is no answer to the deterrence argument to
say that the death penalty cannot prevent a killing during a fight in a
barroom brawl. Such heat of passion offenses are typically punished
as second-degree murders and are not eligible for capital punishment.
The ultimate penalty is reserved for first-degree murders and, indeed,
for a subset of first-degree murders that are especially aggravated. Nor
is it an answer to say that murders continue to be committed in this
country in the face of the death penalty. The salient issue is not
whether the death penalty deters *every* murder, only whether it deters
some murders. Logic suggests that at least some potential murderers
will be deterred.

FIRSTHAND REPORTS OF DETERRENCE

Firsthand reports from criminals and victims confirms our logical intuition that the death penalty deters. Senator Dianne Feinstein recently
recounted her experience in the 1960s sentencing of a women convicted
of robbery in the first degree:

> . . . I saw that she carried a weapon that was unloaded into a grocery
> store robbery. I asked her the question: "Why was the gun un-
> loaded?" She said to me: "So I would not panic, kill somebody, and
> get the death penalty." That was firsthand testimony directly to me
> that the death penalty in place in California in the sixties was in fact
> a deterrent.[15]

Another interesting historical example is Kansas's decision to reinstate
the death penalty for first-degree murder in 1935 after a spate of deliberate killings committed in Kansas by criminals who had previously

committed such crimes in surrounding states. In those states, their punishment, if captured, could have been the death penalty. These criminals admitted having chosen Kansas as the site of their crimes solely for the purpose of avoiding a death sentence in the event that they were captured.[16] A more recent example comes from New York City following the Supreme Court's 1972 *Furman* decision temporarily suspending the death penalty. John Wojtowicz and another criminal held eight bank employees hostage and threatened to kill them before they were thwarted by FBI agents. In threatening the hostages, Wojtowicz said: "I'll shoot everyone in the bank. The Supreme Court will let me get away with this. There's no death penalty. It's ridiculous. I can shoot everyone here, then throw my gun down and walk out and they can't put me in the electric chair. You have to have a death penalty, otherwise this can happen everyday."[17] Also, when the death penalty was suspended, a couple in Kansas was held hostage for three hours during a bank robbery. During this time, the robbers decided to kill the couple rather than leave them alive as potential witnesses. Fortunately, the wife escaped and the husband survived after being shot twice in the head and left for dead. As the couple later wrote, "Thank God that we lived so that we can tell you that capital punishment does make a difference."[18]

Since the restoration of the death penalty in 1976, further evidence confirms the deterrent effect of the death penalty. Harvard Law Professor Alan Dershowitz, a strong opponent of the death penalty, has conceded as much. "Of course, the death penalty deters some crimes," he acknowledged during a debate with me in 1995. "That's why you have to pay more for a hitman in a death penalty state, than a non-death penalty state."[19]

The death penalty's deterrent effect may be an especially important consideration in preventing murders inside prison walls. While Professor Bedau tersely asserts that there is "no evidence" that the absence of a death penalty increases the risk to prisoners or prison guards, in fact experienced prison administrators have observed such a risk. During the 1980s, when the federal death penalty was suspended, at least five federal prison officers were killed, and the inmates in at least three of the incidents were already serving life sentences for murder.[20] Norman Carlson, the widely respected director of the U.S. Bureau of

Prisons, testified that "in the case of someone serving a nonrevokable life sentence, execution is the only sanction which could possibly serve as a deterrent. . . . We must impose the death penalty on prisoners sentenced to life who murder guards or other inmates in order to bring some semblance of security to our Federal prison system."[21] In short, those serving a sentence of life without parole (often offered as a substitute for capital punishment) have a "license to kill" without the availability of a death penalty.

STATISTICAL SUPPORT FOR THE DETERRENT EFFECT

A final support for the death penalty's deterrent effect comes from statistical analysis. Abolitionists appear to have little time for investigating this issue. When they trouble to do so, they typically do little more than assert that the states without the death penalty have lower homicide rates than states with the penalty. Stephen Bright's chapter here can serve as a convenient illustration. Bright quickly dismisses the possibility of a deterrent effect with the factoid that the South has the highest murder rate in the country while the Northwest, with the fewest executions, has the lowest.[22]

This analysis is fundamentally flawed. It fails to account for a variety of regional differences—e.g., educational levels, criminal justice expenditures, economic prosperity—that are well known to have potential effects on homicide levels.[23] Indeed, Bright's observation may prove little more than that the states that most need death penalty laws have been the ones most likely to pass them.

A far better measure of a deterrent effect comes from measuring the experience of states with death penalty laws over time. Thus, we might compare what various states' murders rates were in 1968 to 1976 (a period of time in which no one was executed) with what it was during the years 1995–2000. Senator Hatch and other senators recently collected the relevant data.[24] The five states showing the greatest relative improvements are, in order, Georgia, South Carolina, Florida, Delaware, and Texas. All these states have aggressive application of the death penalty.

Another way of reviewing the data over time is to compare a state's 1999 murder rates to those of 1966, the most recent year in which the national homicide rate equaled that of 1999. In 1999, the national hom-

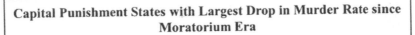

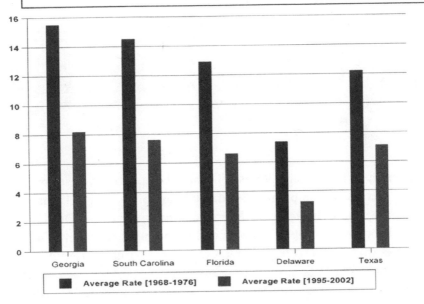

icide rate had fallen to 5.7 murders per 100,000 persons, a 32-year low and the lowest rate since 1966. If death penalty states have simply followed along with the national trend in recent years, one would expect that in 1999 they and the non-death penalty states would all have returned to the low rates they experienced in 1966. But the data reveal a strikingly different pattern: States aggressively using the death penalty have generally seen their murder rates decline while states not using the penalty have generally seen rates increase.

The six leading states measured by total executions are, in order, Texas, Virginia, Missouri, Florida, Oklahoma, and Georgia. Obviously this way of comparing states is biased against the smaller states. An alternative yardstick is to examine the rate of executions per murders in each state. By this measure—executions per total murders since 1976—the most aggressive death penalty state in the country is Delaware, followed by Oklahoma, Missouri, Texas, Virginia, and Arkansas. Taking the eight states that show up on either of these two lists, six have seen their murder rates drop since 1966. Arkansas's murder rate

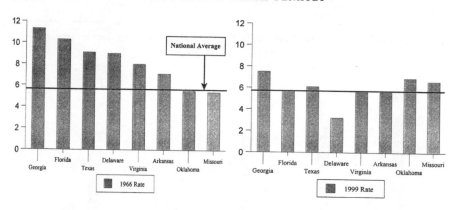

is down by 1.5 percentage points, Virginia's by 2.4 points, Texas by 3.0 points, Georgia by 3.8 points, Florida's by 4.6 points, and Delaware by 5.8 points. The only states whose murder rates went up—Oklahoma and Missouri—went up by only 1.4 and 1.2 points, respectively. Of the six states with declining murder rates (Arkansas, Virginia, Texas, Georgia, Florida, and Delaware), the period between 1997 and 1999 saw all six reach their lowest murder rate since 1960. Indeed, four of these states—Virginia, Florida, Delaware, and Arkansas—went from having murder rates well above the national average in 1966 to rates well below the average in 1999.

In contrast to the general declines in the leading death penalty states, the largest abolitionist states have seen rising homicide rates. Among non-death penalty states, nine are large enough to have two congressmen and have no wild swings in murder rates from year to year. These states are Wisconsin, Minnesota, Massachusetts, Iowa, Michigan, West Virginia, Rhode Island, and Hawaii. Of these, six have seen their murder rates go up since 1966 (Wisconsin, Minnesota, Michigan, West Virginia, Rhode Island, and Hawaii), one has stayed the same (Maine), and two have seen slight reductions (Massachusetts by 0.4 of a percentage point and Iowa by 0.1 point).

These state-by-state comparisons are bolstered by more sophisticated and recent econometric analysis that controls for the variety of demographic, economic, and other variables that differ among the states. The best of these studies suggest that the death penalty has an incremental deterrent effect over imprisonment—in plainer terms, that the death penalty saves innocent lives.

Professors Hashem Dezhbakhsh, Paul Rubin, and Joanna Shepherd of the Department of Economics at Emory University have recently published the most comprehensive analysis of the American death penalty data.[25] Many other studies of capital punishment's deterrent effect relied on antiquated data, developed before the Court's 1976 decision in *Gregg v. Georgia* established the modern American death penalty jurisprudence. The Emory researchers analyzed data for 3,054 American counties over the period 1977 to 1996, controlling for such variables as police and judicial resources devoted to crime, economic indicators, and other potentially confounding influences on the murder rate. The Emory researchers found that, in general, murder rates fell as more murderers were arrested, sentenced, and—most important for present purposes—executed. In particular, they concluded that each additional execution during this period of time resulted, on average, in 18 fewer murders.

Parallel conclusions were reached by H. Naci Mocan, chair of the Department of Economics at the University of Colorado (Denver) and graduate assistant R. Kaj Gottings.[26] In an article that will be published in the October 2003 *Journal of Law and Economics*, they report the results of multiple regression analysis of a newly available data set concerning all 6,143 death sentences between 1977 and 1997. Controlling for numerous variables, the University of Colorado researchers found "a statistically significant relationship between executions, pardons and homicide." In particular, they found that each additional execution deters five murders. Of particular relevance to Governor Ryan's recent actions in Illinois, they also studied the effect of commutations of death sentences. They found that each commutation reduces deterrence and produces five murders, a finding suggesting that Governor Ryan's decree will cause the deaths of dozens of innocent persons.

Late in 2002, Paul Zimmerman, a statistician with the Federal Communications Commission, derived further support for the death penalty. He conducted an econometric study of state data over the years 1978 to 1997 to determine the deterrent effect of the probability of execution on the per capita rate of murder. Zimmerman controlled for a wide range of possibly confounding factors. He concluded that each state execution deters somewhere between 3 and 25 murders a year (14 being the average). Zimmerman also found that the "announcement" effect of a capital sentence, as opposed to the existence of a death penalty provision, is the mechanism actually driving the deterrent effect associated with state executions.[27]

Finally, Professors Dale Cloninger and Roberto Marchesini of the University of Houston reached similar conclusions with a different methodology, investigating the number of homicides committed in Texas during 1996 and 1997.[28] Before 1996, Texas executed about 17 convicted murderers per year. In 1996, the number of executions fell to near zero because of a temporary stay on actually carrying out the sentence entered by the Texas Court of Criminal Appeals. Then, in the following year, Texas executed 37 murderers. Using a model that compared the actual number of homicides with the "expected" number of homicides, Cloninger and Marchesini found that the suspension in executions produced a statistically significant increase in homicides in Texas. They estimated that the suspension resulted in about 220 additional murders that would have otherwise been deterred—or, put more bluntly, the deaths of 220 innocent people. They explained: "The unexpected homicides occurred despite the fact that arrests continued to be made for homicide, scheduled trials for both capital and non-capital offenses went on, sentencing capital and non-capital verdicts went uninterrupted, and there were no known, dramatic changes in the state's demographics. The only change relevant to the crime of homicide was the suspension of executions."[29] In the understated words of social scientists, they concluded that "politicians may wish to consider the possibility that a seemingly innocuous moratorium on executions could very well come at a heavy cost."

The abolitionist response to such sophisticated deterrence studies is revealing: They essentially duck the issue. Professor Bedau's chapter exemplifies this approach. Bedau acknowledges that the abolitionist position is "vulnerable to evidence" of a deterrent effect; he contends, however, that "since there is so little reason to suppose that the death penalty is a marginally superior deterrent over imprisonment, or that such superiority (if any) can be detected by the currently available methods of social science, this 'what-if' counter-argument can be put to the side and disregarded."[30] Professor Bedau forthrightly acknowledges that recent research from the Emory professors shows a deterrent effect, but "predicts" that subsequent studies will reach the opposite conclusion.

The abolitionists are remarkably sanguine. If the deterrence argument is correct, innocent people will die when we rely solely on imprisonment and fail to carry out executions. Deterrence is supported by logic, firsthand reports, and statistical studies. All these sources suggest a specific, incremental saving of lives from implementing the death penalty over and above long-term imprisonment. To those who might die at the hands of emboldened murderers, we are compelled not to casually "put to the side and disregard" this very real possibility.

The abolitionists really appear to be seeking safety in the proposition that a deterrent effect cannot be (as Bedau puts it) "detected" by the currently available methods of social science. This point contains a kernel of truth: social science research is often uncertain. Yet indisputable social science evidence has never been the *sine qua non* of criminal justice policy. To cite but one obvious example, if ironclad evidence of a deterrence effect were required to justify prison sentences, then we would have to put every violent offender in the country back on the streets. After all, we lack indisputable evidence that prisons incapacitate and deter. Of course, no one would urge such a policy, as we have a reasonable intuition—bolstered by logic, reports from criminals and victims, and social science research—that flinging open all prison doors would be catastrophic. The parallel evidence concerning the death penalty likewise suggests that emptying the nation's death rows would be quite dangerous.

Just Punishment

A final justification for the death penalty is that it constitutes just punishment for the most serious homicides. Capital punishment's retributive function vindicates the fundamental moral principles that a criminal should receive his just deserts. Even if capital punishment had no incapacitative or deterrent utility, its use would be justified on this basis alone. As Immanuel Kant persuasively explained, "[e]ven if a civil society resolved to dissolve itself...the last murderer lying in the prison ought to be executed."[31] This act of punishment, which can provide no utilitarian benefit, is required because of the "desert of [the murderer's] deeds." More contemporary philosophers have echoed the argument. Noted philosopher Michael Moore, for example, asks us whether we would punish a brutal rapist, even if he has gotten into some sort of accident so that his sexual desires are dampened and we are certain that he no longer poses a threat by recidivism—no need for specific deterrence—and if we could pretend that he was punished, so that others would not be encouraged to commit crimes—no need for general deterrence. Moore suggests that our intuitions still would demand punishment—an intuition that reflects the need for our criminal justice system to impose just punishment.

Through the imposition of just punishment, civilized society expresses its sense of revulsion toward those who, by violating its laws, have not only harmed individuals but also weakened the bonds that hold communities together. Certain crimes constitute such outrageous violations of human and moral values that they demand retribution. It was to control the natural human impulse to seek revenge and, more broadly, to give expression to the deeply held view that some conduct deserves punishment, that criminal laws, administered by the state, were established. The rule of law does not eliminate feelings of outrage, but it does provide controlled channels for expressing such feelings. As the Supreme Court has recognized, society has withdrawn "both from the victim and the vigilante the enforcement of criminal laws, but [it] cannot erase from people's consciousness the fundamental, natural yearning to see justice done—or even the urge for retribution."[32]

The law's acceptability and effectiveness as a substitute for vigilantism depends, however, on the degree to which society's members perceive the law as actually providing just punishment for particularly serious offenses. Determining what sanction is proportionate and, therefore, what constitutes just punishment for committing certain types of murder is admittedly a subjective judgment. Nevertheless, when there is widespread public agreement that the death penalty is a just punishment for certain kinds of murders—as there is in this country today—and when a jury acting under constitutional procedures determines that a defendant has killed another under circumstances for which the legislature has prescribed death as an appropriate penalty, the resulting judgment is no less "just" because its validity cannot be objectively verified.

Capital punishment is proportionate to the offense of the intentional and unjustified taking of an innocent person's life. Murder does not simply differ in magnitude from other crimes like robbery and burglary; it differs in kind. As a result, the available punishments for premeditated murder must also differ in kind. The available punishment must reflect the inviolability of human life. As Professor Walter Berns has explained:

> In a country whose principles forbid it to preach, the criminal law is one of the few available institutions through which it can make a moral statement. . . . To be successful, what it says—and it makes this moral statement when it punishes—must be appropriate to the offense and, therefore, to what has been offended. If human life is to be held in awe, the law forbidding the taking of it must be held in awe; and the only way it can be made awful or awe inspiring is to entitle it to inflict the penalty of death.[33]

Faced with the clear public acceptance of the death penalty as just punishment in this country, abolitionists frequently retreat to the claim that other parts of the world condemn the penalty. Professor Bedau, for example, notes that "opponents of the death penalty are cheered by the knowledge that the rest of the civilized world openly and increasingly condemns our death penalty practices."[34] In our post-modern age, where many academics denounce the "alleged" superiority of "western civilization," the use of the term civilized seems almost quaint. It would be interesting, for example, to see how many death penalty abolitionists would employ this term in other contexts to describe such countries as Japan, Thailand, and China, all of whom retain the death penalty. But it is true that Canada and the Western European countries do not authorize the ultimate sanction. Is this because, as the abolitionists would have it, a moral consensus exists against the penalty?

In fact, the death penalty is abolished in these countries primarily because these countries are less democratic than we are.[35] A majority of Canadians want the death penalty reinstated in their country.[36] In Britain, about two-thirds to three-quarters of the public support the death penalty. In France, a majority of the population backed capital punishment long after it was abolished in 1981. And even in Italy, where the Colosseum is bathed in light whenever a death sentence is commuted, roughly half the population supports capital punishment. Liberal columnist Joshua Marshall nicely summarized things recently: "Basically, then, Europe doesn't have the death penalty because its political systems are less democratic, or at least more insulated from populists' impulses, than the U.S. government."[37]

ADMINISTRATIVE OBJECTIONS

Because their general objections to the death penalty have found so little support, abolitionists have largely abandoned these claims. Even if the death penalty is justified in principle, they maintain, in practice it is unfairly administered. The collection of essays here is typical of the modern debate. Three of the four abolitionist chapters (by Governor Ryan, Bright, and Stevenson) rest almost exclusively on administrative challenges to the penalty.

The abolitionists most frequently raise three particular administrative challenges to the death penalty: first, that it is infected with racism; second, that innocent persons have been executed; and finally, that capital defendants do not receive effective assistance of legal counsel. This section explains why each of these objections cannot justify nationwide abolition of the penalty. But before turning to the details of these objections, an opening observation is in order.

No responsible supporter of the death penalty holds any brief for inadequate defense attorneys, racist prosecutors, or inattentive judges. If problems arise in a particular case, they should be corrected. And, indeed, in many of the cases cited by the abolitionists here, the problems in particular cases were in fact corrected. The issue debated in this volume, however, is whether such problems are sufficiently widespread to justify completely depriving the federal government and 38 states of the option of imposing a capital sentence on a justly convicted offender. These are global questions that cannot be resolved by reciting isolated instances of abuse in a single jurisdiction (e.g., Alabama, where Bryan Stephenson conducts most of his work, or Illinois, where Governor Ryan conducted a review). Rather, these questions are appropriately resolved by examining the data about the system as a whole. With the big picture in view, it is clear that the administrative objections provide no grounds for abolishing capital punishment.

Racism

Capital punishment in America is racist, its opponents claim. The arguments about racism come in two forms: a "mass market" version and a "specialist" form.[38] Both versions are seriously flawed.

In the "mass market" version, we are told that the death penalty discriminates against African American defendants. For instance, the Reverend Jesse Jackson, in his book *Legal Lynching*, argues that "[n]umerous researchers have shown conclusively that African American defendants are far more likely to receive the death penalty than are white defendants charged with the same crime."[39] The support for this claim is said to be the undisputed fact that when compared to their percentage in the overall population African Americans are overrepresented on death row. For example, while 12 percent of the population is African American, about 43 percent of death row inmates are African American, and 38 percent of prisoners executed since 1977 are African American.[40]

Such simple statistics of overrepresentation fail to prove racial bias. The relevant population for comparison is not the general population, but rather the population of murderers. If the death penalty is administered without regard to race, the percentage of African American death row inmates found at the end of the process should not exceed the percentage of African American defendants charged with murder at the beginning. The available statistics indicate that is precisely what happens. The Department of Justice found that while African Americans constituted 48 percent of adults charged with homicide, they were only 41 percent of those admitted to prison under sentence of death.[41] In other words, once arrested for murder, blacks are actually less likely to receive a capital sentence than are whites.

Critics of these data might argue that police may be more likely to charge African Americans than whites with murder at the outset of the process. No such claim is advanced in the abolitionist chapters of this book and in any event, the data do not support it. One way of investigating this claim is to analyze crime victim reports of the race of those who commit crimes against them. While it is obviously impossible to talk to murder victims, it is possible talk to victims of armed robberies, who are reasonable surrogates. When victim reports for armed robbery are compared with criminal justice processing, there is no evidence of racial discrimination in charging decisions.[42]

The overrepresentation of African Americans on death row to which Reverend Jackson refers is, indisputably, of great public concern. Policy makers must certainly examine the causes of that overrepresentation— for example, differences in economic or educational opportunities— and address them. But given such societal factors, racial bias cannot be inferred from such simplistic calculations.

To confirm or dispel concern about black defendants being singled out for the death penalty, one must conduct more sophisticated social science research. Various researchers (often of an abolitionist bent) have set out to prove such racial discrimination. They have been disappointed. The studies of the post-*Furman* death penalty in America have generally found that African American defendants are not more likely than white defendants to receive the death penalty. Summarizing all the data in 1990, the General Accounting Office concluded that evidence that blacks were discriminated against was "equivocal."[43] Similarly, in a comprehensive study Professor Baldus and his colleagues reported that "regardless of the methodology used" studies show "no systematic race-of-defendant" effect.[44]

This ought to be treated as good news of progress in the American criminal justice system. One could draw the following conclusion: That while African American defendants in capital cases were previously treated unfairly (especially in the South), modern statistics reveal considerable progress. This conclusion, of course, is anathema to the agenda of abolitionists. Thus, when pressed by someone who is familiar with the social science data finding no discrimination against African American offenders, more sophisticated abolitionists often abandon the mass market version of their racism argument and shift to the specialist version. In his chapter in this book, for example, Bryan Stevenson argues that data demonstrate the existence of "racial bias in Georgia's use of the death penalty"—by which he means statistics suggesting that blacks who kill whites are more likely to receive a death penalty than are other victim/offender combinations.[45]

These specialist statistics are no less misleading than the mass market statistics. But before turning to them, it is important to note the implications of this retreat to a race-of-the-victim claim. It seems implausible, to say that least, that a racist criminal justice system would look past minority defendants and discriminate solely on the more attenuated basis of the race of their victims. If racists are running the system, why wouldn't they just discriminate directly against minority defendants?

In any event, the race-of-the-victim claim cannot withstand close scrutiny. It is first important to understand that the claim cannot be proven by the kind of seat-of-the-pants anecdotes recounted here at considerable length by Bryan Stevenson and Stephen Bright. Of necessity, a race-of-the-victim claim involves comparison—that is, comparing the facts of comparable cases in different victim and offender combinations to see whether unexplainable disparities emerge. Thus, the anecdotes tell us little; the question belongs in the realm of statistical analysis.

Statisticians Stanley Rothman and Stephen Powers have offered the best review of the relevant data.[46] As they explain, the vast majority of homicides (no less than other offenses) are intraracial: about 95 percent do not cross racial lines. The small minority of inter-racial homicides have vastly different characteristics. Black-on-black homicides and white-on-white homicides are most likely to occur during altercations between persons who know one another—circumstances often viewed as inappropriate for the death penalty. On the other hand, black-on-white homicides are much more often committed during the course of a serious felony—a classic case for the death penalty. For example, in Georgia, only 7 percent of the black-defendant-kills-black-victim cases involve armed robbery, compared to 67 percent of the black-defendant-kills-white-victim cases. Similarly, black-defendant-kills-white-victim cases more often involve the murder of a law enforcement officer, kidnaping and rape, mutilation, execution-style killing, and torture—all quintessential aggravating factors—than do other combinations. Finally, white-defendant-kills-black-victim cases are so rare that it is difficult to draw meaningful statistical conclusions from them.

Given these obvious differences between, on the one hand, intra-racial homicides and, on the other, black-on-white homicides, the simple comparison of the percentage of death sentences within each classification reported in this volume by Bryan Stevenson and Stephen Bright is unilluminating. To put the point in more precise statistical terms, an alleged race-of-the-victim effect will be an obvious "spurious" correlation. To cite but one example, a significant number of death penalty cases involve murder of law enforcement officers, about 85 percent of whom are white. Unless there are statistical controls for this fact, it is virtually certain that a simple eyeballing of statistics will show a race-of-the-victim effect that is instead immediately explainable by this fact (among many others).

The issue about spurious correlations and the alleged race-of-the-victim effect was put on trial in 1984 before United State District Court Judge J. Owen Forrester. Judge Forrester took testimony from Professor Baldus and other statisticians who purported to have identified a genuine race-of-the-victim effect in Georiga. In an opinion that spans 65 pages in the federal reporter, Judge Forrest squarely rejected the claim. Judge Forrester first observed that Baldus found no race-of-the-*defendant* effect—that is, black defendants were not directly discriminated against. With respect to the race-of-the-*victim*, only his "summary" models (i.e., models including just a few control variables) purported to demonstrate the effect. The effect in fact disappeared entirely as additional control variables were added. When Baldus ran his regression equations with all the 430 control variables for which he had collected data, no statistically significant evidence of discrimination remained. Judge Forrester accordingly held: "The best models which Baldus was able to devise which account to any significant degree for the major non-racial variables ... produce no statistically significant evidence that races play a part in either [the prosecution's or the jury's capital decisions]."[47]

Judge Forrester's carefully reasoned and detailed opinion should have put an end to race-of-the-victim claims. It is, after all, the only review of the claim by a neutral decision maker. Moreover, Judge Forrester's findings about the Baldus study—that a purported race of the victim effect in "summary" models gradually disappears as more control variables are added into the equations—apply equally to the other race-of-the-victim studies cited in this volume. Without exception, the studies purporting to demonstrate a race-of-the-victim effect control for only a few relevant variables (nowhere approaching the 430 variables ultimately analyzed by Judge Forrester), producing a spurious correlation rather than any casual connection. But abolitionists—including all of the contributors to this volume—never discuss his findings. Instead, they refer to the later U.S. Supreme Court decision reviewing Judge Forrester's opinion. The Supreme Court, perhaps unwilling to dive into the statistical subtleties of multiple regression analysis, decided to proceed on the "assumption" that the Baldus race-of-the-victim figures were *factually* accurate. The Court found that the figures were nonetheless *legally* insufficient to establish a cognizable claim of discrimination. Because it proceeded on this assumption, the Supreme Court could affirm Judge Forrester without needing to reach the statistical question of whether a race-of-the-victim effect actually existed. But Judge Forrester's opinion might well serve as an emblematic example of abolitionist claims: When put to the test before a fair-minded observer, they cannot withstand scrutiny.

Innocent Defendants

Perhaps the most successful rhetorical attack on the death penalty has been the claim that innocent persons have been convicted of, and even executed for, capital offenses. The claim about innocents being executed is a relatively new one for abolitionists. Nowhere is this rhetorical shift better exemplified than in the writings by Professor Bedau. In 1971, Professor Bedau took the position that it is "false sentimentality to argue that the death penalty ought to be abolished because of the abstract possibility that an innocent person might be executed, when the record fails to disclose that such cases occur."[48] Now, however, Professor Bedau apparently takes the view that such cases happen frequently enough that capital punishment must be abolished in this country. More generally, the claim that innocents have actually been executed has been repeated by abolitionists so often that it has become something of an urban legend. But (like other abolitionist arguments) the claim does hold up under scrutiny.

A note is important at the outset; *None* of the chapters in this book advances a claim that any factually innocent person has been executed in this country in the modern death penalty era. Given the prominence of these contributors, perhaps their silence on this point should end debate on the matter. But because such claims have been loudly advanced elsewhere, it may be worth saying a few words about the issue.

The claim that innocent defendants have been executed was most notably advanced in a 1987 article by Professor Bedau and his co-author, Michael Radelet.[49] In their article, they claimed that 23 innocent persons had been executed in this country in this century. Their article has been widely cited.

Of course, the immediate question that springs to mind is how precisely did Bedau and Radelet determine the "innocence" of these executed persons. Stephen Markman (then an assistant attorney general in the Justice Department and currently a justice on the Michigan Supreme Court) and I began looking carefully at the 23 cases and published our response in the 1988 *Stanford Law Review*.[50] We found that most of the cases came from the early part of this century, long before the adoption of the extensive contemporary system of safeguards in the death penalty's administration. Moreover, Bedau and Radelet could cite but a single allegedly erroneous execution during the past 30 years—that of James Adams, convicted in 1974. A dispassionate review of the facts of that case demonstrates, however, that Adams was unquestionably guilty. To find Adams "innocent," Bedau and Radelet ignored such compelling evidence of guilt as money stained in blood matching that of the victim found in Adams's possession and the victim's eyeglasses found in the locked trunk of his car. A full recitation of the evidence against Adams is set out in a footnote,[51] but the compelling evidence of guilt raises the question of how Professors Bedau and Radelet wound up making so many mistakes in their analysis of the case. Perhaps the reason is the source they used. The *only* source cited in their article is Adams's Petition for Executive Clemency, a document written by his defense lawyers. An objective review of the claims by the Florida Clemency Board found the petition to be without merit, a finding Bedau and Radelet do not discuss. In short, James Adams was a murderer and was justly convicted.[52]

Bedau and Radelet's other alleged instances of "innocent" persons executed in earlier parts of this century are equally questionable. In our 1988 article, we reviewed all 11 cases of alleged executions of innocent persons in which appellate opinions set forth facts proved at trial in detail sufficient to permit a neutral observer to assess the validity of Bedau and Radelet's claims, including all of the cases since 1940. While a full review of all of those cases would unduly extend this chapter,[53] a few highlights will suffice to make the point. To prove the "innocence" of one defendant, Everett Appelgate who was executed for murdering his wife with rat poison in 1932, Bedau and Radelet cited two sources; those sources in fact actually believed that Appelgate was guilty.[54] In another case, that of defendant Sie Dawson, the authors stated, falsely, that there were no eyewitnesses to the crime. In fact, there was an eyewitness: the victim's four-year-old son, Donnie, who had been beaten and left to die at the scene of the crime. When found a day later, Donnie told his father, the police chief, and a family friend that Sie Dawson had committed the murder with a hammer.[55] As another example, Bedau and Radelet cite a book to prove generally the innocence of Charles Louis Tucker, executed in Massachusetts in 1906 for stabbing a young girl to death during a robbery; the book actually says that the governor's rejection of Tucker's clemency petition was "conscientious and admirable."[56]

Finally, my favorite example of Bedau and Radelet's research comes from my home state of Utah and involves one of their sources cited "generally" to prove that Joseph Hillstrom was innocent. That source was a book published by Wallace Stegner entitled *Joe Hill: A Biographical Novel.* The foreword explained that the book "is *fiction*, with fiction's prerogatives and none of history's limiting obligations. . . . Joe Hill as he appears here—let me repeat it—is an act of the imagination." While citing a work of fiction is bad enough, even more startling is the fact that the novel strongly suggests that its protagonist, Joe Hill, is in fact a guilty murderer! This is not surprising, since Wallace Stegner published two magazine articles in which he gave his view that the real-life Joseph Hillstrom was a killer.[57]

The questionable examples in the Bedau-Radelet article make an important point about the debate over mistaken executions. It is easy for opponents of the death penalty to allege, despite a unanimous jury verdict, appellate court review, and denial of executive clemency, that an "innocent" person has been executed. Such an assertion costs nothing and will help abolitionists advance their cause. As this review demonstrates, such claims should be reviewed with a healthy dose of skepticism.

While abolitionists have been unable to find a credible case of an innocent person who has actually been executed in recent years, they have provided some credible "close call" cases—that is, examples of innocent persons sentenced to death who were exonerated shortly before the execution. Such miscarriages of justice are, to be sure, very troubling. These cases deserve careful study to determine what went wrong and what kinds of reforms can correct the problem. But when offered as justification for abolishing the death penalty, these close call cases are unpersuasive.

To justify abolishing the death penalty on grounds of risk to the innocent, abolitionists would have to establish that innocent persons are jeopardized more by the retention of the death penalty than from its absence. In fact, the balance of risk tips decisively in favor of retaining the death penalty. On the one hand, abolitionists have been unable to demonstrate that even a single innocent person has been executed in error. On the other hand, there are numerous documented cases of innocent persons who have died because of our society's failure to carry out death sentences. Earlier in this chapter, for example, I discussed the deaths of Colleen Reed and many other women because of society's failure to execute a single dangerous murderer—Kenneth Allen McDuff. The victims of McDuff were no "close calls" but rather fatalities directly resulting from abolition of the death penalty in 1972. Today, thousands of killers no less dangerous than McDuff are currently incarcerated on the nation's death rows. If they are not executed, they will remain serious threats to kill again—either inside prison walls or outside them following an escape or a parole. Clearly, on any realistic assessment, the innocent are far more at risk from allowing these dangerous convicts to live than from executing them after a full and careful review of their legal claims.

Effective Representation of Counsel

A last attack on the death penalty concerns the quality of counsel appointed to represent indigent defendants charged with capital offenses. Abolitionists argue that inexperienced and even incompetent counsel are routinely appointed in capital cases. In this book, for example, Stephen Bright argues that the death penalty is imposed "not upon those who commit the worst crimes, but upon those who have the misfortune to be assigned the worst lawyers."[58] Citing various anecdotal examples of ineffective assistance of counsel, Bright concludes that the death penalty ought to be abolished.

The conclusion does not follow from the factual premises. Ineffective assistance of counsel in a particular case calls for reversal of the conviction—something already required by Supreme Court precedents.[59] But to make a persuasive argument for completely abolishing capital punishment, the abolitionists would need to demonstrate that defendants in capital cases are represented by inadequate counsel (1) frequently (2) throughout the United States (3) under current appointment procedures. The abolitionists cannot begin to make such a showing on any of these three points.

For starters, the abolitionists do not show that the ineffectiveness is widespread. Instead, their inevitable tactic (well exemplified in this volume) is to recite various anecdotal examples of defense ineffectiveness. The reader should assess those few examples against the backdrop of about 3,500 persons currently on death row[60]—all of whom have had, or will soon have, their cases reviewed by appellate courts to insure that their trial counsel was effective. The abolitionists never explain why a handful of anecdotes justify setting aside literally thousands of capital sentences.

The abolitionists also fail to justify abolition through the United States. It is hard to understand, for example, why my home state of Utah should have its capital sentencing statute invalidated because of concerns over the quality of appointed counsel in, say, Alabama. Utah has a carefully developed procedure for appointing counsel in capital cases. The court must appoint at least two attorneys for the accused. At least one of the attorneys must meet stringent requirements for experience in criminal cases generally and capital cases in particular.

The court is further required to make specific findings about the capabilities of the lawyers to handle a capital defense.[61] These new procedures have worked well to insure high quality representation for capital defendants in Utah. Indeed, the only vocal complaints have come from county treasurers, who complain about the sizable cost of hiring defense lawyers from the small pool that meets the stringent certification requirements. In Utah, payments to defense attorneys in capital cases often exceed $100,000.[62] Josh Marquis has made a similar point in this book about his state of Oregon.[63] The abolitionist contributors to this book have been asked for examples of ineffectiveness of counsel in Utah and Oregon but have not produced any.

Indeed, in another striking example of a mismatch between their evidence and their claims, the abolitionists seek to strike not merely 38 state statutes authorizing capital punishment but also numerous federal statutes. Current federal law authorizes death penalties for such extremely serious offenses as terrorist bombings, espionage involving the nation's nuclear weapon systems, treason, and assassination of the president or members of Congress. In a death penalty case, federal law requires appointment of extremely well-qualified counsel and provides them with seemingly unlimited resources. The federal government spent in excess of $13.8 million to pay for attorneys and cover other costs of McVeigh's defense until his execution.[64] Yet even with what may have been the most expensive defense in the history of the world, McVeigh was sentenced to death and ultimately executed—disproving Stephen Bright's claim here that the ultimate penalty falls only on those who have "the misfortune to be assigned the worst lawyers." To be sure, McVeigh's case was the most costly in federal history, but defendants faced with death in the federal system receive generous financial support, with payments well in excess of $100,000 commonplace. The abolitionists offer no explanation as to why these federal provisions fail to assure effective representation.

The evidence of inadequacy of counsel suffers another serious flaw: It is grossly outdated. In reading the contributions to this book, it is striking how many of the examples are more than 10 and even 20 years old. Perhaps such timeworn anecdotes would be instructive if attorney appointment procedures had remained the same. They have not. In recent years, nearly all the states authorizing capital punishment have created specific competency standards for appointed counsel.[65] Most of those standards exceed the exacting qualifications that Congress require for appointment of counsel in federal cases.[66]

Recent reforms in the leading death penalty state of Texas will serve to illustrate the point. In 1995, Texas created local selection committees to handle appointment of counsel in capital cases and set a variety of competence standards for capital defense attorneys.[67] As part of the continuing effort to monitor defense counsel in capital cases, in 2001 Texas established a Task Force on Indigent Defense to develop further standards and policies for the appointment of defense counsel.[68]

Illinois provides another illustration. Governor Ryan's remarks in commuting previously imposed death sentences obscured (perhaps by design) the extent to which significant recent reforms have been made. For example, in 2001, the Illinois Supreme Court established a Capital Litigation Trial Bar, which set demanding standards for attorneys representing capital defendants. It required that indigent defendants be appointed two attorneys and that prosecutors give notification of their intent to seek the death penalty no later than 120 days after arraignment in order to give the defense more time to prepare. After putting these new rules into effect, the high court emphasized that it would continue to monitor closely all death penalty cases and add additional reforms as appropriate.

These recent reforms make one last point about questions of adequacy of counsel: Any deficiencies are not inherent in the death penalty. The abolitionist contributors to this book have not even chosen to discuss the recent changes in Texas, Illinois, and elsewhere. Instead, they engage in little more than rhetorical posturing. That is disappointing, because it would be informative to hear suggestions from experienced capital defense attorneys like Bryan Stevenson and Stephen Bright as to how the latest wave of improvements could be further improved. But the abolitionists apparently have little interest in incremental progress in the capital punishment system. Indeed, Hugo Bedau in his essay forthrightly reports that it is "troubling" to abolitionists that reforms "might succeed," thereby giving "an even more convincing seal of approval to whatever death sentences and executions were imposed under their aegis."[69] Abolitionists are certainly entitled to single-mindedly pursue their attack on the death penalty. But without squarely addressing the recent reforms made (for example) in providing counsel to capital defendants, their arguments for abolition will remain unconvincing.

CONCLUSION

This chapter has tried to briefly but comprehensively present the arguments for the death penalty and respond to the claims lodged against it. In closing, it may be appropriate to step back from the specifics of the fray and look at the debate as a whole.

Those of us who support the death penalty do not pretend to have clairvoyant vision. Instead, we recognize that decisions about the death penalty, no less than many other social policies, must be made on the basis of imperfect information. At the same time, however, we recognize the extreme importance of the social choices that are being made. We understand that human lives are held in the balance whenever death penalty decisions are made—whether the decision is to impose the penalty on a defendant who might later prove to be innocent or withhold it from a defendant who might later kill again or serve as a deterrent example. It is because of the value that we place on innocent human life that we find the choice an agonizing one. In this volume, for example, both Judge Alex Kozinski and District Attorney Joshua Marquis have talked openly about the conflicts that they experience in handling death penalty cases.

In contrast, those opposed to capital punishment have a surety that we find surprising. Abolitionists are certain that the death penalty does not deter—indeed, that it has not ever deterred anyone, anywhere, at any time. They are certain that it has never incapacitated anyone and prevented a subsequent killing. Finally, they are certain that it is not just punishment, despite the contrary views of the majority of their fellow citizens in this country (and in many others).

At the debate that preceded the publication of these essays, I probed this confidence. I asked the abolitionists, assuming for a moment that the death penalty deters, whether they would nonetheless continue to oppose it. They refused to answer what they viewed as a speculative question. Hugo Bedau, however, has given a straightforward response on other occasions. As Louis Pojman points out in his chapter here, Bedau has frankly stated that he would oppose capital punishment even if it increased the homicide rate by 100 percent or more.[70] Most abolitionists probably hold the same view but are unwilling to admit it quite so forthrightly.

This difference is, perhaps, the starkest contrast between the abolitionists and the penalty's supporters. Those of us who support the death penalty find the anguish and destruction resulting from any murder too much to tolerate. We could never dream of society standing by while the homicide rate unnecessarily rose even 1 percent, let alone 100 percent. We know that behind the homicide "rate" are flesh and blood individuals, like Colleen Reed described in the introduction to this chapter.

We are confident of only one thing—that society must do everything reasonably within its power to prevent such tragedies. To be sure, the benefits of the death penalty are not always certain. But we are unwilling to risk innocent lives on the speculative chance that the death penalty will turn out not to deter and not to incapacitate. The last time abolitionists succeeded in invalidating capital punishment in this country, they released brutal murderers to kill again—ultimately causing the deaths of Colleen Reed and many others. That was too high a price then. It is too high a price now.

NOTES

1. With apologies for borrowing a metaphor to Bernard Weisberg, *Police Interrogation of Arrested Persons: A Skeptical View*, 52 J. Crim. L. & P.S. 21 (1961).

2. *See generally* BOB STEWART, NO REMORSE (1996) Gary M. Lavergne, Bad Boy from Rosebud: The Murderous Life of Kenneth Allen McDuff (1999) *McDuff v. State*, 939 S.W.2d 607 (Tex. Ct. Crim. App. 1997).

3. Kozinsky, chapter 1 this volume.

4. Bedau, chapter 2 this volume.

5. Stevenson, chapter 4 this volume.

6. Bright, chapter 6 this volume.

7. *Gregg v. Georgia*, 428 U.S. 153 (1976).

8. Gallup Poll 2003, Poll Analyses, March 12, 2003.

9. Gallup Poll, June 8–10, 2001, found at *www.gallup.com/poll/indicators/inddeath_pen.asp* (19% identify themselves as opposing the death penalty and support

McVeigh's execution; 17% identify themselves as opposing the death penalty and opposing McVeigh's execution).

10. In preparing this chapter, I am in debt to the very interesting Web site maintained by Dudley Sharp of Justice for All, a Texas-based crime victims organization.
See www.prodeathpenalty.com.

11. Memorandum from Lawrence A. Greenfeld to Steven R. Schlesinger 2 (Dec. 18,
1985). The numbers do not appear to have been updated recently, but there is no
reason to think that the current statistics would be any different.

12. Bedau, chapter 2 this volume.

13. JAMES Q. WILSON, THINKING ABOUT CRIME 121 (rev. ed. 1983).

14. 428 U.S. 153, 186 (1976) (plurality opinion).

15. 141 CONG. REC. S7662 (June 5, 1995).

16. REPORT OF THE ROYAL COMMISSION ON CAPITAL PUNISHMENT 1949–53, at 375,
in 7 REPORTS OF COMMISSIONERS, INSPECTORS, AND OTHERS 677 (1952).

17. RECOUNTED IN FRANK CARRINGTON, NEITHER CRUEL NOR UNUSUAL 96 (1978).

18. *Id.* at 99.

19. Debate among Professor Paul Cassell, Professor Alan Dershowitz, and Wendy
Kamenar on the death penalty (Harvard Law School, March 22, 1995).

20. William F. Weld & Paul G. Cassell, Report to the Deputy Attorney General on
Capital Punishment and the Sentencing Commission at 28 (Feb. 13, 1987).

21. Hearings Before the Sen. Subcom. on Criminal Law, Prison Violence and Capital
Punishment, Comm. Serial No. J-98-80 (Nov. 9, 1983), at p. 3.

22. Bright, chapter 6 this volume.

23. *See generally* Paul G. Cassell & Richard Fowles, *Handcuffing the Cops? A Thirty-
Year Perspective on* Miranda's *Harmful Effects on Law Enforcement,* 50 STAN. L. REV.
1055, 1074–82 (1998) (collecting variables that affect criminal justice systems).

24. These data and my discussion of them draw heavily on the excellent report and
accompanying charts prepared by Senator Hatch. *See* S. Rep. 107–315, The Innocence
Protection Act of 2002, 107th Cong., 2d Sess. 47 ff. (Oct. 16, 2002) (views of Senator
Hatch).

25. Hashem Dezhbakhsh et al., *Does Capital Punishment Have a Deterrent Effect?
New Evidence from Post-Moratorium Panel Data,* SSRN xxx. (January 2001).

26. H. Naci Mocan & R. Kaj Kittings, *Getting Off Death Row: Commuted Sentences
and the Deterrent Effect of Capital Punishment,* forthcoming in the *Journal of Law and
Economics,* Oct. 2003, available on http://econ.cudenver.edu/mocan/papers/KajPaper
August2002.pdf.

27. The paper is available at http://papers.ssrn.com/sol3/papers.cfm?abstract_id=
354680.

28. Dale O. Cloninger & Roberto Marchesini, *Execution and Deterrence: A Quasi-
Controlled Group Experiment,* 33 APPLIED ECONOMICS 596 (2001).

29. Dale Cloninger, *Scientific Date Support Executions' Effect,* WALL ST. J., June 27,
2002, at A21.

30. Bedau, chapter 2 this volume.

31. IMMANUEL KANT, THE PHILOSOPHY OF LAW (W. Hastie translation 1887).

32. *Richmond Newspapers, Inc. v. Virginia*, 448 U.S. 555, 571 (1980).

33. Walter Berns, *Defending the Death Penalty*, 26 CRIME & DELINQ. 503, 509 (1980).

34. Bedau, chapter 2 this volume.

35. This argument is developed in Joshua Micah Marshall, *Death in Venice: Europe Death-Penalty Elitism*, THE NEW REPUBLIC, JULY 31, 2002, at 14.

36. Josephin Mazzuca, *The Death Penalty in North Amercia*, Gallup Tuesday Briefing (Oct. 15, 2002) (available at www.gallup.com/poll/tb/religValue/20021015b.asp).

37. Marshall, *supra* note 15, at 14.

38. *See* John C. McAdams, *Racial Disparity and the Death Penalty*, 61 LAW AND CONTEMP. PROBLEMS 153 (1998).

39. JESSE JACKSON, LEGAL LYNCHING: RACISM, INJUSTICE, AND THE DEATH PENALTY 100 (1996).

40. U.S. DEPT. OF JUSTICE, BUREAU OF JUSTICE STATISTICS, SOURCEBOOK OF CRIMINAL JUSTICE STATISTICS 1999 (2000), tables 6. 84 6.95.

41. U.S. DEPT. OF JUSTICE, BUREAU OF JUSTICE STATISTICS, BULLETIN: CAPITAL PUNISHMENT, 1984, Tables A-1, A-2, and A-3.

42. Patrick Langan, *Racism on Trial: New Evidence to Explain the Racial Composition of Prisons in the United States*, 76 J. OF CRIMINAL L. & CRIMINOLOGY 666 (1985).

43. U.S. GENERAL ACCOUNTING OFFICE, DEATH PENALTY SENTENCING: RESEARCH INDICATES PATTERN OF RACIAL DISPARITIES (1990).

44. DAVID C. BALDUS ET AL., EQUAL JUSTICE AND THE DEATH PENALTY: A LEGAL AND EMPIRICAL ANALYSIS 254 (1990).

45. Stevenson, chapter 4 this volume.

46. Stanley Rothman & Stephen Powers, *Execution by Quota?* PUBLIC INTEREST, Summer 1994, at 3. To simplify the exposition, I will track Rothman and Powers in referring to African Americans as blacks in the discussion of race-of-the-victim issues.

47. *McCleskey v. Zant*, 580 F. Supp. 338, 368 (N.D. Ga. 1984).

48. Hugo Bedau, *The Death Penalty in America*, FED. PROBATION, June 1971, at 32, 36.

49. Hugo Bedau and Michael Radelet, *Miscarriages of Justice in Potentially Capital Cases*, 40 STAN. L. REV. 21 (1987).

50. Stephen J. Markman & Paul G. Cassell, *Protecting the Innocent: A Response to the Bedau-Radelet Study*, 41 STAN. L. REV. 121 (1988).

51. James Adams was convicted of killing, then robbing a Florida rancher in 1974. Adams was executed in 1984. Bedau and Radelet claim that Adams was innocent, but do not mention the following salient facts:

- Adams was arrested shortly after the murder with money stained with blood matching the victim's;
- Adams claimed that the money was stained because of a cut on his finger, but his blood did not match the blood on the money;

- Clothes belonging to Adams were found in the locked trunk of his car stained with blood matching the victim's;
- Eyeglasses belonging to the victim were also found in the locked trunk of Adams' car;
- Adams told the police when arrested that the clothing and eyeglasses found in his trunk were his, but at trial changed his story and denied owning any of the items.
- A witness, John Tompkins, saw Adams driving his car to and from the victim's house at the time of the murder;
- Another witness saw Adams's car parked at the victim's house at the time of the murder;
- A few hours after the murder, Adams took his brown car to an auto shop and asked that it be painted a different color.
- Adams's principal alibi witness contradicted him on the critical issue of his whereabouts at the time of the crime.

While ignoring all of this evidence, Bedau and Radelet offer the following to "prove" Adams's innocence:

- A witness who identified Adams's car leaving the scene of the crime was allegedly mad at Adams—but Bedau and Radelet do not mention that three other witnesses also saw Adams at or near the scene of the crime;
- A voice that sounded like a woman's was heard at the time of the murder—but the trial transcript reveals that this was the strangled voice of the victim pleading for mercy;
- A hair sample was found that did not match Adams's hair—but Bedau and Radelet state inaccurately that it was found "clutched in the victim's hand" when in fact it was a remnant of a sweeping of the ambulance and could have come from any of a number of sources.

52. A full review of the Adams case, including citations to the original trial transcript and other court documents is found in Markman & Cassell, *supra* note 47, at 128–33, 148–50.

53. *See* Markman & Cassell, *supra* note 47, at 133–45.

54. *Compare* Bedau & Radelet, *supra* note 46, at 92 n. 362, *with* DOROTHY KILGALLEN, MURDER ONE 190–91, 230 (1967) (Appelgate "very nearly got away" with the murder); L. LAWES, MEET THE MURDERER 334–35 (1940) ("Frankly, I do not doubt the culpability" of Appelgate).

55. *Compare* Bedau & Radelet, *supra* note 46, at 109, *with Dawson v. State*, 139 So. 2d 408, 412 (Fla. 1962); ST. PETERSBURG TIMES, Sept. 24, 1977, at 12A col. 1; Markman & Cassell, *supra* note 47, at 136 N.75. Interestingly, Bedau himself indicated in 1982 that the Dawson case "remain[ed] in the limbo of uncertainty" because "[t]he original news story [regarding Dawson's supposed innocence] merely reported allegations and

was inconclusive; no subsequent inquiry known to me has established whether Dawson was really innocent." Bedau, *Miscarriages of Justice and the Death Penalty*, in THE DEATH PENALTY IN AMERICA 236–37 (H. Bedau, ed. 1982) (citing the same sources later cited in the *Stanford Law Review* as somehow "proving" Dawson's innocence).

56. *Compare* Bedau & Radelet, *supra* note 46, at 164 n. 869, *with* E. PEARSON, MASTERPIECES OF MURDER 171 (1963); Markman & Cassell, *supra* note 21, at 143 n.116.

57. *Compare* Bedau & Radelet, *supra* note 46, at 126 n. 588, *with* W. STEGNER, JOE HILL: A BIOGRAPHICAL NOVEL 13–14 (1969); Stegner, *Joe Hill: The Wobblies Troubadour*, NEW REPUBLIC, Jan. 5, 1948, at 20; Stegner, *Correspondence: Joe Hill*, NEW REPUBLIC, Feb. 9, 1948, at 39. *See also* Markman & Cassell, *supra* note 47, at 138–39,

58. Bright, chapter 6 this volume.

59. *See Strickland v. Washington*, 466 U.S. 668 (1984).

60. U.S. DEPT. OF COMMERCE, STATISTICAL ABSTRACT OF THE UNITED STATES 205 (2002).

61. Utah R. Crim. Pro. 8(b).

62. *Inmate Legal Fees Could Deplete Sanpete Coffers*, SALT LAKE TRIB., August 16, 1994, at A1, 1994 WL 7363933.

63. *See* Marquis, chapter 5 this volume.

64. *Defending McVeigh*, THE JOURNAL RECORD (OKLAHOMA CITY), July 2, 2001, 001 WL 4525208.

65. Herman, Indigent Defense & Capital Representation (National Center for State Courts, No. IS01-0407, July 17, 2001).

66. *See* S. Rep. 107–315, The Innocence Protection Act of 2002, 107th Cong., 2d Sess. 89 (Oct. 16, 2002) (views of Senator Hatch).

67. Tex. Crim. Pro. R. 26.052.

68. Tex. Gov't Code Ann. § 71.060.

69. Bedau, chapter 2 this volume.

70. Pojman, Draft at chapter 3 this volume (citing correspondence from Bedau, among other sources).

8

———— • ————

"I Must Act"

George Ryan

The following is the prepared text of Governor George Ryan's speech delivered at Northwestern University College of Law on January 11, 2003, announcing his commutation of all of Illinois's death sentences.

Four years ago I was sworn in as the 39th governor of Illinois. That was just four short years ago; that's when I was a firm believer in the American System of Justice and the death penalty. I believed that the ultimate penalty for the taking of a life was administrated in a just and fair manner.

Today, three days before I end my term as governor, I stand before you to explain my frustrations and deep concerns about both the administration and the penalty of death. It is fitting that we are gathered here today at Northwestern University with the students, teachers, lawyers and investigators who first shed light on the sorrowful condition of Illinois' death penalty system. Professors Larry Marshall, Dave Protess, and their students along with investigators Paul Ciolino have gone above the call. They freed the falsely accused Ford Heights Four, they saved Anthony Porter's life, they fought for Rolando Cruz and Alex Hernandez. They devoted time and effort on behalf of Aaron Patterson, a young man who lost 15 years of his youth sitting among the condemned, and LeRoy Orange, who lost 17 of the best years of his life on death row.

It is also proper that we are together with dedicated people like Andrea Lyon who has labored on the front lines trying capital cases for many years and who is now devoting her passion to creating an innocence center at De Paul University. You saved Madison Hobley's life.

Together you spared the lives and secured the freedom of 17 men, men who were wrongfully convicted and rotting in the condemned units of our state prisons. What you have achieved is of the highest calling. Thank you!

Yes, it is right that I am here with you, where, in a manner of speaking, my journey from staunch supporters of capital punishment to reformer all began. But I must tell you, since the beginning of our journey, my thoughts and feelings about the death penalty have changed many, many times. I realize that over the course of my reviews I had said that I would not do blanket commutation. I have also said it was an option that was there and I would consider all options.

During my time in public office I have always reserved my right to change my mind if I believed it to be in the best public interest, whether it be about taxes, abortions or the death penalty. But I must confess that the debate with myself has been the toughest concerning the death penalty. I suppose the reason the death penalty has been the toughest is because it is so final, the only public policy that determines who lives and who dies. In addition it is the only issue that attracts most of the legal minds across the country. I have received more advice on this issue than any other policy issue I have dealt with in my 35 years of public service. I have kept an open mind on both sides of the issues of commutation for life or death.

I have read, listened to and discussed the issue with the families of the victims as well as the families of the condemned. I know that any decision I make will not be accepted by one side or the other. I know that my decision will be just that—my decision, based on all the facts I could gather over the past three years. I may never be comfortable with my final decision, but I will know in my heart, that I did my very best to do the right thing.

Having said that I want to share a story with you:

I grew up in Kankakee which even today is still a small midwestern town, a place where people tend to know each other. Steve Small was a neighbor. I watched him grow up. He would babysit my young children, which was not for the faint of heart since Lura Lynn and I had six children, five of them under the age of three. He was a bright young man who helped run the family business. He got married and he and his wife had three children of their own. Lura Lynn was especially close to him and his family. We took comfort in knowing he was there for us and we for him.

One September midnight he received a call at his home. There had been a break-in at the nearby house he was renovating. But as he left his house, he was seized at gunpoint by kidnappers. His captors buried him alive in a shallow hole. He suffocated to death before police could find him.

His killer led investigators to where Steve's body was buried. The killer, Danny Edward was also from my hometown. He now sits on death row. I also know his family. I share this story with you so that you know I do not come to this as a neophyte without having experienced a small bit of the bitter pill the survivors of murder must swallow.

My responsibilities and obligations are more than my neighbors and my family. I represent all the people of Illinois, like it or not. The decision I make about our criminal justice system is felt not only here but the world over.

The other day, I received a call from former South African President Nelson Mandela who reminded me that the United States sets the example for justice and fairness for the rest of the world. Today the United States is not in league with most of our major allies: Europe, Canada, Mexico, most of South and Central America. These countries rejected the death penalty. We are partners in death with several third world countries. Even Russia has called a moratorium. The death penalty has been abolished in 12 states. In none of these states has the homicide rate increased. In Illinois last year we had about 1,000 murders, only 2 percent of that 1,000 were sentenced to death. Where is the fairness and equality in that? The death penalty in Illinois is not imposed fairly or uniformly because of the absence of standards for the 102 Illinois state attorneys, who must decide whether to request the death sentence. Should geography be a factor in determining who gets the death sentence? I don't think so but in Illinois it makes a difference. You are five times more likely to get a death sentence for first-degree murder in the rural area of Illinois than you are in Cook County. Where is the justice and fairness in that? Where is the proportionality?

The Most Reverend Desmond Tutu wrote to me this week stating that "to take a life when a life has been lost is revenge, it is not justice." He says justice allows for mercy, clemency and compassion. These virtues are not weakness. "In fact the most glaring weakness is that no matter how efficient and fair the death penalty may seem in theory, in actual practice it is primarily inflicted upon the weak, the poor, the ignorant and against racial minorities." That was a quote from Former California governor Pat Brown. He wrote that in his book *Public Justice, Private Mercy*; he wrote that nearly 50 years ago, nothing has changed in nearly 50 years.

I never intended to be an activist on this issue. I watched in surprise as freed death row inmate Anthony Porter was released from jail. A free man, he ran into the arms of Northwestern University Professor Dave Protess who poured his heart and soul into proving Porter's innocence with his journalism students. He was 48 hours away from being wheeled into the execution chamber where the state would kill him.

It would all be so antiseptic and most of us would not have even paused, except that Anthony Porter was innocent of the double murder for which he had been condemned to die.

After Mr. Porter's case there was the report by Chicago *Tribune* reporters Steve Mills and Ken Armstrong documenting the systemic failures of our capital punishment system. Half of the nearly 300 capital cases in Illinois had been reversed for a new trial or resentencing.

Nearly half!

Thirty-three of the death row inmates were represented at trial by an attorney who had later been disbarred or at some point suspended from practicing law. Of the more than 160 death row inmates, 35 were

African American defendants who had been convicted or condemned to die by all-white juries. More than two-thirds of the inmates on death row were African American. Forty-six inmates were convicted on the basis of testimony from jailhouse informants. I can recall looking at these cases and the information from the Mills/Armstrong series and asking my staff: How does that happen? How in God's name does that happen? I'm not a lawyer, so somebody explain it to me.

But no one could. Not to this day.

Then over the next few months. There were three more exonerated men, freed because their sentence hinged on a jailhouse informant or new DNA technology proved beyond a shadow of doubt their innocence. We then had the dubious distinction of exonerating more men than we had executed: 13 men found innocent, 12 executed.

As I reported yesterday, there is not a doubt in my mind that the number of innocent men freed from our death row stands at 17, with the pardons of Aaron Patterson, Madison Hobley, Stanley Howard, and Leroy Orange. That is an absolute embarrassment. Seventeen exonerated death row inmates is nothing short of a catastrophic failure. But the 13, now 17 men, is just the beginning of our sad arithmetic in prosecuting murder cases. During the time we have had capital punishment in Illinois, there were at least 33 other people wrongly convicted on murder charges and exonerated. Since we reinstated the death penalty there are also 93 people, 93, where our criminal justice system imposed the most severe sanction and later rescinded the sentence or even released them from custody because they were innocent.

How many more cases of wrongful conviction have to occur before we can all agree that the system is broken?

Throughout this process, I have heard many different points of view expressed. I have had the opportunity to review all of the cases involving the inmates on death row. I have conducted private group meetings, one in Springfield and one in Chicago, with the surviving family members of homicide victims. Everyone in the room who wanted to speak had the opportunity to do so. Some wanted to express their grief, others wanted to express their anger. I took it all in.

My commission and my staff had been reviewing each and every case for three years. But, I redoubled my effort to review each case personally in order to respond to the concerns of prosecutors and victims' families. This individual review also naturally resulted in a collective examination of our entire death penalty system.

I also had a meeting with a group of people who are less often heard from, and who are not as popular with the media. The family members of death row inmates have a special challenge to face. I spent an afternoon with those family members at a Catholic Church here in Chicago. At that meeting, I heard a different kind of pain expressed. Many of these families live with the twin pain of knowing not only that, in some cases, their family member may have been responsible for inflicting a terrible trauma on another family, but also the pain of knowing that society has called for another killing. These parents, siblings and children are not to blame for the crime committed, yet these innocent stand to have their loved ones killed by the state. As Mr. Mandela told me, they are also branded and scarred for life because of the awful crime committed by their family member.

Others were even more tormented by the fact that their loved one was another victim, that they were truly innocent of the crime for which they were sentenced to die.

It was at this meeting that I looked into the face of Claude Lee, the father of Eric Lee, who was convicted of killing Kankakee police officer Anthony Samfay a few years ago. It was a traumatic moment, once again, for my hometown. A brave officer, part of that thin blue line that protects each of us, was struck down by wanton violence. If you will kill a police officer, you have absolutely no respect for the laws of man or God.

I've known the Lee family for a number of years. There does not appear to be much question that Eric was guilty of killing the officer. However, I can say now after our review, there is also not much question that Eric is seriously ill, with a history of treatment for mental illness going back a number of years. The crime he committed was a terrible one, killing a police officer. Society demands that the highest penalty be paid.

But I had to ask myself: Could I send another man's son to death under the deeply flawed system of capital punishment we have in Illinois? A troubled young man, with a history of mental illness? Could I rely on the system of justice we have in Illinois not to make another horrible mistake? Could I rely on a fair sentencing?

In the United States the overwhelming majority of those executed are psychotic, alcoholic, drug addicted or mentally unstable. They frequently are raised in an impoverished and abusive environment.

Seldom are people with money or prestige convicted of capital offenses, even more seldom are they executed.

To quote Governor Brown again, he said, "Society has both the right and the moral duty to protect itself against its enemies. This natural and prehistoric axiom has never successfully been refuted. If by ordered death, society is really protected and our homes and institutions guarded, then even the most extreme of all penalties can be justified.

"Beyond its honor and incredibility, it has neither protected the innocent nor deterred the killers. Publicly sanctioned killing has cheapened human life and dignity without the redeeming grace which comes from justice metered out swiftly, evenly, humanely."

At stake throughout the clemency process, was whether some, all, or none of these inmates on death row would have their sentences commuted from death to life without the possibility of parole.

One of the things discussed with family members was life without parole . . . seen as a life filled with perks and benefits.

Some inmates on death row don't want a sentence of life without parole. Danny Edwards wrote me and told me not to do him any favors because he didn't want to face a prospect of a life in prison without parole. They will be confined in a cell that is about 5-feet-by-12 feet, usually double-bunked. Our prisons have no air conditioning, except at our supermax facility where inmates are kept in their cell 23 hours a day. In summer months, temperatures in these prisons exceed one hundred degrees. It is a stark and dreary existence. They can think about their crimes. Life without parole has even, at times, been described by prosecutors as a fate worse than death.

Yesterday, I mentioned a lawsuit in Livingston County where a judge ruled the state corrections department cannot forcefeed two corrections inmates who are on a hunger strike. The judge ruled that suicide by hunger strike was not an irrational action by the inmates, given what their future holds.

Earlier this year, the U.S. Supreme Court held that it is unconstitutional and cruel and unusual punishment to execute the mentally retarded. It is now the law of the land. How many people have we already executed who were mentally retarded and are now dead and buried? Although we now know that they have been killed by the state unconstitutionally and illegally. Is that fair? Is that right?

This court decision was last spring. The General Assembly failed to pass any measure defining what constitutes mental retardation. We are a rudderless ship because they failed to act.

This is even after the Illinois Supreme Court also told lawmakers that it is their job and it must be done.

I started with this issue concerned about innocence. But once I studied, once I pondered what had become of our justice system, I came to care above all about fairness. Fairness is fundamental to the American system of justice and our way of life.

The facts I have seen in reviewing each and every one of these cases raised questions not only about the innocence of people on death row, but about the fairness of the death penalty system as a whole.

If the system was making so many errors in determining whether someone was guilty in the first place, how fairly and accurately was it determining which guilty defendants deserved to live and which deserved to die? What effect was race having? What effect was poverty having?

And in almost every one of the exonerated 17, we not only have breakdowns in the system with police, prosecutors and judges, we have terrible cases of shabby defense lawyers. There is just no way to sugar coat it. There are defense attorneys that did not consult with their clients, did not investigate the case and were completely unqualified to handle complex death penalty cases. They often didn't put much effort into fighting a death sentence. If your life is on the line, your lawyer ought to be fighting for you. As I have said before, there is more than enough blame to go around.

I had more questions.

In Illinois, I have learned, we have 102 decision makers. Each of them ... [is] politically elected, each beholden to the demands of their community and, in some cases, to the media or especially vocal victims' families. In cases that have the attention of the media and the public, are decisions to seek the death penalty more likely to occur? What standards are these prosecutors using? Some people have assailed my power to commute sentences, a power that literally hundreds of legal scholars from across the country have defended. But prosecutors in Illinois have the ultimate commutation power, a power that is exercised every day. They decide who will be subject to the death penalty, who will get a plea deal or even who may get a complete pass on prosecution. By what objective standards do they make these decisions? We do not know, they are not public. There were more than 1,000 murders last year in Illinois. There is no doubt that all murders are horrific and cruel. Yet, less than 2 percent of those murder defendants will receive the death penalty. That means more than 98 percent of victims' families do not get and will not receive whatever satisfaction can be derived from the execution of the murderer. Moreover, if you look at the cases, as I have done, both individually and collectively— a killing with the same circumstances might get 40 years in one county and death in another county. I have also seen where co-defendants who are equally or even more culpable get sentenced to a term of years, while another less culpable defendant ends up on death row.

In my case-by-case review, I found three people that fell into this category, Mario Flores, Montel Johnson, and William Franklin. Today I have commuted their sentences to a term of 40 years to bring their sentences into line with their co-defendants and to reflect the other extraordinary circumstances of these cases.

Supreme Court Justice Potter Stewart has said that the imposition of the death penalty on defendants in this country is as freakish and arbitrary as who gets hit by a bolt of lightning.

For years the criminal justice system defended and upheld the imposition of the death penalty for the 17 exonerated inmates from Illinois death row. Yet when the real killers are charged, prosecutors have often sought sentences of less than death. In the Ford Heights Four case, Verneal Jimerson and Dennis Williams fought the death sentences imposed upon them for 18 years before they were exonerated. Later, Cook County prosecutors sought life in prison for two of the real killers and a sentence of 80 years for a third.

What made the murder for which the Ford Heights Four were sentenced to die less heinous and worthy of the death penalty 20 years later with a new set of defendants?

We have come very close to having our state Supreme Court rule our death penalty statute—the one that I helped enact in 1977—unconstitutional. Former State Supreme Court Justice Seymour Simon wrote to me that it was only happenstance that our statute was not struck down by the state's high court. When he joined the bench in 1980, three other justices had already said Illinois's death penalty was unconstitutional. But they got cold feet when a case came along to revisit the question. One judge wrote that he wanted to wait and see if the Supreme Court of the United States would rule on the constitutionality of the new Illinois law. Another said precedent required him to follow the old state Supreme Court ruling with which he disagreed.

Even a pharmacist knows that doesn't make sense. We wouldn't have a death penalty today, and we all wouldn't be struggling with this issue, if those votes had been different. How arbitrary.

Several years after we enacted our death penalty statute, Girvies Davis was executed. Justice Simon writes that he was executed because of this unconstitutional aspect of the Illinois law—the wide latitude that each Illinois state's attorney has to determine what cases qualify for the death penalty. One state's attorney waived his request for the death sentence when Davis's first sentencing was sent back to the trial court for a new sentencing hearing. The prosecutor was going to seek a life sentence. But in the interim, a new state's attorney took office and changed directions. He once again sought and secured a death sentence. Davis was executed.

How fair is that?

After the flaws in our system were exposed, the Supreme Court of Illinois took it upon itself to begin to reform its rules and improve the trial of capital cases. It changed the rule to require that state's attorneys give advance notice to defendants that they plan to seek the death penalty to require notice before trial instead of after conviction. The Supreme Court also enacted new discovery rules designed to prevent trials by ambush and to allow for better investigation of cases from the beginning.

But shouldn't that mean if you were tried or sentenced before the rules changed, you ought to get a new trial or sentencing with the new safeguards of the rules? This issue has divided our Supreme Court, some saying yes, a majority saying no. These justices have a lifetime of experience with the criminal justice system and it concerns me that these great minds so strenuously differ on an issue of such importance, especially where life or death hangs in the balance.

What are we to make of the studies that showed that more than 50 percent of Illinois jurors could not understand the confusing and obscure sentencing instructions that were being used? What effect did that problem have on the trustworthiness of death sentences? A review of the cases shows that often even the lawyers and judges are confused about the instructions—let alone the jurors sitting in judgment. Cases still come before the Supreme Court with arguments about whether the jury instructions were proper.

I spent a good deal of time reviewing these death row cases. My staff, many of whom are lawyers, spent busy days and many sleepless nights answering my questions, providing me with information, giving me advice. It became clear to me that whatever decision I made, I would be criticized. It also became clear to me that it was impossible to make reliable choices about whether our capital punishment system had really done its job.

As I came closer to my decision, I knew that I was going to have to face the question of whether I believed so completely in the choice I wanted to make that I could face the prospect of even commuting the death sentence of Daniel Edwards, the man who had killed a close family friend of mine. I discussed it with my wife, Lura Lynn, who has stood by me all these years. She was angry and disappointed at my decision like many of the families of other victims will be.

I was struck by the anger of the families of murder victims. To a family they talked about closure. They pleaded with me to allow the state to kill an inmate in its name to provide the families with closure. But is that the purpose of capital punishment? Is it to soothe the families? And is that truly what the families experience?

I cannot imagine losing a family member to murder. Nor can I imagine spending every waking day for 20 years with a single-minded focus to execute the killer. The system of death in Illinois is so unsure that it is not unusual for cases to take 20 years before they are resolved. And thank God. If it had moved any faster, then Anthony Porter, the Ford Heights Four, Ronald Jones, Madison Hobley, and the other innocent men we've exonerated might be dead and buried. But it is cruel and unusual punishment for family members to go through this pain, this legal limbo for 20 years. Perhaps it would be less cruel if we sentenced the killers to TAMS to life, and used our resources to better serve victims.

My heart ached when I heard one grandmother who lost children in an arson fire. She said she could not afford proper grave markers for her grandchildren who died. Why can't the state help families provide a proper burial? Another crime victim came to our family meetings. He believes an inmate sent to death row for another crime also shot and paralyzed him. The inmate he says gets free health care while the victim is struggling to pay his substantial medical bills and, as a result, he has forgone getting proper medical care to alleviate the physical pain he endures.

What kind of victims services are we providing? Are all of our resources geared toward providing this notion of closure by execution instead of tending to the physical and social service needs of victim families? And what kind of values are we instilling in these wounded families and in the young people? As Gandhi said, an eye for an eye only leaves the whole world blind.

President Lincoln often talked of binding up wounds as he sought to preserve the Union. "We are not enemies, but friends. We must not be enemies. Though passion may have strained, it must not break our bonds of affection." I have had to consider not only the horrible nature of the crimes that put men on death row in the first place, the terrible suffering of the surviving family members of the victims, the despair of the family members of the inmates, but I have also had to watch in frustration as members of the Illinois General Assembly failed to pass even one substantive death penalty reform. Not one. They couldn't even agree on ONE. How much more evidence is needed before the General Assembly will take its responsibility in this area seriously? The fact is that the failure of the General Assembly to act is merely a symptom of the larger problem. Many people express the desire to have capital punishment. Few, however, seem prepared to address the tough questions that arise when the system fails. It is easier and more comfortable for politicians to be tough on crime and support the death penalty. It wins votes. But when it comes to admitting that we have a problem, most run for cover. Prosecutors across our state continue to deny that our death penalty system is broken, or they say if there is a problem, it is really a small one and we can fix it somehow. It is difficult to see how the system can be fixed when not a single one of the reforms proposed by my Capital Punishment Commission has been adopted. Even the reforms the prosecutors agree with haven't been adopted. So when will the system be fixed? How much more risk can we afford? Will we actually have to execute an innocent person before the tragedy that is our capital punishment system in Illinois is really understood? This summer, a United States District court judge held the federal death penalty was unconstitutional and noted that with the number of recent exonerations based on DNA and new scientific technology we undoubtedly executed innocent people before this technology emerged.

As I prepare to leave office, I had to ask myself whether I could really live with the prospect of knowing that I had the opportunity to act, but that I failed to do so because I might be criticized. Could I take the chance that our capital punishment system might be reformed, that wrongful convictions might not occur, that enterprising journalism students might free more men from death row? A system that's so fragile that it depends on young journalism students is seriously flawed.

"There is no honorable way to kill, no gentle way to destroy. There is nothing good in war. Except its ending."

That's what Abraham Lincoln said about the bloody war between the states. It was a war fought to end the sorriest chapter in American history—the institution of slavery. While we are not in a civil war now, we are facing what is shaping up to be one of the great civil rights struggles of our time. Stephen Bright of the Southern Center for Human Rights has taken the position that the death penalty is being sought with increasing frequency in some states against the poor and minorities.

Our own study showed that juries were more likely to sentence to death if the victim were white than if the victim were black—three-and-a-half times more likely to be exact. We are not alone. Just this month Maryland released a study of their death penalty system and racial disparities exist there too.

This week, Mamie Till died. Her son Emmett was lynched in Mississippi in the 1950s. She was a strong advocate for civil rights and reconciliation. In fact just three weeks ago, she was the keynote speaker at the Murder Victims' Families for Reconciliation Event in Chicago. This group, many of whom I've met, opposes the death penalty even though their family members have been lost to senseless killing. Mamie's strength and grace not only ignited the civil rights movement—including inspiring Rosa Parks to refuse to go to the back of the bus—but inspired murder victims' families until her dying day. Is our system fair to all? Is justice blind? These are important human rights issues.

Another issue that came up in my individual, case-by-case review was the issue of international law. The Vienna Convention protects U.S. citizens abroad and foreign nationals in the United States. It provides that if you are arrested, you should be afforded the opportunity to contact your consulate. There are five men on death row who were denied that internationally recognized human right. Mexico's President Vicente Fox contacted me to express his deep concern for the Vienna Convention violations. If we do not uphold international law here, we cannot expect our citizens to be protected outside the United States. My Commission recommended the Supreme Court conducted a proportionality review of our system in Illinois. While our appellate courts perform a case-by-case review of the appellate record, they have not done such a big picture study. Instead, we tinker with a case-by-case review as each appeal lands on their docket.

In 1994, near the end of his distinguished career on the Supreme Court of the United States, Justice Harry Blackmun wrote an influential dissent in the body of law on capital punishment. Twenty years earlier he was part of the court that issued the landmark Furman decision. The Court decided that the death penalty statutes in use throughout the country were fraught with severe flaws that rendered them unconstitutional. Quite frankly, they were the same problems we see here in Illinois. To many, it looked like the Furman decision meant the end of the death penalty in the United States.

This was not the case. Many states responded to Furman by developing and enacting new and improved death penalty statutes. In 1976, four years after it had decided Furman, Justice Blackmun joined the majority of the United States Supreme Court in deciding to give the states a chance with these new and improved death penalty statutes. There was great optimism in the air. This was the climate in 1977, when the Illinois legislature was faced with the momentous decision of whether to reinstate the death penalty in Illinois. I was a member of the General Assembly at that time and when I pushed the green button in favor of reinstating the death penalty in this great State, I did so with the belief that whatever problems had plagued the capital punishment system in the past were now being cured. I am sure that most of my colleagues who voted with me that day shared that view.

But 20 years later, after affirming hundreds of death penalty decisions, Justice Blackmun came to the realization, in the twilight of his distinguished career that the death penalty remains fraught with arbitrariness, discrimination, caprice and mistake. He expressed frustration with a 20-year struggle to develop procedural and substantive safeguards. In a now famous dissent he wrote in 1994, "From this day forward, I no longer shall tinker with the machinery of death."

One of the few disappointments of my legislative and executive career is that the General Assembly failed to work with me to reform our deeply flawed system.

I don't know why legislators could not heed the rising voices of reform. I don't know how many more systemic flaws we needed to uncover before they would be spurred to action.

Three times I proposed reforming the system with a package that would restrict the use of jailhouse snitches, create a statewide panel to determine death eligible cases, and reduce the number of crimes eligible for death. These reforms would not have created a perfect system, but they would have dramatically reduced the chance for error in the administration of the ultimate penalty.

The governor has the constitutional role in our state of acting in the interest of justice and fairness. Our state constitution provides broad power to the governor to issue reprieves, pardons and commutations. Our Supreme Court has reminded inmates petitioning them that the last resort for relief is the governor.

At times the executive clemency power has perhaps been a crutch for courts to avoid making the kind of major change that I believe our system needs. Our systemic case-by-case review has found more cases of innocent men wrongfully sentenced to death row. Because our three-year study has found only more questions about the fairness of the sentencing; because of the spectacular failure to reform the system;

because we have seen justice delayed for countless death row inmates with potentially meritorious claims; because the Illinois death penalty system is arbitrary and capricious—and therefore immoral—I no longer shall tinker with the machinery of death.

I cannot say it more eloquently than Justice Blackmun.

The legislature couldn't reform it.

Lawmakers won't repeal it.

But I will not stand for it.

I must act.

Our capital system is haunted by the demon of error, error in determining guilt, and error in determining who among the guilty deserves to die. Because of all of these reasons today I am commuting the sentences of all death row inmates. This is a blanket commutation. I realize it will draw ridicule, scorn, and anger from many who oppose this decision. They will say I am usurping the decisions of judges and juries and state legislators. But as I have said, the people of our state have vested in me to act in the interest of justice. Even if the exercise of my power becomes my burden I will bear it. Our constitution compels it. I sought this office, and even in my final days of holding it I cannot shrink from the obligations to justice and fairness that it demands.

There have been many nights where my staff and I have been deprived of sleep in order to conduct our exhaustive review of the system. But I can tell you this: I will sleep well knowing I made the right decision.

As I said when I declared the moratorium, it is time for a rational discussion on the death penalty. While our experience in Illinois has indeed sparked a debate, we have fallen short of a rational discussion. Yet if I did not take this action, I feared that there would be no comprehensive and thorough inquiry into the guilt of the individuals on death row or of the fairness of the sentences applied. To say it plainly one more time—the Illinois capital punishment system is broken. It has taken innocent men to a hair's breadth escape from their unjust execution. Legislatures past have refused to fix it. Our new legislature and our new governor must act to rid our state of the shame of threatening the innocent with execution and the guilty with unfairness.

In the days ahead, I will pray that we can open our hearts and provide something for victims' families other than the hope of revenge. Lincoln once said: "I have always found that mercy bears richer fruits than strict justice." I can only hope that will be so. God bless you. And God bless the people of Illinois.

Contributors

—————— • ——————

Hugo Adam Bedau is professor emeritus of philosophy at Tufts University and the editor of the *The Death Penalty in America: Current Controversies*. Bedau is one of the leading and most widely recognized opponents of the death penalty.

Stephen B. Bright is director of the Southern Center for Human Rights and teaches courses on the death penalty and criminal law at Harvard and Yale law schools.

Paul G. Cassell is a United States district court judge of Salt Lake City. He is a former clerk for Judge Antonin Scalia (when he was a judge on the U.S. Court of Appeals) and for former Supreme Court Chief Justice Warren Burger. Cassell also served as an associate deputy attorney general with the U.S. Justice Department and was professor of law at the University of Utah. He has lectured frequently and been called on often to testify as an expert in the areas of criminal justice reform and the rights of crime victims.

Alex Kozinski is a federal judge on the United States Court of Appeals for the Ninth Circuit.

Joshua K. Marquis is district attorney of Clatsop County in Astoria, Oregon. He has been a prosecutor for more than 17 years and was a defense lawyer for 18 months. He is past president of the Oregon District Attorneys' Association and a board member of the National District Attorneys' Association, where he serves as co-chair of the Capital Litigation Committee. He speaks, writes, and debates frequently across America on criminal justice issues. He has successfully argued for a death sentence and also worked as lead defense counsel on three capital murder cases.

Louis P. Pojman (D. Phil. Oxford University) is professor of philosophy at the United States Military Academy, and has been a visiting professor at Brigham Young University in Utah and a visiting fellow at Oxford University. He has written on a host of ethical topics pertaining to life and death issues and has authored *Life and Death: Grappling with the Moral Issues of Time*. He is the co-author with Jeffrey Reiman of *The Death Penalty: For and Against*.

George Ryan is a former governor of Illinois.

Bryan Stevenson is the executive director of the Equal Justice Initiative in Montgomery, Alabama, and professor of clinical law at New York University School of Law. He has won national acclaim for his work challenging bias against the poor and people of color in the criminal justice system. He has assisted in securing relief for dozens of condemned prisoners.

Acknowledgments

———— • ————

This book and the public symposium that preceded it would not have transpired without support from several sources. Martha Elliott deserves and has our thanks for managing the symposium. She made all the arrangements for the participants and helped frame the debate. Both the debate and the book owe much of their form and substance to Martha's tireless efforts. Jack Beatty, senior editor at the *Atlantic Monthly*, was a superb moderator, keeping the discussion moving forward and allowing the participants to express their views in a manner that disentangled the several threads of argument. David Levine attended to the logistics at the CUNY Graduate Center, and we are grateful for his help. We are most grateful to the Annenberg Public Policy Center of the University of Pennsylvania for providing the grant that supported the symposium as well as this book, and our thanks go to Kathleen Hall Jamieson of the Center. Without that support neither the public discussion nor this book would have been possible, and we are much in her debt. Robert Tempio, assistant editor at Oxford University Press helped keep us on schedule. Finally, the authors are delighted to acknowledge the patient help and wise advice from the very beginning given by our editor at Oxford University Press, Tim Bartlett. We could not have asked for more patience from Tim, and thanks to his gentle prodding our written contributions in this book are far superior to what they would have been without his counsel and advice from start to finish.

Index

26⁰⁰